The Personal Success
Handbook—Unabridged

Also by Antony J. Iozzi

The Personal Success Handbook
- How to achieve personal excellence,
and lead yourself to wealth, health and happiness-

The Sales Success Handbook
- Your guide to the systems and strategies
of highly effective sales people-

The Nine Pillars of Happiness
- The suspense thriller for the new millennium -
(a novel)

The Personal Success Handbook—Unabridged

Your personal guide for achieving a wealthy, happy and successful life

Tony Iozzi

Authors Choice Press

San Jose New York Lincoln Shanghai

The Personal Success Handbook—Unabridged

Authors Choice Press
an imprint of iUniverse.com, Inc.

For information address:
iUniverse.com, Inc.
620 North 48th Street, Suite 201
Lincoln, NE 68504-3467
www.iuniverse.com

Originally published by Business and Professional Publishing

Originally published as You Can Succeed Anywhere

ISBN: 0-595-12852-1

Printed in the United States of America

Contents

Preface

You can succeed anywhere! And this book shows you how. But what does success mean to you?

When many people think of success they usually think of money—lots of it. To be sure, money is essential, and it is our duty to acquire it. Having it shows we have succeeded in the financial sphere of life. But what of the family, personal, work, community and spiritual spheres? And in our emerging global community, what of the global sphere?

We cannot all be billionaire entrepreneurs and no person or system should claim otherwise. However to the extent that we wish to strive for it everyone is empowered to achieve and live a successful life limited only by their highest and best efforts—a life of success with achievement, balance and harmony with ourselves and with our environment.

This book for your personal success outlines the philosophy and skills of holistic success. Wealth? Certainly! But with health and happiness too!

By tapping the centuries-old vein of success experience, *You Can Succeed Anywhere* shows the method, not just the theory, of achieving a Self-led, personally successful life.

It is a work with a mission. Its reason for being is to foster and help you on your journey of success through Self-leadership and Personal Excellence; not with bold, sweeping statements, but step by step so you can enrich your life and enjoy the process. This book could be one of your life's best friends.

Until now you might have been living a storyline written for you by someone else. You might need to script your own destiny; to live life by your design, not by default; by plan, not by accident. What kind of storyline would you write for your life if you knew you couldn't fail?

This success book includes a model to help you design your Life Blueprint for success. It is a step-by-step guide that will form the road map for your personal success journey. It is serious about helping you achieve your success goals because it is certain that, given skill, time and effort, you can succeed anywhere.

The best of everything could lie ahead of you.

Let this success book help you fulfil the promise of your better future.

About the author

Tony Iozzi spent the first ten years of his life in Caraffa, a mountain-top village in Calabria, southern Italy. As one of a family of five children, he learned about poverty and deprivation. He also learned about the dignity that belongs to all people, about caring and the value of a supportive family. After emigrating to Australia he had to make major adjustments in language and culture, and experienced the hostility of many people who did not take kindly to immigrants.

Joining the Royal Australian Air Force at age 18, he completed his education and was commissioned, attaining the rank of Flight Lieutenant (Captain). His varied postings in the Air Force included stints as Administrator, RAAF School of Languages, and Lecturer, Officers' Training School.

After resigning his commission, he worked in various managerial positions in the retail and insurance industries, including five years as Public Relations Manager for one of Australia's largest insurance companies. He started his own public relations consultancy firm and soon listed clients such as the Premier of Western Australia as well as the Western Australian Week Council, a body responsible for organising over 2000 State-wide events each year.

In the past five years, Tony Iozzi has been managing his own marketing and training consultancy accepting a number of assignments throughout Australia and Asia. His activities now include international public speaking, motivation, project management, training and personal development courses.

Acknowledgments

You Can Succeed Anywhere is a work based on research. Its knowledge has been applied by many people in many countries and in many ages, and consistently found to be highly effective.

In compiling this important work I owe much to the countless individuals dating from the year 2200 BC to the present era. These include religious leaders, captains of business and commerce, artists, philosophers and teachers. I owe much to them because they have pioneered the concept of cataloguing and sharing success experiences and skills to help others achieve a high level of personal success.

You Can Succeed Anywhere also reflects my own philosophy and success experiences.

Those who have contributed to my knowledge of the dynamics of personal success are far too many to list individually. Nevertheless I offer them my heartfelt thanks, which can best be expressed by passing on their success know-how—to you.

Part 1

Laying the foundations for personal success

1

The moment you change your life forever

THE rich citizens of City X have a strong interest in maintaining the status quo because it protects their privileged lifestyle. Many of them made their wealth through nepotism, corruption and 'deals' with officials who award their 'partners' lucrative contracts.

The vast majority of the population would consider themselves fortunate if they earned US$50 per week. In this capital city of about 10 million people (officially 6 million) no one can drink the water unless it is purified and supplied in sealed bottles. The road toll is so horrific that the United Nations has asked its leaders to take steps to lower it. Air pollution is so bad that it claws at your throat and one rarely sees a patch of blue sky.

Maimed beggars who cannot stand crawl along the gutters of busy roadways lifting their hands to cars for alms. There are many whose emaciated feet or stumps are wrapped in blood-stained bandages—the result of injuries caused by the nipping of careless wheels.

It is a country with no 'free' social services, no unemployment benefits and no free medical care. (Even in an emergency people are refused treatment unless they can pay first.)

Pensions are provided only to government workers, and even then payment is so minimal that many have to work in old age to survive. Everyone contrives to exist in any way they can.

Cannot the State help them? The country's religion, which is deeply rooted in 95 per cent of the population and supported by the State, certainly enjoins all citizens to practise charity—to help those in need. As in many societies, hypocrisy is alive and well in City X.

At nearly all levels of public and business life, corruption is endemic. Officials fleece the population by skimming much of the net wealth from each transaction for themselves, rather than risk letting it find its way to benefit this tragically overpopulated and poverty stricken people.

How easy would it be for the people of City X to change their life forever? For the emaciated beggars and for most of the beggar children who walk in and out of traffic chanting songs in a plea for alms, it would almost be impossible without systematic and organised help. For the majority of the people, it would be difficult unless the country's political system, people's work attitudes and general passivity changed.

However, for many individuals, changing their life forever is possible provided they are willing to educate themselves on success knowledge and skills, practice Self-leadership and make the effort required. But they would still have to struggle against a system that works to hinder progress.

In developed countries changing your life forever and achieving personal success in all the major spheres of life is a much easier undertaking. Yet many people whine about their lack of success, putting it down to a 'lack of opportunity' when, comparatively speaking, opportunity is all around them. And what about you?

Compared with people in City X, do you think you have more opportunity to achieve and maintain the level of personal success you want within your own community? If so, what are the *real* obstacles preventing you from achieving your personal success goals? Is it possible that most of those are self-made?

We do not have secret police keeping people from success and happiness. We do not have a 'Bureau for Failure Enforcement' to prevent citizens from achieving their personal share of wealth. What we have is a stream of opportunities and a river of money flowing all around us.

Yet amid this wealth people like Tom and Mary spend hours foraging for specials to save $1! They buy a second rate item to save ten cents. Rather than work out ways to increase their standard of living, they lower it. They acquiesce. They might be honest, loyal and good taxpayers but live from day to day in dread of the next bill—paupers in the midst of wealth. Despite living in a world where developed countries create more wealth daily than at any time in human history, in the end Tom and Mary would retire at the mercy of a State pension. Were Tom and Mary conditioned into accepting this relative poverty? Were they given storylines on how to live their life—storylines written by others?

In City X 'the system' conditions people into poverty. But there are many other ways of conditioning. Nearly everywhere verbal conditioners such as 'Money can't buy happiness,' 'There are more important things than money' and 'Money is the root of all evil' (which should be 'The love of money is the root of all evil' (i.e. greed)) contribute to many people's financial downfall because they establish a belief system. They condition people. And negative conditioning, because of its life-long drag, can kill many splendid plans and stifle the quest for personal success.

In City X the majority of the people have few choices. But from the time they left school Tom and Mary had a smorgasbord of choices yet saw life as something that 'happened to them', not as a menu of things they could achieve. Were Tom and Mary unique? Let's see.

An Australian Bureau of Statistics government demographic survey showed that in 1988 of every 100 citizens starting work, by age 65, 30 are already dead. Only seven live on more than $653 per week (gross); 50 live on incomes between $125 per week and $653 per week (the median is $253 per week); and 13 live on less than $125 per week (poverty level).

Yet the June 1992 issue of the Australian *Business Review Weekly* showed that of Australia's wealthiest 400 families, only some 2 per cent inherited their wealth. The others powered through obstacles and created their own wealth. What made the difference?

Given the choice, most people would choose wealth over poverty. But most people don't realise wealth *is* a matter of choice.

For those who live in developed countries and even for many people in developing countries, it isn't society, God, the government, the 'system', the weather, anyone or anything that prevents people from living a successful life.

What shapes people's destiny are the choices and decisions they make each day.

Bill and Helen lived in a country were achieving personal success was much easier than for the people of City X. They saw their opportunities and grabbed them with both hands. They knew how lucky they were materially and never stopped to whine that life did not give them any breaks. They saw, planned, applied themselves and achieved the success *they* wanted.

They devoted most of their energy to the pursuit of wealth. Both had professional careers and were taken in as full partners of their respective practices within a relatively short time (which unfortunately reduced the time they could spend with their children).

Bill became adept at investing in shares and property. By the time they were in their early forties they had accumulated enough money to generate an independent income for life. But they had even bigger goals.

By now their two boys were 18 and 21 and had lived away from home ever since that terrible row a year ago. Bill and Helen simply don't understand young people these days. Hadn't they provided their boys with the best that money could buy? Were Bill and Helen successful?

Brenda and Jason would not think so. They doted on their family. In their fifties, they enjoy a close relationship with all their children regardless of age (the youngest is 11). Brenda believes that being a wife and mother is the most important job in the world. Jason earns a modest income as an electrician. His plans for securing his future will come to fruition at retirement. Financially, he will have put away enough money to supplement his pension, but not more. Are Brenda and Jason successful?

Terence Lewis might not think so. He seemed to have everything—wealth, power, position, respect and a high regard as a valued member of the community of Queensland, Australia. He was Commissioner of Police—the State's top police officer. In 1991 he was found guilty of corruption and is serving a long prison sentence. Was he successful?

Brian Epstein, the man who created Beatlemania and launched the Beatles as the most famous pop group in history, added great wealth to his already full purse. He had an impeccable upbringing, fame, youth, glamour and wealth, and managed three of the most successful pop groups in the world.

Yet he 'lived on pills'—pills to help him sleep, pills to wake him up, pills to cheer him up. At the early age of 32, the man envied by the world's impresarios, died from a self-administered accidental overdose of drugs. Was Brian Epstein successful?

Elvis Presley was idolised and adored by millions. Referred to as 'The King', his legend refuses to die. He achieved fame, wealth and power, yet in 1967 Elvis tried to take his own life by swallowing a whole bottle of barbiturates.

Bloated and unhappy, Elvis was dependent on drugs to the end. The biochemist who investigated Elvis's death said he had never seen so many drugs in one specimen. Was Elvis Presley successful?

John Spencer would certainly not think so. John is a lay preacher and part-time missionary. All his work is devoted to charitable causes and, hence, produces little income for himself. John has a deep conviction that God will provide for his needs. Is John successful?

Terry White might think so. Terry was encouraged by all his friends and his wife to become a salesperson because people liked him and sought his advice. However, all he knew was how to be a good sheet-metal worker. He dreaded paperwork and 'wasn't any good with numbers'. Persuaded, Terry became a life insurance sales-person. His wife Laura helped with administration and the two made a great team.

Everyone was right! In his first year Terry won all the awards and trebled his former income. Then one night he attempted sui-cide, saved only by a chance visit from a friend he hadn't seen for two years. Was Terry a success?

These are questions for you to answer. But before you do it's important to remember that we all live in a number of spheres, and judging anyone by taking into account only one part of their life simply doesn't provide a complete answer.

Also, looking at the way others live and at what they achieve can only serve as pointers because our own definition of success depends on what we value individually and on what we want to achieve.

For all of us there comes a moment when we are given or we create the opportunity to change our life forever—for the better. If you reflect on your life you will probably recall some opportunity or moment in the past that, had you taken a different course, your life could be quite different.

In City X, for the majority of its people such opportunities are few. But it is much easier for you. The moment you change your life forever by stepping off on your success journey may be very close. But in which sphere of your life do you most want success?

How many lives do you live?

Imagine that a trusted friend made arrangements for you to visit a television studio as a member of an audience.

You sit in the front row, casting your eyes at the props, the lights, the cables strewn on the floor linking the television cam-eras ... The audience erupts with applause. The popular host—whose face you recognise at once—walks briskly to centre stage in front of an elaborate settee. His trained voice fills the studio as he looks straight at you and cries: 'This is your life!'

You freeze. Why you? Your friend pats you on the back and smiles, joining the audience in even louder applause as you are encouraged to take your place before the cameras. The host walks towards you with an outstretched hand.

'My God!' you exclaim as you walk to the settee. You sit self-consciously for what seems an eternity as the host calls your friends, acquaintances and family members, each to tell their version of your life story to the world.

■ In your *personal life* would you want them to speak of your honesty, integrity, caring and Self-leadership? Your success through Personal Excellence?

■ In your *family life* would you want them to tell the world about a loving friend, parent and partner who nurtured a happy home?

■ In your *financial life* would you want them to glow with admiration at the security you achieved for yourself and for those you love?

■ In your *business/work life* would you want them to tell the world about the example you set, the diligence, and the support you give to others?

■ In your *community life* would you want everyone to know of your support for worthy causes, of your work for youth, sport and for a caring community?

■ In your *global life* would you like them to tell the world how you were among those who could see the emerging global community and interdependent economies? How you understood that your country's prosperity depended on the prosperity of international communities? About your efforts to help people such as those in City X; to encourage international understanding and peace by helping less fortunate communities achieve a measure of dignity, self-reliance and independence? Would you want them to know about the personal example you set in pollution reduction, your purchase of environmentally friendly products, conservation and recycling, beginning in your own home?

■ In your *spiritual life* would you want them to say how your beliefs, philosophy and work enriched the community in which you live? How your example provided a role model for others?

Your answers will help you determine the level of personal success you want for each sphere of your life. They will help you strive for goals that are ennobling, rewarding and achievable. They will invigorate every day of your personal success journey.

A major shift in perception

In City X differences in the way various strata of its society perceive the world are quite marked. The sun-lined faces of men pulling wood and corrugated iron barrows laden with household rubbish reinforce their perception of a world of hardship, struggle and unrelenting drudgery.

Now and then prestige motor cars whisper by with their tinted windows, air conditioning, chauffeur and privileged passengers.

The barrow people may look up but can have little perception of the lifestyle enjoyed by the wealthy few. They live their life according to a paradigm of desperation.

We too live our lives according to the way we perceive the world around us. Some of us go beyond this limitation and try to change the world we see, for the better. Unfortunately, not all of us succeed.

Consider the ageless story of *The Adventures of Don Quixote De La Mancha* by Miguel De Cervantes. The hero is a pathetic yet lovable character on a 'mission'. He sets out to right the 'unrightable wrong', 'defend the helpless', 'reach the unreachable star'.

The legend of knights, chivalry, purity and great deeds were Don Quixote's 'virtual reality'. Through his mind's eye he transfigures a windmill into a monster and charges at it with tilted lance (with predictable results). A scullery maid and prostitute become his 'Dulcinea' to whom he will dedicate awesome victories and noble deeds. A run-down inn becomes a castle; a barber's bowl becomes the mystical 'Helmet of Mandrino'.

Despite heroic efforts, Don Quixote fails to realise his splendid vision and dies in delusion. He was the very embodiment of a *positive mental attitude*, but that did not improve the outcome.

He put in *'That extra effort'*, yet failed just the same. He 'read all the books' but died a broken—yet lovable—old fool. He was a paragon of *self-motivation,* yet he might as well have brooded silently at home. Even though he changed his life forever by taking the step to become a 'Knight Errant', those vital success disciplines failed him. Why?

From the start Don Quixote's quest was doomed because his perception was based on 'virtual reality' rather than on reality itself. Through his mind's eye he saw the world as he thought it was or as he wished it to be, not as it really existed. All his positive mental attitude, extra effort, self-motivation and study simply ensured he got to the wrong place faster.

On the other hand Tom and Mary, Bill and Helen, Brenda and Jason, Terence Lewis, John Spencer, Terry White, Brian Epstein and Elvis Presley might well have seen the world as it really was, yet achieved success in only one or a few spheres of life.

To succeed in all the major spheres of life (personal, family, business/work, financial, community, global and spiritual) could require a major shift in perception. You might need to develop *a different way of seeing things.*

During the 'Cold War' many people in the West were extremely concerned about the possibility of a Soviet nuclear strike. Yet in that period the same people would not have been concerned at all about US, British or French nuclear weapons.

Were Western nuclear weapons any less horrific?

Westerners perceived the Soviets as the enemy, and the United States, Britain and France as allies. What they saw, their attitudes and feelings towards it and what they did about it depended on their perceptions.

For many centuries people perceived the world as flat. Mediterranean seamen refused to sail past the 'Pillars of Hercules' (the Straits of Gibraltar) for fear of falling off the Earth. What happened once the flat Earth perception changed? Was not a new world discovered?

You may know the story of a mother whose face was terribly disfigured by fire. Her teenage daughter was ashamed of her. She was embarrassed to bring her friends to her house and did not want to be seen with her mother in public.

Eventually the shame and embarrassment erupted into an argument where the daughter told her mother how 'ugly' she was and that she wished she had no mother at all.

One day she learned how her mother became disfigured. When the daughter was only two years old the house caught fire. Her mother risked her life again and again to save her daughter, and in the process suffered horrible burns.

This new perception transformed each scar on her mother's face into a testament of love, courage, self-sacrifice and devotion. Once the daughter's perception changed, so did her attitude, feelings and behaviour. By changing *how* she saw, she changed *what* she saw.

When I lived in an apartment I was frequently disturbed by the noise coming from what I thought was the apartment above. I put up with it for months without complaint. One day the noise of a masonry drill reverberated through the entire block, beginning at 7 a.m. That was too much!

I took the elevator to the upper floor and marched angrily down the corridor. The noise of the drill grew louder and even more irritating. I pounded on the door, ready to blast away.

When the door opened, a frail old man in a wheelchair answered: 'Yes?'

All I could say was: 'Sorry, I'm from the apartment below. Do you know where that terrible noise is coming from?'

He replied: 'I thought it was coming from you.'

Many 'born again' Christians tell of the moment when all at once everything made sense—when they saw the 'big picture'. Their perception of the world changed and with it they changed their life forever.

Yet an accurate perception of the world and your place in it will not, of itself, create the moment you change your life forever. It will, however, give you an accurate platform from which to begin your personal success journey.

The power of dissatisfaction

Many people who do not succeed might fail because they become too satisfied with what they have. They think: 'We're doing OK.' Somehow they adjust and accept a mediocre condition despite the life of stress, hardship and frustration it brings. They give up.

When they become dissatisfied they empower *reactive dissatisfaction* to hurt them. They grumble, mumble and complain, but keep living a storyline written by others and by circumstances.

As you sharpen your perception and see the world as it really is, you too could be dissatisfied. You might realise all your hard work has been railroading you towards the wrong destination. You could become very dissatisfied. That can be good. It could empower you to achieve greatness. Use dissatisfaction to fuel positive change by transforming it into a *proactive* rather than a *reactive* force. To make this transformation work for you requires *Self-leadership*.

Together they can wrench victory from defeat, a positive from a negative, a challenge from a problem, and success from failure.

Many less successful people recognise they have an urgent need for change but want to achieve it with minimal personal effort. If they attend success seminars they are drawn by the hope of learning the secret of creating wealth quickly—without work.

Like Tom and Mary, they do not empower *proactive dissatisfaction* to change their life for the better. They have not yet reached the point of anguish and frustration in their lives where they have cried 'Enough!'

Violeta Chamorro cried 'Enough!' when the violence that swept her country took her husband's life and threatened anarchy. Never imagining she would be anything but a housewife and mother, she became President of Nicaragua and the first female national leader in the history of Central America.

Professor Fred Hollows cried 'Enough!' when he visited Watti Creek in outback Australia and saw how appalling eye health was among Aborigines. 'Third World stuff! Nineteenth century!' he exclaimed. Two years and 250,000 kilometres later his trachoma program had already made a great difference, benefiting over 100,000 Aborigines. He established eye care hospitals and lens factories in war-torn Eritrea and restored sight to countless people.

Josiah Wedgwood cried 'Enough!' when the father of the woman he loved declared Sarah would never marry a potter from the then nondescript town of Burslem, England. Despite a painful limp, pock-marked face and nothing but years of toil as his heritage, Josiah determined to wed his beloved Sarah and to achieve Personal Excellence.

Eventually he transformed his poverty-afflicted village into a prosperous haven for artisans, was appointed potter to the Queen of England, married Sarah, became known as the finest potter in all England and amassed a fortune. Today 'Wedgwood' is synonymous with finest quality porcelain.

Charles Dickens cried 'Enough!' when his parents were put into a debtors' prison and he had to work under appalling conditions packaging shoe blackener. He never forgot the humility his family endured; nor was the memory of the exploitation of children far from his mind. Through books such as *Oliver Twist* he pricked the conscience of England and changed the world forever. His works have been ranked as second only to those of Shakespeare.

James L. Kraft cried 'Enough!' when his debt-ridden parents could not pay the mortgage on their farm and the bank threatened to foreclose. All young James had was an old horse and some meagre savings. Yet he was determined to achieve success and Personal Excellence. He peddled cheese to pay off his parent's mortgage and built the foundation for the giant Kraft Foods Group.

George Washington Carver cried 'Enough!' when he saw a racist mob beat a black American to death and burn the body in the public square. The son of slaves, George never knew his family. Yet his proactive dissatisfaction with the lot of American blacks inspired him to refuse offers of comfort and wealth so he could advance the cause of his people. Among other things he discovered how to make rubber from peanuts, plastic from soybeans and flour from sweet potatoes. He was known as the wizard of farm chemistry.

Gustav Dalen cried 'Enough!' when he refused to live the storyline of a farmer written for him by his parents. Winner of the Nobel Prize for Physics, he revolutionised lighthouses around the world, saving countless lives.

Jane Addams cried 'Enough!' when she saw for the first time how the poor really lived. Crippled with typhoid, tuberculosis and a curved spine, Jane won a Nobel Peace Prize. She founded Hull House in Chicago's slums and devoted her life to working with the poor.

Florence Nightingale cried 'Enough!' when she saw the shocking conditions of hospital treatment and hygiene. Single-handedly she set about establishing the nursing profession and provided the foundation of today's hospital nursing system.

These are but a few examples of people who achieved success and Personal Excellence through empowering *proactive dissatisfaction*. Every day in your own community there are people who are transforming their future by crying out in anguish 'Enough!', and then doing something about it.

Dr Donald A. Laird, author of *The Technique of Getting Things Done*, discovered that dissatisfaction tied to a specific goal is a powerful incentive to action. The power to change is always within us. It cannot be taken from us unless we surrender it.

Unfortunately, for many people the impetus of dissatisfaction is fleeting. Before long they adjust, they accept, they acquiesce and live the storyline written by others or by circumstances. And that is easy to do.

Just as in a sealed room one gets accustomed to stale air, after a while you don't notice it at all and you forget about it. Eventually you think this is the way it is; you don't believe anything else. You will actually defend it.

All it takes is for a crack to let in a breath of fresh air. Only then do you realise what fresh air is. As a result you become dissatisfied with what you have and yearn to breathe fresh air and freedom.

In City X and in countless cities like it, the barrow people and the stall keepers who stay open 18 hours each day, seven days each week *just to keep themselves in poverty*, may not have the opportunities open to you. Only rarely do they enjoy that breath of fresh air let in by a crack in the wall of their conditioning—of their social system.

They too may become dissatisfied and want to improve their lot—to achieve personal success. But they can only dream about such heights and hope that one or more of their children can do better so they can support them in old age.

In developed countries achieving personal success is so much easier for the vast majority of those prepared to strive for it.

The starting point needs to be an unyielding dissatisfaction with the current situation, the willingness to stop griping about it and the energy to transform dissatisfaction into a powerful, proactive force for change.

Even so, the moment of dissatisfaction alone is not the moment you change your life forever. It is the starter motor that gets your engine for change going.

The moment you change your life forever

It is most likely that the moment you change your life forever will be an experience unique to you.

Realising the importance of creating wealth, of itself, will not bring the moment about. Most humans run deeper than placing all their values on money. We also need social contact, affection, respect, to be appreciated, a sense of importance and more.

Identifying your spheres of life and determining to succeed in all or some of them will not bring the moment of change either. Recognising the various lives you live and the influence you have on those around you is a fine beginning, but not a result.

Gaining accurate perceptions to change your frame of reference is important too, but not of itself because knowledge unapplied is of little value.

Empowering proactive dissatisfaction gets us very close, but dissatisfaction can pass, then we might adjust, acquiesce, accept, surrender. Rounding your life's goal with a mission will provide purpose, direction and self-esteem, but will not be the moment you change your life forever.

As an example, consider the moment when a young man destined to become known throughout the world changed his life forever.

Wearing a smart business suit and a turban he bought a first class rail ticket in 1893 South Africa and took his seat. The burly conductor looked aghast. He demanded the young man go to the third class carriage. When the young man refused, showing the conductor the first class ticket, the conductor threw him bodily from the train.

Angry and frustrated, the young lawyer wanted to leave that country. Then he asked himself the question: 'Should I run away, or stay to fight injustice even though it will mean personal harm?'

Dusting off his suit he walked back to the platform, sat down and waited for the next train. He had *committed* to stay and fight and in so doing changed his life—and the history of South Africa and India—forever. His name? Mohandas Gandhi. He too cried in anguish: 'Enough!'

The moment you begin to change your life forever will follow a sequence of self-discoveries—when they coalesce and enable you to see the big picture. In an instant you *commit,* deep down in your heart, to a set of core values and a path for your life's work that you will follow regardless of the frustrations, setbacks and pain along the way. W. N. Murray of the 1951 Scottish Himalayan Expedition has this to say about commitment:

> *'Until one is committed there is hesitancy, the chance to draw back, always ineffectiveness. Concerning all acts of initiative (and creation) there is one elemental truth, the ignorance of which kills countless ideas and splendid plans.*
>
> *'The moment one definitely commits oneself, then providence moves too. All sorts of things occur to help one that would never otherwise have occurred. A whole stream of events issues from the decision, raising in one's favour all manner of unforeseen incidents and meetings and material assistance, which no man could have dreamt would have come his way.*
>
> *'I have learned a deep respect for one of Goethe's couplets: "Whatever you can do, or dream you can, begin it. Boldness has genius, power and magic in it."'*

The moment you commit to live your life by your own design and in a way that enriches you and the community is the moment you *begin* to change your life forever.

You *want* success! True success! The kind of success that cannot be measured by dollars alone! Intuitively you have recognised that *you* are the major key to your better future—that there is no Aladdin's lamp, tooth fairy or benevolent genie who will give you success because you feel you deserve it.

But do you need to compare yourself to the great men and women of history? Do you need to aim for lofty goals and great deeds? Do you need to become a billionaire entrepreneur before you can say of yourself 'I'm a successful person'?

Frankly, I don't know. And that's because I don't know your specific *Major Life Goal*. The success journey needs to be plotted by individuals according to their own aspirations, dreams, needs and wants. If you want to become the Secretary General of the United Nations, that's fine. If that's what you really want, then that's what your friends and family should also want for you.

On the other hand, if your aspirations are to nurture a happy family life and to provide them with financial and emotional security, that's great! If that's what you want, it's what I want for you too.

In City X a labourer's Major Life Goal might be to devote as much of his monthly pittance as possible to ensuring a university education for one or more of his children and thus break his family's poverty cycle.

If you are not living in a place like City X you have a great advantage in life. You can aim for loftier levels of personal success because through an accident of birth you were given an easier road to travel. You have the wind at your back.

You can write a far more challenging and rewarding storyline and know that, compared to the majority of people in cities like City X, your circumstances will present you with a vastly better opportunity to achieve it.

Yet many people hesitate. The factor that prevents them from living a storyline written by themselves is that parents, society and experience have written a storyline *for* them. They have been conditioned. They are victims of 'conditioning drag'.

Personal success can only begin when *we* write our own storyline and live it through Self-leadership and Personal Excellence. So if you are going to change *your* life forever, when is the best time to start? When will be the right moment? What about right now? Let this be the moment you cry: 'Enough!'

Let now be the moment you commit yourself deeply and wholly to achieving success in all the major spheres of your life. Then *begin* to live it! Because the very moment you *actually begin to live* your own storyline will be the very moment you change your life forever.

KEY POINTS

- We can be 'conditioned' into poverty by society, family or by living a storyline written by others. Success requires Self-leadership. It requires us to burst through 'conditioning drag'.

- Acquiring wealth is essential for financial security. However, of itself it is a hollow achievement unless it is accompanied by health and happiness.

- We face the choice of wealth or poverty daily. Our success depends on the choices that we make—on achieving Personal Excellence.

- Many outwardly successful people succeed only in one or a few spheres of life.

- We all live many lives: a personal life, a family life, a work life, a financial life, a community life, a global life and a spiritual life. How successful do you want to be in each of those? Additionally, we need a sense of mission to provide direction and purpose, especially in our chosen field.

- We need correct perceptions of the world to avoid following the wrong blueprint. A positive mental attitude and motivation will help get us to the wrong place faster unless we have an accurate blueprint. If we change how we see we will change what we see, our attitude and feelings towards it and what we do about it.

- The power of proactive dissatisfaction—of crying 'Enough!'—can be the most powerful impetus for change.

- You are the major key to your better future. There is no Aladdin's lamp, tooth fairy or benevolent genie who will give you success because you feel you deserve it.

- When your self-discoveries converge and you commit—deeply and wholly—to a set of core values and a path for your life's work, the moment you change your life forever will be the moment you take the first step and begin to live the storyline written by you, and only by you.

2

The 'success book of rules'

S UCCESS experiences from 2200 BC to the present era established one overriding truth—there is no secret for achieving success without work. Nature's Law of Growth forbids it.

Other laws of success have been known for millennia. Yet rather than study and apply them, many people choose to suffer the misery of want—to accept, to adjust, to surrender their life to circumstances, and to live by default rather than by design. Is that too far fetched? Let's see.

In a survey by Napoleon Hill of 16,000 American men and women only 5 per cent were regarded as successful. Yet they all had the same government, the same economy, the same language, the same 24 hours per day, and the same weather.

Their world too was bursting with opportunities, ready to welcome anyone who could make a better shoe, dig a better hole, invent a cleaner fuel, think a better thought, write a better book, or make themselves more valuable.

What was the 5 per cent factor that made all the difference? If the survey were carried out today, in which group would it find you?

Are there fewer opportunities for you now than there were before? If you think so, 92 per cent of all scientists who ever walked the Earth would probably disagree with you. How do I know? Because 92 per cent of all scientists who ever lived are alive today! Such is the promise of the future!

Yet only a few people see gold where many see only rock and hard work! What are the secrets of success that make the difference between triumph and defeat, wealth and poverty, and success and failure?

Is there a 'book of rules' for success? A set of laws enabling all to succeed to their fullest potential? In ancient Greece they got it down to seven 'Pillars of Wisdom':

■   Know thyself (Euclid).
■   Look to the end of life (Chilo).
■   Seize occasion (Pittacus).
■   The mean is best (Cleobulus).
■   The most of men are evil (Bias).
■   In industry is all (Periander).
■   Haste, if thou woulds't fail (Thales).

Thomas J. Watson, founder of IBM, tried to help his employees succeed by inspiring them to:

> *'. . . think, observe, discuss, listen.'*

He had these injunctions printed on the steps of the IBM office so they would be seen every day.

Whether you are lucky enough to live in a developed country with its myriad opportunities, or in a place like City X with its far greater challenges and obstacles, the fundamentals for personal success are the same.

You need to know these fundamentals because, taken as a whole, they could be said to form a 'book of success rules'. If you know the rules for achieving and maintaining a life of personal success you can avoid the pain of failure. Eventually you might want to form your own 'book of rules', which might include some or all the rules shown here. That will be a great moment for you. It will mark the moment when you will have truly arrived as a strong leader of self.

Susan Mitchell, Australian author of *Tall Poppies* and *Tall Poppies Too*, says of the women leaders she has studied:

> *'What really unites them is a common framework for viewing themselves and the world.'*

They too have a set of 'rules' in common, even if not written down. They learned them through the college of experience, where the fees are very high.

The following success 'rules' provide vital roadsigns for anyone embarking on a personal success journey. You don't have to *like* the rules. But I believe you would be wise to know them.

The 30 'rules' for success

Rule 1   Know the formula for success

Rule 2   Determine your specific Major Life Goal

Rule 3   Identify the areas in which you want success

Rule 4   Define what success means for you

Rule 5   Understand the laws of growth and change

Rule 6   Put in that extra effort

Rule 7   Use nature's law of increasing returns

Rule 8   Apply Self-leadership

Rule 9   Develop a pleasant personality

Rule 10   Apply clear, accurate thinking

Rule 11   Develop co-operation and synergy

Rule 12   Know you can't fail

Rule 13   Be tolerant of others

Rule 14   Show a humane regard for people

Rule 15   Think and apply a win–win philosophy

Rule 16   Manage time effectively

Rule 17   Put quality in, get quality out

Rule 18   Turn your back on 'excusitis'

Rule 19   See difficulties as opportunities

Rule 20   Prevent erosion of achievement

Rule 21   Accept that you are the only one who can succeed for you

Rule 22   Be prepared for success

Rule 23   Have specific reasons for wanting success

Rule 24   Think and see yourself how you want to be

Rule 25   Be happy

Rule 26   Use it or lose it

Rule 27   Anticipate and prepare for tough times

Rule 28   Save and invest

Rule 29   Nurture a positive world view

Rule 30   Tap into your spiritual strength

Rule 1: Know the formula for success

The formula for achieving and maintaining holistic success is:

$$S \;=\; \frac{Asl^2}{PE}$$

where S equals Success, A equals Attitude, sl equals Self-leadership and PE equals Personal Excellence. So, the formula is Success equals Attitude times Self-leadership squared over Personal Excellence.

The emphasis is on the power of Self-leadership—on doing things, because *success does not depend on our ability to follow or to lead others, but on our ability to lead ourselves into positive action.* It includes the ability to self-discipline and to self-reward. It takes us out of the passenger seat and places us at the steering wheel.

We need not wait to be prodded or cajoled, or forced or threatened. We take our own lead. We manage our own day-to-day business. We accept the responsibility for setting and achieving our own goals.

Some people find Self-leadership the most difficult part of the personal success formula. This is not surprising because it demands organisation, energy, application, courage, and working to a specific Major Life Goal. But if you love what you do, deeply believe in what you do and are wholly committed to it, Self-leadership will be a pleasure, not a task.

The biggest challenge of success is more than running our own business, and more than earning independence and wealth. It means accepting responsibility for our own life and, having done so, fulfilling the promise of our better future.

The other major determinant for attaining holistic success is Personal Excellence. Without this quality you might *accomplish* (i.e. obtain wealth), but what is the good of wealth without personal honour, health and happiness?

Rule 2: Determine your specific Major Life Goal

Do you remember the time in your teens when the world was a place to conquer? There were dreams to fulfil. Energy was boundless. Nothing was impossible. You were going to live forever!

Given the same feelings and the knowledge that you couldn't fail, what *could* you be? Forget difficulty. Forget present constraints. Let your mind soar. What *could* you be?

What happened to the dream? To the teenager who was full of hope for the future? What were your detours? Are you doing what you want to do? If income were not a consideration, what would you be doing instead? What *could* you be?

The Australian biographer of *Montgomery*, Alan Moorehead, refused to continue along a detour from his Major Life Goal. Early in his life he decided to become a writer. However, he felt pressured to study law and even paid for his university education by selling freelance stories.

Realising that becoming a lawyer was a detour he decided not to sit for his final exam—making that decision the day before it was to be held. Instead he accepted a post as a journalist to develop his writing skills. He achieved his specific Major Life Goal.

People who know what they want achieve it despite the storyline others might have written for them. (When I left school, my mother's great hope for me was that I should 'learn a trade'.)

Michelangelo's father beat him because he wanted to be a sculptor and painter. Playwright Henrik Ibsen was intended to be a chemist; Isaac Newton was meant to be a farmer; Rubens was meant to be a lawyer; Nikola Tesla and Charles Darwin were meant to be priests . . . and so the list goes on.

Find a dream. What *could* you be? Write a clear, concise statement of your mission in life. Write it down! Know what you want, when you want it, why you want it, how you plan to achieve it and what you are prepared to do (discipline) to get it.

Here is an example of a specific Major Life Goal:

'By my fifty-fifth birthday, to own my house, buy a house for each of my children, have $1 million to invest so I can live comfortably on the interest, and to devote my remaining years to work in my local community in aged-care programs.'

To achieve such a Major Life Goal would require a number of steps or sub-goals. It might require further education, setting up a business, earning constant promotion up the corporate ladder, and so on, to generate the type of income necessary to make it all possible.

Here is another example:

'To make a breakthrough in the treatment of Multiple Sclerosis

leading directly to a cure by the time I reach my sixtieth birthday.'

This Major Life Goal would require a great deal of education, training, experimentation and hard work. Breaking the mission into steps would make its achievement much more likely, and easier.

Here is a final example:

'By my sixty-fifth birthday to have written and published 10 books that will contribute to obtaining equality for women in developing countries.'

As for the previous goals, this too will require preparation and planning. Firstly, there is an interim income requirement. What type of work will give the income you need with the free time required to research and produce such a body of work?

For the majority of people a specific Major Life Goal does not go much further than financial security in old age. This too can be limited to a modest house and an age pension. However this goal is not sufficiently inspiring to motivate them to achieve those things their abilities will allow. Indeed, unless we test ourselves we rarely can determine what we are capable of achieving.

The idea of a Major Life Goal is to set your sights on achieving something that will give you a great sense of satisfaction and accomplishment when you get there, and purpose and direction in the meantime. Without a Major Life Goal, where are you heading?

So many people limit their life's purpose to their work that when that work is taken away they become lost. This is because they do not see their work as only one means of achieving a higher, personal goal—that is, a Major Life Goal.

Even 'average' people can find a goal worth striving for. We do not all have to achieve great deeds and noble purposes to justify our existence. However it needs to be said that the goals that provide the most satisfaction are those that benefit others as well as enriching ourselves. For example, a humble factory worker can aim for a more modest financial security goal while working in the Scout movement, for a charity or for homeless youth. This person's Major Life Goal could easily be expressed as:

'By age 65, to own my house, have enough money put aside to augment my age pension and to have raised $1 million for homeless youth in my community.'

For others their Major Life Goal could be that, by retirement at age (65?) to own their house, to have money set aside for investment and to have travelled to (one or more specific countries). That too will require planning, money management and preparation.

Most people don't have a Major Life Goal because they don't know what they want to achieve with their lives. For so many, their thinking rarely extends past their immediate needs for money and entertainment. Consequently they can rarely get enough money to satisfy their needs.

The idea that they should aim at achieving something specific with their lives, then set goals and plan to reach them, rarely occurs to them. When it does, it frightens them. They don't know where they are going, and so any road will take them there.

Goals are simply a road map. It charts your journey one achievement at a time. The sum of those achievements can be your specific Major Life Goal.

My Major Life Goal is that by my fifty-fifth birthday I will have acquired $5 million to enable me to devote the rest of my life to helping people—particularly young people—achieve *holistic* success.

My sub-goals in the meantime? This book is one of them. I also make available personal development programs to individuals and to companies, hold seminars, train managers and employees alike in my own country and overseas and generally am progressing towards my Major Life Goal one success at a time.

To achieve even that which I have already, I have had to outline my specific goals and work towards them. That's how I know what to accept or to reject. That is, I reject any work or business opportunity that does not contribute to the achievement of my Major Life Goal.

Some people say that goal setting does not work for them. But that's not because setting goals is a waste of energy—quite the contrary. It's mostly because they set goals that, deep in their hearts, they don't want to achieve. Or they set goals related to their job which, in the majority of cases, they would rather not be doing.

A Major Life Goal that sets you ablaze with enthusiasm will empower your life with the might of purpose.

If you don't have a Major Life Goal you'll be part of someone else's plan for theirs. Can you guess how much someone else will provide for you?

Clearly, a happy and balanced life is enjoyed by people who live a storyline written by themselves. A happy ending is the achievement of your Major Life Goal. A happy journey is enjoying the process, savouring each achievement and relishing each step that takes you closer to where *you* want to go. (There is a Life Blueprint in Chapter 14 that will help you determine and plan your specific Major Life Goal.)

Rule 3: Identify the areas in which you want success

To be attained, success must be defined for each sphere of your life. What specific success do you want to achieve in your:

- *Personal life?* This is your own private life. What do you want for you? It includes personal, private goals as well as your program for relaxation, maintenance of health and personal growth.
- *Family life?* What type of family life do you want? It is not enough to say 'A happy family'. What are you prepared to do to achieve it? What activities will you set aside for them? What will you contribute? What are you prepared to give up? What standard of living will you provide? How much of your time will you devote to them each day? Who will come first—work or family? These are issues you will need to consider.
- *Community life?* No one lives in a vacuum. Our own health, safety and standard of living depend on the standards and resources of the community that nurtures us. How will you support your community? In what areas will you be active in fostering its well being?
- *Business/work life?* So many people place the major part of their effort, energy and devotion to this sphere of life that often they wreck their family life in doing it. What do you want to achieve in business? How far up the corporate tower do you want to climb? What limits will you set?
- *Financial life?* We all want financial independence, yet few achieve it. The paradox is that most of us will earn a fortune in our lifetime. What goals will you set? What yearly income will you want and at what age?

  How far are you prepared to go in getting the money you want? How will you manage the money you earn to ensure it grows?

■ *Global life?* In the globalisation of humankind new issues are emerging. Our increasing numbers are threatening life on the planet. In developed countries our continued prosperity depends in large part on the markets in developing countries. We need to accept individual responsibility and to play a part, regardless of how small, in setting things right for the sake of present and future generations.

We need to conserve, recycle and become active in helping peoples in developing countries increase their prosperity, because in doing so they will not need to destroy forests and will be more able to control their population growth. How will you play your part?

■ *Spiritual life?* Many successful men and women have gained enormous strength and support in achieving their personal success objectives. They achieved this through connection with their spiritual dimension.

Yet many 'modern' people scoff at the idea. Each of us needs to examine this sphere of life and come to our own conclusions. However if there is a power that will help you achieve holistic success (health, wealth *and* happiness) wouldn't you want to know it?

Rule 4: Define what success means for you

Defining success is not as simple as it might appear to someone whose concept of it is limited to money. To some, success can mean freedom from mortgages and debts; freedom to buy what they need whenever they need it; freedom to help others; and freedom to change jobs.

The great H. G. Wells held that:

'Wealth, notoriety, place or power are no measure of success whatever. The only true measure of success is the ratio between what one might have been and done on one hand, and the thing we have made and made of ourselves on the other.'

For example, to Mother Teresa success might mean living a life of service to the poor and needy.

How would you define success? If you don't have a clear idea of what it is, how will you know when you have it? How will you know to achieve it?

In forming our personal definition of success we need to acknowledge that success is not a future event, nor is it a destination. The holistic view is that:

'Success is in Life as it is lived. It is a perpetual "now".'

For example, what is the point of accumulating wealth to age 65, retiring and virtually waiting for . . . what? The holistic philosophy maintains that success is a dynamic of life. It must be, or we would still be living in trees. Success grows with each achievement throughout life. It does not simply fall into place at some single, distant point.

You are living success to your individual extent right now. By wanting 'success' you probably mean that you want to increase the level of success you have already.

Rule 5: Understand the laws of growth and change

The Qur'an (Koran) equates personal success with personal growth. A property of growth is sequence. For example: you must be a baby before you can be a child; or you must be a child before you can be an adult. The law of growth affects all living things. It also affects our understanding and provides us with knowledge, experience and maturity of judgment.

Can total knowledge be acquired in an instant? If a person were kept in a totally dark room for years and the blind were suddenly lifted, would not the glare of sunlight daze that person? Is it not more effective to lift the blind little by little so the light can be absorbed gradually?

We all grow at different rates. We need to 'fail' several times before we begin to succeed (as in learning to walk). We grow through trial, error and success. We acquire knowledge through experience and study—all of which takes time.

As success is a process of living, some people will succeed more quickly than will others. It is nonsense to be crest-fallen over the fact that at 30 years of age you might not have achieved the success you want. The law of growth affects everyone differently.

Measure success against the progress you have made since your last measure—not against someone else's achievements.

Linked to the law of growth is the law of change. Did you ever consider the many bodies in which you have lived? You lived in a seven year old body; a teenager's body; and there is the body in which you live now. Without change you would stay as helpless as you were at birth.

To life's certainties of death and taxes we could add change as another sure bet. Change occurs in every sphere of life. Many of the opinions you held as a child might have changed. You change your mind, your clothes, your car, your school and house.

One would think that having practised and lived through change all our lives, we would respond to change in a positive manner. Yet only a minority adapt to and succeed through change. Most people cope and survive while about a third of those affected go under.

This is quite surprising when you consider that we ask for change when we ask for more success. The key to succeeding through change, therefore, must lie in how we choose to respond. The thing to remember is: It's only change.

Tragically, Mick T. could not cope with sudden change. He had worked as a truck driver in the Melbourne Water Works for 15 years. His wife and friends say that his work was his life. Shortly after he received a redundancy notice, he committed suicide.

Change does not always bring good. Whenever it comes with whatever it portends, we can choose either to respond or to react to it. (There is a world of difference. When we go to a doctor we can respond to the treatment and get better, or react to it and get worse.)

A successful formula for dealing with change is:

- Acknowledge that change is coming.
- Accept the change that is coming your way.
- Look for the opportunities that change will bring.
- Achieve that change and profit from its opportunities by helping to drive the process.

When I was consulting in Hong Kong during 1994 there was a great expectation of change. Since the British colony was to revert to China in 1997, some citizens were so apprehensive about that prospect that they emigrated. Others remained, but to hedge their bets they squirrelled much of their wealth in investments abroad.

However the majority saw only opportunity and transformed Hong Kong into a place for manufacturing wealth. Virtually swimming in billions of investment dollars, full employment and seemingly unlimited potential, the Hong Kong miracle left the weaker Western economies gasping in its wake.

The people who succeeded were those who acknowledged that change was coming, looked for the opportunities and helped steer the process in the direction that would benefit themselves and Hong Kong.

Of course, some change can be disastrous (e.g. to health or the environment). However it's important to know the difference between fighting change for a noble cause and resisting it because it will dislodge you from your comfort zone.

Don't count yourself among those who think that progress would be wonderful 'if only it would stop!' Life itself is movement. The whole universe is in motion. Nothing stands still—not even rocks. To live means to live with change.

Rule 6: Put in that extra effort

The reward for making that extra effort is opportunity. Decide how hard you should work—eight hours per day five days per week? Six days per week? 12 hours per day? You must decide for yourself. This decision will form a vital part of your personal success philosophy.

Kemmons Wilson, the founder of Holiday Inns, never graduated from high school. Addressing students at a graduation ceremony he said:

> *'I really don't know why I'm here. I never got a degree, and I've only worked half days my entire life. I guess my advice to you is to do the same. Work half days every day. And it doesn't matter which half . . . the first 12 hours or the second 12 hours.'*

Over 75 per cent of millionaires in the United States are people who have worked six to seven days per week, up to 10–12 hours per day for 20–30 years. It is the effort they have been willing to make for financial success.

Arguably the world's most versatile genius, Leonardo Da Vinci, had it all worked out centuries ago with this prayer:

'O Lord, You give us everything for the price of effort.'

The famous French artist Toulouse-Lautrec insisted on supervising every phase of printing his works. After a night out he would sleep in a cab outside the print shop waiting for it to open so he could be on hand to ensure the work was done to his satisfaction. That's extra effort!

Rule 7: Use nature's law of increasing returns

Sow one grain of wheat and it brings forth a bushel; sow one apple seed and it produces an orchard. That's how life works. But the law of increasing returns applies to negative as well as to positive sowing. If you are the type who lives in the past, resists change, hands out bad news or 'pukes' your problems onto others, your negativity will come back to you a hundredfold.

Negative sowers are morale saboteurs. They are masters at transferring their conditioning drag onto others. Over time others lose respect for them, enjoy themselves more and are happier when they're not around.

With whom are you associating? What are you letting them do to you? What are you becoming? Associate with people who have high expectations of their future. Sow positive thoughts so you harvest a bounty of respect, recognition, achievement and reward. Do it with enthusiasm, cheerfulness and a positive mental attitude.

Rule 8: Apply Self-leadership

E. M. Gray spent most of his life looking for the one denominator common to all successful people. To paraphrase what he said:

'Successful people have the habit of doing things failures don't like to do, of leading themselves to do them.'

All great leaders are great Self-leaders. Successful people might not like to do everything they have to do, but their dislike is subordinated to their strength of purpose.

Self-leadership includes adherence to a set of values and code of behaviour. It is also thought control, emotion control and laziness control. There is excitement in the ability to make ourselves do things, especially those things we thought we could never do.

Many well-known people had to learn to lead themselves before they could become successful. One method that has worked well for them is to set a daily goal. Author W. Somerset Maugham declared:

> *'Wherever I've gone and whatever I've done I have kept in mind that each day I must write from 1000 to 1500 words.'*

Emile Zola's motto for Self-leadership was:

> *'Not a day without a line.'*

Scientist Sir Thomas Huxley believed that:

> *'Duty is to the thing we ought to do, at the time we ought to do it, whether we feel like doing it or not.'*

Famous composer Rossini had himself locked in for three days to force himself to write the opera *Othello*.

The great Russian composer, Tchaikovsky, said:

> *'One cannot afford to sit waiting for inspiration; she is a guest that does not visit the lazy, but comes only to those who call her. Very often one must first conquer laziness and lack of inclination.'*

Even talent needs strong Self-leadership to learn how it can be used. Famed tenor Luciano Pavarotti told Dr Germaine Greer that it takes him three years to learn a role. He vocalises throughout the day before a performance.

Self-leadership gets us moving whether we feel like it or not. How can you learn if you can't lead yourself? How can you persist? How can you be single-minded in achieving your goals?

Ray Kroc, founder of the McDonald's Corporation, says:

'The essential factor that lifts one man above his fellows in terms of achievement and success is his capacity for greater self-discipline.'

If you can't lead yourself you'll be led by others.

Rule 9: Develop a pleasant personality

Studies in the United States suggest that 10 seconds is all it takes to form a first opinion of someone new—55 per cent of this opinion is based on what we wear; 37 per cent on body language and attitude, and only 7 per cent on what we actually say.

Our character, the clothes we wear, our facial expressions, the way we smile and shake hands—all help to create an impression. There must be hundreds of thousands of people who have little or no idea what is in their insurance policies. They bought the sales-person's personality as much as they bought anything else.

If people like you, they will be more likely to help you. A pleasant personality is the key to rapport. Taking a 'human interest' in other people's welfare is its cornerstone. Buddha's view was that:

'To conquer oneself is a greater task than conquering others.'

Rule 10: Apply clear, accurate thinking

Not that long ago people believed steel ships couldn't float; that only birds could fly; that if a train sped at 30 kilometres per hour passengers would suffocate; and that London would be made impassable by 'mountains' of horse droppings. Other examples of unclear thinking are:

■ blaming others or circumstances for our own shortcomings ('excusitis')
■ waiting for others to lead us instead of leading ourselves
■ wishing things were easier, instead of making ourselves better

- wanting fewer challenges instead of developing more skills to handle them
- wanting to be a millionaire without first becoming a thousandaire
- saying things cost too much, instead of admitting we can't afford that ·

Clear, accurate thinking is vital to success. Here are some tips:

- learn to separate facts from information
- deal only with relevant facts
- don't exaggerate or over-react
- don't act on gossip
- look for evidence before drawing conclusions
- question everything, including your own assumptions
- concentrate your effort and thought.

I have a young friend who is a computer programmer and talented in a variety of other fields. However he suffers from an attraction to detours. He wants to live in Japan for 12 months so he can further his study of martial arts, and is in the process of selling his house to fund that aim. He is also studying the Japanese language to make his mission easier.

In the meantime he 'does cars up', assembles computers, writes programs (he has been writing a small program for me for two years and it is still not finished), holds down a very busy job, builds Japanese gardens, assembles model aeroplanes, and so on. In and around his home are the skeletal remains of many 'projects in progress'.

Were he to focus his considerable energy, enthusiasm and skill on one project until it is finished, there would be no holding this man back. However, he constantly succumbs to detours and unless he learns to concentrate his effort and thought he will be unlikely to achieve his full potential.

The way of personal success also has many side roads and detours. They can take the form of job offers with more pay. If you don't concentrate your effort towards your Major Life Goal you could easily fall for the temptation of a job that leads you away from it—a detour with more pay, but a detour!

Charles Goodyear worked for 10 years to find a way of vulcanising rubber. Despite poverty and hardship he refused to take any detours.

Napoleon Bonaparte said:

'When you have an enterprise on hand concentrate upon it wholly; forget that anything else in the world exists.'

Learn to focus your mind on the issues at hand until you .ecide on a definite course. Make thought concentration a habit. You'll develop an increased ability to solve problems, see weaknesses in arguments and possibly save thousands of dollars by avoiding errors.

Years ago Russell Conwell made $6 million dollars from one lecture, 'Acres of Diamonds'. On concentration he says:

'Whatever you have to do at all, put your whole mind into it and hold it there until that is all done. This principle can be adopted by nearly all . . . This principle makes men great almost anywhere.'

Victorious General Ulysses S. Grant would spend hours hunched over his desk thinking about his military strategies. It was said that his concentration was so complete that if he needed a document from somewhere else in his room he would walk over to fetch it without straightening up and return to his desk—all the while maintaining the same posture.

Rule 11: Develop co-operation and synergy

Co-operation makes organised effort possible and creates synergy—that unique phenomenon where 2 + 2 can equal 8, or 50, or 100. Synergy is where the total of the whole is greater than the sum of its parts.

You have probably experienced it many times—perhaps at a meeting or in a field trip where you had to surmount an obstacle. Everyone contributed and came up with a better solution than any individual could have found alone.

In his life study of success Napoleon Hill struggled to identify this phenomenon. He called it 'The Master Mind Alliance' and gave it an almost spiritual quality. He found that when people gather in a spirit of harmony to solve a problem for the common good, a 'Master Mind' formed that was greater than the sum of each individual mind.

The truth is that to succeed we need the co-operation of other people. The synergy of personal success within a group results from the willing co-operation of its members. Without co-operation work could be transformed into chaos through 'malicious obedience'. This happens when staff do not use their judgment in how they apply instructions. They interpret everything literally then say 'That's what you told me to do.' Genuine interest in people's welfare and a sympathetic appreciation of their viewpoint helps greatly to win co-operation.

Rule 12: Know you can't fail

There is no such thing as failure, only outcome. We gain from every experience and grow stronger and wiser from every defeat.
  Henry Ford said:

'Failure is the chance to start again more intelligently.'

Many people are so afraid of failure they never get started. Yet Thomas Edison 'failed' almost 10,000 times before he was able to make his new invention, the gramophone, play the words 'Mary had a little lamb'. His reply was:

'I didn't fail 9999 times. I discovered 9999 ways it wouldn't work.'

Sir Henry Parkes 'failed' many times. He was bankrupted three times, having to sell his tools as an ivory turner to buy food. He emigrated from England to Australia where he worked as a labourer and generally proved to be totally inept in business. Yet he became an accomplished politician, the premier of New South Wales and father of Australian Federation.
  Author Leon Uris 'failed' his English examination three times. Abraham Lincoln was thought a failure when he entered the Black Hawk war as a captain, but came out a private.
  No one is a failure. Everyone succeeds to some extent. For example, you might earn $35,000 per year. You have been successful to the extent of $35,000 per year. However what you might want is to increase the extent of your success to earn more.

It is pointless determining success by comparison with others because there will always be someone more and someone less successful than yourself. It is far better to measure your success against your previous successes. For example, by earning more this year than last year you have increased your success in the financial sphere of life. Napoleon Hill discovered there are few, if any, successful people on Earth who have not 'failed' many times before they began to succeed. Setbacks merely defer success. We have to be around when that later time comes. We can't be around if we quit.

Rule 13: Be tolerant of others

Time shows that much of what we hold true is false, based on incomplete knowledge or on misunderstanding.

An extreme case of intolerance is found in the saga of Australian explorer Robert O'Hara Burke. Dying of starvation as he proceeded along the bed of Cooper's Creek towards Mount Hopeless, he refused food from friendly Aborigines because he regarded them as 'below his station'. Consequently he and fellow explorer, William John Wills, perished. Their companion, a more sensible man named King, accepted the food and survived.

Dr Samuel Johnson said:

> *'If God Himself does not propose to judge a man until the end of his days, how can I?'*

Rule 14: Show a humane regard for people

US billionaire George Soros is probably the greatest single contributor to humanitarian causes. His contributions to organisations in Eastern Europe alone totalled over US$700 million in 1994.

He earns US$2 million a day, and gives it all away to charities, needy causes and freedom movements. In an interview with QTQ9 television on 22 December 1993, he said:

> *'I see it [wealth] as a kind of obligation to use that money in a socially useful way . . . I care about what I stand for while I'm alive.'*

Was he born into wealth? Far from it. He was a Jewish refugee from Hungary who emigrated to the United States and succeeded through hard work, investment skill, Self-leadership and Personal Excellence.

Andrew Carnegie was a great humanitarian. After his death a note stating his Major Life Goal was found. It read:

'To spend half my life accumulating wealth and the other half in giving it away.'

He succeeded in giving away what would amount to billions of dollars in today's value. We who do not have such great wealth can apply their philosophy in a more modest way. Whatever we do, we can ask ourselves:

'How will my actions in achieving my Major Life Goal create a win–win situation for myself and for others?'

You might remember the story of a man who wanted money so much he betrayed his best friend to get it. In the end he bitterly regretted his action, but what he had become could not be erased by the money his betrayal had earned. He lost his self-respect. Instead of happiness his treasure brought misery and despair.

He tried to return the money, but those who paid him quickly rebuked him: 'You got what you wanted and we got what we wanted. So keep your blood money.' He threw the money away but it was too late. Within a few days he hanged himself from a tree. His name? Judas Iscariot.

Holistic success means achieving our goal without compromising Personal Excellence (integrity, honour, self-respect), and without causing harm to others. How can we achieve this unless our goal is obtained in a way that serves others honestly and creates opportunities also for them?

Rule 15: Think and apply a win–win philosophy

In the words of Stephen R. Covey:

'Win–win is not a technique, it is a total philosophy of human interaction. To win doesn't have to mean "to beat".'

If others don't win when we do, what sort of community will we create? Here's a glimpse:

■ In Rio de Janeiro, and other cities like it, wealthy citizens barricade themselves behind high walls. Some employ armed guards to protect themselves from their own community. Is that win–win? Is that success?

■ In Bophal, the environment is so polluted that life expectancy is drastically cut and community health has been described as a disaster. Why? Because some locally based multinationals strive for dollar success despite the enormous damage they inflict on the world—and people—around them. Is that success?

■ In City X, cigarette companies have no restrictions on advertising. Faced with a declining market in developed countries they peddle their affliction in a manner that will appeal to the young, knowing that if people don't take up the habit by age 21, they will not be smokers.

The result is that some 90 per cent of men in City X are smokers. They smoke standing, walking, eating, in lifts—at every chance they get. In City X cigarettes are cheap. So is life.

What kind of society do we create when we allow greedy multinationals to damage the health of our young? Yet the executives of those companies will pride themselves on increasing market share and no doubt will regard themselves as successful people.

But is that win–win? Is it Personal Excellence when you know that according to the Word Health Organization, six million people will die of smoking-related diseases by the year 2000 because of your product?

Personally we might not be able to do very much for Rio, Bophal or City X, but we can embrace and apply a win–win philosophy in our personal totem (i.e. the code by which to live).

Rule 16: Manage time effectively

We've all met perpetually busy people who gasp: 'If only I had more time!' But regardless of what we do, beg, steal or borrow, 24 hours a day is all we are entitled to and all we get. So doesn't it make sense to manage it?

A national cliche of the people in City X is that: 'Time is elastic.' Few people attend appointments on time. Often they arrive hours late, causing delay and a chain of disruption right across the business and private community.

Time certainly is not elastic where results are required. And the world requires results, not cliches.

We are paid for what we achieve with time. The more value time we put in, the higher our income. If we want more income, we need to become more valuable. When you get your next 24 hour ration, how much of it will you convert to value time? How much of it will you control? How much of it will control you?

Rule 17: Put quality in, get quality out

Your mind is a vast, wonderful library. It stores information that you and others put into it. It employs a faithful 'librarian'. When you want to recall a fact or feeling your librarian will sift through many years of data to make it available to you.

However faithful and efficient your librarian might be, it can only retrieve what you have collected. If you put quality in, your mental 'librarian' will get quality out!

Consider the TV you watch and the books you read. Ask yourself:

> *'Is this information I am storing in my mental library positive or negative? Will it help me achieve wealth, health and happiness?'*

Rule 18: Turn your back on 'excusitis'

Accurate knowledge, when organised and applied, is the fuel that powers our modern world. Success or the lack of it results from the choices we make based on the knowledge we have.

To apply knowledge takes Self-leadership, effort, energy and determination. Simply knowing how to be successful will not make you so unless you lead yourself to achieve it.

How many people do you know who have a wooden leg (a ready excuse for not trying)? They say they are too old, too ill, too unschooled, don't know how, and so on. They might have 'excusitis', the affliction of low-achievers. Here are some common forms of excuse, and some people who turned their back on 'excusitis':

■ *Excuse: Too old*. After 26 years in a South African prison, Nelson Mandela continued to lead his people's struggle for freedom. As secretary of the African People's Congress he led South Africa—blacks and whites—to their first democratic election and became the first black president of his country. His age at the time? 75 years.

Konrad Adenauer was Chancellor of West Germany. Under his leadership West Germany became an economic giant, rebuilt its defence force and provided a cornerstone for European unity. He began his 14 year term of office at age 73.

Dr Dennis Wheatley, sports psychologist, author, motivator and speaker admitted he didn't get started until he was 45. Abraham Lincoln didn't begin to succeed in the presidential stakes until he was over 50. J. P. Morgan—the power in world finance—made his vast fortune after 60. Miguel De Cervantes, author of *Don Quixote*, didn't do anything of any substance until after he was 48.

Leonardo Da Vinci was over 60 when he painted the *Mona Lisa*. P. T. Barnum, the great circus owner and showman, didn't start his circus until he was over 60. President Woodrow Wilson was still a college professor at 50. Aristotle, one of the world's great philosophers, started his work at 50.

■ *Excuse: Too ill*. Professor Fred Hollows helped save the sight of countless thousands of people even though he was suffering from cancer.

Chopin suffered from severe lung disease. Despite his illness, which amounted to a slow death, he wrote preludes, fantasies, waltzes and ballads that have enriched the world forever.

Frederick Schiller, a consummate poet, was devastated by illness when aged 30. He was in constant pain, weak and breathed with difficulty because one lung was stuck to his chest wall, yet he worked 14 hours each day on happy hymns and beautiful poetry.

Julius Caesar, William of Orange, William Van Loon (painter), William Pitt (British prime minister), James Watt, Sir Walter Scott—all were debilitated by constant, severe headaches. Countless others also achieved greatness by writing their own storyline despite personal suffering—such as poet Alexander Pope, composer Sir Arthur Sullivan, and writers Eugene O'Neill, Robert Louis Stevenson and Helen Keller.

■ *Excuse: No place to work.* Johann Strauss wrote waltzes while eating at a restaurant. Harriet Beecher Stowe, author of *Uncle Tom's Cabin*, wrote while working in her kitchen.

Founder of the Methodist Church and charismatic preacher John Wesley wrote his sermons as he walked. Marie Curie used a store room in a basement for her early experiments on uranium.

The father of bacteriology and Nobel Prize winner Robert Koch carried out experiments on his front porch because he had no room in his house. Charles Goodyear experimented with vulcanising rubber while in prison for being unable to pay his debts. Marco Polo wrote his *Travels* while in prison.

Giorgio Vassari reminds us:

'No man distinguishes himself in any art who is not ready to beat the cold, heat, hunger and thirst. He who imagines that he can become great by taking his ease in pleasant surroundings is much mistaken.'

Apparently Dr Henry Wieman didn't agree with him. It was said of Dr Wieman by Howard Crago in *Spare a Minute*:

'Wishing to improve his intellectual life, he procured a large, comfortable chair, slippers and cosy jacket. A book rest was attached to his chair to hold the book under a special reading lamp at the correct angle before his eyes. A revolving bookcase stood alongside.

'He equipped himself with pens, paper and eyeshade. After the evening meal he would come into the study, put on his jacket and slippers, adjust the lamp and place the book on its rest.

'When everything was arranged, he would recline in the chair with eyeshade over his eyes and . . . go to sleep!'

■ *Excuse: Too broke.* Before she achieved international success,

Madonna, the undisputed Pop Queen of the 1990s, often had to borrow money just to buy enough food to survive.

The woman who built one of the world's great business houses, Coco Chanel, was raised in poverty. So were Pierre Cardin and Rudolph Nureyev.

Famous author and humanist Emile Zola lived mostly on sparrows that he caught and roasted on the end of a curtain rod. Vincent Van Gogh, Mozart, George Washington Carver, Andrew Carnegie and countless others achieved the life they designed for themselves even though, initially, they were broke.

One of America's great businesspeople, former chairman of IBM Thomas J. Watson Jr, said of his father, the founder of IBM, in *Father, Son and Co.* that he:

'. . . *was once reduced to sleeping on a pile of sponges in the basement of a drugstore. He had only one suit to his name, and when he could afford to get it pressed he had to wait in the back of the tailor shop in his underwear until it was ready.*'

(He rose to become the most highly paid man in America.)

I know a talented young architect in City X who dreamed of building a business empire. Aged 21 he borrowed $9000 to start his first business. Only nine years later he controls a group of companies that turns over $200 million per year. Despite the comparative difficulties of life in City X his is a success story that would be the envy of many entrepreneurs anywhere.

■ *Excuse: Not schooled.* Neither were the great bulk of the world's achievers. Schooling might get you a job, but self-education can make you rich!

If you lack schooling you have joined the famous company of Jesus, Thomas Jefferson, Benjamin Franklin, Thomas Edison, Henry Ford and many thousands of others who didn't have enough 'schooling'. They taught themselves because they were Self-leaders.

In the end excusitis is a 'wooden leg'—a reason to excuse lack of effort. Every day in many ways 'ordinary' men and women are turning their backs on excusitis.

It takes a specific Major Life Goal built on Personal Excellence, a determination to succeed, a blueprint for achieving the life you want, heartfelt commitment to take the steps that will change your life forever and the Self-leadership to get it done.

Rule 19: See difficulties as opportunities

In 1979 the Arab oil exporters initiated a world economic crisis through massive increases in the price of crude oil. Among the countries worst affected was Japan, who imported 85 per cent of its oil from the Middle East. Overnight, there was panic. Japan's trading position worsened instantly and it seemed the crisis would devastate its economy.

The government took immediate steps. It launched a nationwide economy drive to reduce its use of energy. It restructured its economy and replaced old technology with new, energy-efficient and productive equipment. It launched whole-heartedly into automation and became the first to use industrial robots to build cars.

The result? Japan converted enormous difficulty into great opportunity. The economy's restructure and automation transformed Japan into an economic superpower. So complete was Japan's success that when a similar price hike was inflicted on the world some years later, its economy hardly missed a beat. The crisis was only opportunity dressed as difficulty.

Josiah Wedgewood experienced great difficulty. As a result of his limp (which led to amputation) he could not turn the potter's wheel so he experimented with vases, plates, cameos and fine quality porcelain. Eventually a statue was erected in his honour, unveiled by Prime Minister William Gladstone who travelled from London to Burslem to honour a 'common potter'.

Opening new doors is not difficult when you have the keys. Ann Landers said that:

> *'Opportunities are usually disguised as hard work, so most people don't recognise them.'*

Opportunity searches for people who are prepared for it and moves on when it does not find them.

Popular singer Engelbert Humperdinck's opportunity to achieve stardom came when Alec Fyne, Head of Light Entertainment Casting at ATV, phoned Lew Grade to say their star for that night's episode of *Sunday Night at the London Palladium* had missed his plane. Alec suggested a relatively unknown singer, Engelbert Humperdinck. What would have happened if Engelbert Humperdinck had said 'I'm not ready'?

The great tenor Luciano Pavarotti drew a London crowd of 100,000 including prime ministers and princes who stood in pouring rain for over two hours to hear him sing. How did Luciano get his opportunity? Again, at the London Palladium the opera star Giuseppe di Stefano could not appear because of illness. Luciano Pavarotti was at the beginning of his career and had spent years in preparation.

What would have happened to that opportunity if he had asked: 'Please give me a few more years to prepare'?

Do not be surprised if highly paid jobs or opportunities are relatively difficult to execute successfully. It has been so for past generations and will be so for your generation too. By preparing for them you will develop the skill to convert difficulties into opportunities; opportunities into successes; and successes into achievement of your specific Major Life Goal.

Rule 20: Prevent erosion of achievement

The overall aim of holistic success is to achieve—through Self-leadership and Personal Excellence—wealth, health and happiness, to keep it and to enrich your community through it. However everything in life is subject to erosion. Through decisions we do or do not take we can lose or diminish our success.

Success requires maintenance. We need to mend our fences; live off our interest not our capital; increase our knowledge and acquire new ideas; manage expenses; watch cash receipts; attend to daily Self-leadership; weigh, measure, count and be prepared for tough times.

Success is rarely a case of 'have arrived, sit back and enjoy gourmet living'. It happens a day at a time, growing as we grow, living as we live. It is a dynamic of life. Life itself is the product of a string of biological successes. Yet is it not subject to quick death and decay if unattended?

Rule 21: Accept that you are the only one who can succeed for you

There are many things that others can do for us. However, achieving personal success on our behalf is not one of them.

People who spend their time dreaming of their 'big day', hoping that a lottery win might rescue them or wishing a 'rich uncle' would give them enough income so they can concentrate on 'becoming great', are heading for disillusionment.

The responsibility for achieving success will always fall on us individually. If we don't reach out to where it is, it will snap back to where we are. There is no magic wand or secret that will change this fundamental principle.

Jim MacDonald, award-winning sales manager for one of the largest insurance companies in Australia, says:

> 'At the ripe "young age" of 49, I am convinced that the "real" secret is that there is no secret—no easy way, no short cut that will guarantee "success".
>
> 'Rather there is a range of views, ideas, experiences, teachings, lessons, methods and systems that have worked well for others and that are deserving of trial to find what works for you.'

The familiar saying 'If it is to be, it is up to me' speaks volumes. *You* need to strive for success—to find the way that suits you best. No one else can do it for you.

Rule 22: Be prepared for success

Time. Effort. Maintaining a positive mental attitude. Study. Avoiding negativity. Practising daily Self-leadership. Persistence. Steadily moving towards your Major Life Goal. That is what is meant by preparation. The effort is not a price you have to pay. You pay the price of failure, not of success. Success brings benefits, not bills.

Too many people are content to pay the price of failure. They want success but are slaves to routine. They wait on the dock for their 'ship to come in', but don't send any ships out. They go to work, come home, eat, watch television and go to sleep.

Most people spend so much time watching television that, if they applied that time productively, they could earn a fortune. Instead, they watch television five or more days a week year in, year out. What if people were to cut their television time in half and used the time saved to study success?

Could their outlook change? Could that change lead to a better life? A life of personal success based on Self-leadership and Personal Excellence? With a new focus could they become wealthier? Happier?

Rule 23: Have specific reasons for wanting success

Many people want success because of their strong disgust; their frustration with their life; with having to beg for every small pay increase; with having to go without things they need; with saying 'no' to their children because they can't afford what they want. They are disgusted and frustrated with living in the shadow of debt and worry.

For some people philanthropy is their chief reason for striving to succeed. Others want to succeed to provide a comfortable, secure life for themselves and for those whom they love.

Why do you want success? List your specific reasons. Make sure they are good enough to motivate you; to inspire you to act; to change your life forever. By listing your specific reasons for wanting success in a 'Positive Self-Awareness' file you'll stay true to yourself. You will motivate your spirit every time you read them. You will be in less danger of losing your sense of self, of forgetting where you want to be and why you want to be there. You will be strengthened against conditioning drag.

Rule 24: Think and see yourself how you want to be

The discipline of psycho-cybernetics is built upon the maxim: 'We become how we think and see ourselves to be.' The human race has known about this great truth for thousands of years! Yet how many people have read such phrases over and over without giving them more than a few seconds of thought?

Visualisation of success achievement is not new. In the battle of Zama in 202 BC the Roman general Scipio defeated Hannibal and saved Rome. Before the battle he inspired his legionnaires by reminding them of their recent successes in Africa. He asked them to visualise the success that surely would be theirs now.

The way it works is this: think and believe success and you'll be successful; think and believe failure and you will surely fail.

Zig Ziglar tells the story of a boy who was born to an unwed mother in a time when the stigma of illegitimacy could be unbearable. Women would whisper within earshot: 'Do they know who the father is?' Some of them would not let their children play with a 'bastard son'. Mother and son were ostracised.

The boy felt as if he were an outcast—valueless and rejected. He avoided mixing with people and withdrew into himself.

Then something happened that changed his life. One Sunday just as the church service ended and the boy was about to leave, the minister stepped down from the pulpit and with a loud booming voice asked him: 'And whose child are you?'

Everyone held their breath. The minister walked up, looked him in the eye and said: 'I know whose child you are! The family resemblance is unmistakable! You are a child of God! That's quite a heritage you have there, boy! See you live up to it!'

Eventually that boy became governor. His self-perception as someone rejected and valueless had changed to that of someone special.

It has much to do with the godlike human quality—imagination. Our imagination can take us to the vast reaches of the universe; create poignant musical phrases; capture a soul on canvas; lift our hearts with sweetest poetry; build great nations.

When Dr Charles Garfield studied peak performers in NASA, business and sport he found that they were all 'visualisers'. They imagine and see the success they will achieve *before* they attempt to achieve it.

Sports psychologists in the United States carried out an interesting imagination exercise involving two basketball teams. They asked one team to carry on with their physical training. The second team was to train only with imagination.

The second team won.

Rule 25: Be happy

We become happy from the moment we decide to feel and act happy,
just as we begin to succeed from the moment we decide to be successful. In the book *Tall Poppies Too* by Susan Mitchell, Carmel
Niland writes:

> '*Happiness comes from knowing that what you are is not
> dependent on titles, or degrees, or job descriptions. It's not
> dependent on anything other than your intrinsic worth, which
> is incalculable.*'

Unhappiness is ugly—a cancer of the spirit. We can't wait for others
or other things to make us happy. (What would we be in the
meantime?) Think success and happiness! Imagine success and
happiness! Believe success and happiness!

A specific Major Life Goal built on Personal Excellence that
also brings value to your community can help you achieve happiness through the power of purpose. If as you have thought and believed, therefore you are, it follows that as you think and believe
from now on, so you will be.

Rule 26: Use it or lose it

The powers to imagine, to love, to think clearly and positively need
constant use. If you don't use them, you'll lose them.

Here is one example. Australian Rod Laver was one of the
world's great tennis champions. As a boy he had a weak left arm. To
strengthen it he kept a squash ball in his left pocket and squeezed it
almost continuously. Eventually his left arm grew almost twice as
large as his right. The law of use worked. He won the Wimbledon
Crown four times and in the process became the world's first tennis
millionaire.

Does a musician retain and develop his talent by playing
constantly, or by not playing at all? Do you become a better chess
player, logician or problem solver by applying your mind often, or
seldom? Yet millions of people are content to hand over their mind
to a television for 40 hours each week! Think of it! They put as much
time into watching television as they put into their job!

There is much to be gained by watching television selectively. In Australia we are quite fortunate in having the ABC and SBS channels both of which screen first rate documentaries, informative dramatisations, and so on. I have obtained a lot of general knowledge by watching both channels selectively.

I apply the rule of 'quality in—quality out' to filter out programs that take my mind for an aimless stroll or put it into 'park'.

I don't see how anyone can develop the mind's potential by indiscriminately handing it over to a box that tells us what to think and when to laugh.

As for any other organ, the brain needs exercise if it is to remain useful. As psychologist Dr Susan Jeffers maintains in *Feel the Fear and Do It Anyway*:

> *'I know of no one who has been able to make 'positive' a permanent way of thinking without practice. Such people may exist, I simply haven't met them. In my experience, if you don't practice, you lose the skill. This is the point most people don't seem to understand.'*

Practise and use your success skills and your manager might begin to see you as promotion material. Your colleagues could develop a new respect for the way you throw yourself into your job; for your cheerfulness; your encouraging words; your willingness to share with and help other people; for your Self-leadership and Personal Excellence.

Rule 27: Anticipate and prepare for tough times

There's nothing new about tough times. These always come and go. It is not they that defeat us but the way we see them and what we do—or don't do—about them that decides the outcome.

The key is to accept that most of the time, life is difficult. There may be a problem at work, at home or with your neighbour. When you accept that life is difficult, then you can proceed to make it better through Self-leadership.

The common alternative is to develop the 'martyr complex' (everything happens to me) and look for 'social aspirins' such as alcohol. But that doesn't make tough times any easier.

Even for members of 'The Lucky Sperm Club' (those people born into wealth) life can be difficult. Tough times are opportunities for us to become stronger, wiser, better, more understanding and compassionate, and more humane. They force us to challenge our self-perception, our resourcefulness, our motives, our ties with others, our values, and our personal totem.

Anyone can sail on calm waters but it takes skill to sail on a stormy sea. Learn to anticipate the storms and prepare for them. Well-managed companies do this by keeping a contingency plan. They project ahead five, 10 or even 20 years. They also keep reserves. Prudent investors protect themselves against risk by spreading their investments over a wide range of portfolios.

The principle of anticipating tough times and preparing for them was demonstrated thousands of years ago on the Yang-Tze River in China. The river was notorious for its danger to shipping and exacted a heavy toll on the precious cargo of rice. The capsizing of any boat meant loss of an entire harvest. Each year it visited ruin on scores of farmers. One day an enterprising person suggested that farmers transport only 10 per cent of their harvest in any one boat. That way if a boat sank only a small part of their crop would be lost.

We can prepare by study, by focusing on our specific Major Life Goal, by interpreting the world's challenges through our personal totem, by working at happy, supportive, personal relationships, by persistence, by anticipation, by daily Self-leadership, and by not running down our reserves.

Rule 28: Save and invest

If cash reserves are essential for a well-managed business, then what about for you and me? Businesses exist to produce and share wealth. You are 'You Incorporated'. Your 'stock' is your ability to earn an income. Your duty is to develop that ability.

The following could be a sobering exercise. Answer the questions honestly:

- How long have you worked? _____ years
- In all that time approximately how much have your earned after tax? $ _____

- How much have you saved and invested? (That is, how much money is in your bank account or in assets?) $ _____
- How much would you have now if you had saved and invested only 10 per cent of all your earnings? $ _____

What happened?

When we have saved money it is easier to borrow more. It gives us the opportunity to begin a business venture, expand an existing business, and increase our capital through investment. It also demonstrates a strong discipline and an ability to repay borrowings. Banks will love us! And so will we.

The alternative is to get into debt for a refrigerator! But non-income producing debt is slavery! It steals our freedom! We are 'owned' by money lenders.

As mentioned earlier, preparing for the 'tough times' requires, among other things, a reserve fund. How can we create this fund and enjoy the peace of mind it brings without regular saving and investment? (A sage advice is to live on 80 per cent of your income and save and invest the rest.)

Rule 29: Nurture a positive world view

Attaining holistic success becomes almost impossible if you walk around with a sense of imminent doom. While it is true that we face a plethora of challenges we do not lack the means to meet them.

For example, the world has more than enough space to sustain double our present population even with more living space than we have now. We have enough arable land to feed everyone on Earth twice over. We have the wealth, the technology, and the knowledge. What we lack is the will and the moral strength to remedy our problems in the foreseeable future.

However that does not mean the world will blow itself up, starve itself or return to the dark ages. The key to positive change is attitude. A positive attitude will lead to learning. Learning will lead to understanding, tolerance, a willingness to share and to help. You can be a vital part of that process.

Don't despair at the problems around you—that only makes you part of those problems. Be part of the solution. Think positively.

For the majority of the human race, the world is a wonderful place. A positive world view will help make it wonderful for more people and will create a climate of blue skies and sunshine for your personal success journey.

Rule 30: Tap into your spiritual strength

If your only concern is to make money then this fundamental of holistic success will offer you little if any support. However if you want to achieve the kind of success that gives a balanced, happy life, then I would recommend you re-examine your spiritual connections.

In my research I have found that the majority of holistically successful people are spiritual as well as material in their outlook. The law of spirituality is the law of balanced success. Whether or not you avail yourself of this timeless source of personal strength is a decision for you to take.

As for our personal success journey, for all our learning, struggle and effort, we might not achieve our ultimate goal. So why try at all?

Like me, you are probably lucky enough to live in a developed country or in a country where comparatively few obstacles are placed in your quest for personal success. If so, given the relatively few opportunities of people in places such as City X, it is worth considering that we owe our best efforts to the family and community that has nurtured us as well as to ourselves.

Also, there is the inherent waste in squandering opportunities when they are denied to the majority of the world's population.

In the philosophy of holistic success, the money you make or the goal you attain is only secondary. A more important reason to strive for success is for the person you become in the process.

There are countless stories of people who have made and lost fortunes only to make another soon afterwards. In succeeding the first time they gained the disciplines, knowledge and skill to do it again. They had become new people.

Even if you do not succeed in your ultimate goal you can succeed part way and live much more successfully than if you had not tried at all. In any case you've got to live until you die, and so if you don't lead yourself to holistic success, what else are you going to do with your life?

KEY POINTS

- Success means freedom—a holistic way to live. It is not a destination but a life journey.
- By living your life by the principles of the 30 'rules' for success, you will be able to achieve the health, wealth and happiness that is rightly yours.

The 30 'rules' for success

Rule 1   Know the formula for success:

$$S = \frac{Asl^2}{PE}$$

That is, Success equals Attitude times Self-leadership squared over Personal Excellence.

Rule 2   Determine your specific Major Life Goal. If you don't have one, you'll be part of someone else's plan for theirs.

Rule 3   Identify the areas in which you want success (personal life, family life, community life, business/work life, financial life, global life and spiritual life).

Rule 4   Define what success means for you.

Rule 5   Understand the laws of growth and change.

Rule 6   Put in that extra effort. Growth is achieved through effort. Knowledge alone is of little value unless it is organised and applied.

Rule 7   Use nature's law of increasing returns.

Rule 8   Apply Self-leadership.

Rule 9   Develop a pleasant personality.

Rule 10   Apply clear, accurate thinking.

Rule 11   Develop co-operation and synergy.

Rule 12   Know you can't fail.

Rule 13   Be tolerant of others. An intolerant person is one who has stopped learning.

Rule 14   Show a humane regard for people. We're all pretty much like you!

Rule 15	Think and apply a win–win philosophy.
Rule 16	Manage time effectively. If you don't organise your day, your day will disorganise you.
Rule 17	Put quality in, get quality out. Watch what you or others file into your mental library.
Rule 18	Turn your back on 'excusitis'.
Rule 19	See difficulties as opportunities. Opportunities are often dressed as difficulties. You can overcome difficulties through preparation.
Rule 20	Prevent erosion of achievement. Everything you build will be subject to erosion. Attaining success is not enough. We also have to work at keeping it.
Rule 21	Accept that you are the only one who can succeed for you.
Rule 22	Be prepared for success.
Rule 23	Have specific reasons for wanting success.
Rule 24	Think and see yourself how you want to be.
Rule 25	Be happy.
Rule 26	Use it or lose it.
Rule 27	Anticipate and prepare for tough times. Tough times have always been with us. So have winters. You can survive by preparing for them. Accept the fact that life is difficult, and proceed to improve on it.
Rule 28	Save and invest.
Rule 29	Nurture a positive world view. A gloomy perspective of the world around you is not conducive to success.
Rule 30	Tap into your spiritual strength. Connecting with their spiritual dimension has helped many of the world's holistically successful people. It might be to your advantage to re-examine this timeless source of personal strength.

3

Overcoming attitude barriers

B ATTLE cries such as 'have a positive mental attitude' and 'it's your attitude, not your aptitude, that determines your altitude' are all very well, but when they are touted as *the* major key to success we have to be extra careful about taking them out of context.

A positive mental attitude (PMA) by itself, will not make you successful. What can be said about PMA is that it will help you do almost anything better than you could have done it had you used a negative mental attitude.

For example, if you decide to start a business, PMA will help only if you have done your research, prepared a business plan and know where, how and when you plan to achieve your goal.

If you have the wrong plan, PMA would only help you fail more cheerfully—and quickly. It will help you get to the wrong place faster. However there is more to attitude than PMA.

When most people talk about attitude they usually mean theirs. Yet we are influenced just as much by the attitudes of the people with whom we work, live and play. The only defence against the negative influence of others is to ensure our own attitude is on track.

Champion golfer Greg Norman said (in an interview with John Garrity in the November 1991 issue of *Time*):

'Sometimes focusing on the negatives creates more negatives. I've never been a negative individual. Never. Let's say I'm playing my bunker shots poorly. Instead of going out there and practicing my bunker shots hour after hour, I'll go chip or hit my five iron instead, something I can be positive about.'

Remember the game of 'wooden leg?' People with poor attitudes are those who play this game most often. It is their excuse for not trying. After all, 'What can you expect from someone with a poor attitude/ wooden leg?'

An attitude problem is the entry qualification to 'Low Achievers Inc.'. Members elect to join this club. They may cancel their membership any time—yet choose not to do so. They despair at living a storyline written by others but will not write the storyline *they* want to live because the drag of their conditioning prevents them.

Do not mix with low achievers who live by the law of accident. They can suffocate you. Mix with goal-driven people whose optimism, high expectations, energy and enthusiasm will invigorate you.

Attitude barriers are built block by block. Following are some of the most common.

Wanting a free ride

The latter third of the twentieth century has been dubbed by some as 'The age of Me'. This is meant to describe a self-centred, acquisitive and selfish philosophy. In many places, absenteeism has almost become a right of employment. In Western society generally there is much talk of 'rights' but comparatively little talk of 'personal responsibility' and of 'duty to our community'.

Other symptoms of the 'Me' philosophy are an increasing demand for government to provide more and more welfare payments, rebates, free services, and so on. Is it any wonder, therefore, that so many people want success without effort and Self-leadership?

Consider the case of Maurice, an electrician working in a small business. His philosophy was to work eight hours per day and not a minute more. When the business won large contracts he refused to work overtime despite the employer's offer to pay generous allowances. He was dismissed, but clung to his work ethics. The result?

Maurice is 65 and broke. He lives on an age pension and drives a car that has seen much better days. He cannot afford to replace the car, the very modest house in which he lives, nor anything else for that matter. Yet he is the first to blame the government for his misfortunes and to cry out for extra handouts.

Maurice has lived his life refusing to put in 'that extra effort'. He is reaping what he has sown. He is paying the price of comparative failure. Is Maurice unusual?

If you suggested to colleagues that the best way to be promoted to a senior position was to work hard, produce quality work and do the best for the employer, what sort of reaction do you think you would get? Even if they agreed with you, would they do it? And if they tried, what would other workers say?

In almost any field, success depends in large measure on the effort you are willing to give it—on Self-leadership. If you want success you will need to earn it. You will need to reach out to where it is. No one has invented a way of achieving success without effort. If there is no such thing as a free lunch, there certainly is no such thing as a free ride to success.

Self-doubt

Living with self-doubt is like driving with one foot on the accelerator and the other foot on the brake.

Do you believe you will be successful? Truly successful in all your spheres of life? If your answer is 'yes', that's a good start, but it's not enough. You need to transcend belief; you need to know. Belief implies room for doubt. When you have written your Life Blueprint for your success, adopted a personal totem centred on integrity and committed yourself to achieving your goal, then you will be able to transcend belief and know. When that happens, doubt vanishes.

Here's an example. The manager of the Buenos Aires Opera House was beside himself with worry because the conductor for that evening's performance of *Aida* was too ill to perform. He asked members of the orchestra if any of them knew the score sufficiently well to conduct it. While others hesitated, an unknown by the name of Arturo Toscanini volunteered. Thus was born the career of one of the greatest conductors of all time.

Did he have doubts? Probably, but he banished them to the farthest corner of his mind and did it anyway! Sydney Myer, the poor Russian immigrant who founded the giant Myer department store chain, had the motto:

'When in doubt, move forward.'

Sir Philip Sidney said:

'Either I will find a way or I will make one.'

Self-doubt is a nag we all have to face. Those jittery thoughts that tell you 'perhaps you can't do it' are echoes from the past—that is, conditioning drag. They could be echoes from your teacher, 'Won't you ever get it right?' or from your parents, 'You're useless!'

Unfortunately our education system does not place great emphasis on 'success conditioning'. It does not ensure students are given tasks suited to their individual ability so that they can succeed one step at a time. If this were done, there would be no need for comments like: 'When will you ever learn?', 'Dummy', and so on. There would be no need to grow with self-doubt and a fear of success.

Such memories from our early conditioning are enemies of confidence. They surface whenever we face a moment of truth. Recognising the drag of conditioning can help us to vanquish self-doubt and to leave by the wayside past lessons in mediocrity. Even self-doubt can be used positively if you see it as a signal to reassess the job at hand. But don't be limited by ghosts from the past or by the thoughts of low achievers in the present. Convert 'obstacle thinking' into 'possibility thinking'.

Before Roger Bannister broke the four minute mile experts openly argued whether such a feat was humanly possible. Shortly after his breakthrough, 37 other runners broke the four minute mile too! Roger Bannister had shown it was possible and so others converted doubt into possibility thinking, and achieved!

Two classic gaffes of obstacle thinking were made by Robert Millikan, Nobel Prize winner in Physics (1923) when he said 'There's no likelihood man can ever tap the power of the atom', and Charles Duell, the head of the American Patent Office (1889), when, with all the solemnity of his office he declared: 'Everything that can be invented, has been invented.'

If you have considered your plan for success carefully, researched it, listened to the experiences of those in that field, can transcend the limits of belief and *know* you can do it, why not be a Self-leader and go for it?

Procrastination

This affliction can strike any time. It can lose fortunes. It can cost you your life (e.g. procrastinating on a treatment for illness). No matter how hard you try, you can't put off today. It comes back every morning right on schedule, laden with the extra baggage of yesterday's unfinished tasks.

Procrastination is a habit and like most habits it can be broken by changing attitudes and replacing a bad habit with a good habit—by practising Self-leadership.

Why do so many of us procrastinate? The truth is that laziness is a natural trait of human beings. Even high achievers develop systems to ensure they keep working.

The most famous prayer for procrastination was uttered by St Augustine, a great patriarch of the early Christian Church. He pleaded: 'O Lord, give me continence and chastity. But not yet.' The great philosopher, Immanuel Kant, twice contemplated marriage. He procrastinated for so long that the first woman married someone else and the second woman left town before he completed his deliberations.

Author William James said: 'Nothing is so fatiguing as the eternal hanging-on of an incompleted task.' Procrastination is such a common thief of success—and life—that it merits detailed discussion. There are a number of specific reasons for procrastination.

Unpreparedness
You might procrastinate in painting that wall because you don't have the paint, brushes or ladder, and so it all seems too much of a bother. Likewise you might procrastinate in doing 'that course' because you would have to enrol, pay fees, attend an interview, and so on. The answer here might be to divide the task into two steps: prepare first, execute second.

Unsure how to do it
Sometimes we might be given a task that we find daunting. Perhaps we are not confident how to go about it and so it is easy to put off making a start. However the task seldom becomes easier by avoiding it. It usually becomes more difficult because by then we have additional work to do. The answer could be to divide each task into steps and to do it one step at a time. If you need more knowledge, acquire it! Ask. Read. Discuss. Then proceed.

Lethargy
Feeling tired from over-eating, lack of exercise or unfitness is a great ball and chain for the procrastinator. It's so easy to rationalise by

saying: 'I'm not at my best. I wouldn't do it well just now. I'm too tired to concentrate.' Lethargy is easy to beat. Get up and move.

Unhappy home or work environment
It's easy to put things off if you're still smarting from a problem at home or at work. You're too busy being angry or hurt to bother about anything else. You want to regurgitate everything that was said, add some things that weren't but should have been said, and generally relive the experience.

Author Colleen McCullough (in Susan Mitchell's *Tall Poppies Too*) puts the unhappy work environment in this context:

> *'The thing is that work ought to be enjoyable just because it's work. You should discipline yourself to enjoy what you do. One of the things I notice all the time is that no matter what people do, they want it always to be this, that and the other thing. I try to tell people that no matter what you do for a living, it's 90 percent shit. The most paradisiacal job in the world is still 90 percent shit. You do the 90 percent shit to have the 10 percent gold.'*

Problems at work or at home are not new and will arise whenever humans work and live together. However brooding over them seldom helps—and can worsen them.

We cannot live in compartments where heavy doors seal off one situation from another. Life is not like that because almost everything is interconnected. But we *can* learn to focus on one issue at a time. Procrastinating because of unhappiness is not a suitable response to any challenge. It is mere reaction. You are still relinquishing control of a part of your life. You are following, not leading.

A little tolerance, understanding and co-operation help most unhappy situations. These three elements represent the effort you might have to make whenever you are faced with a personal dilemma.

You might feel that you need to talk to a qualified counsellor. If so, don't let your ego or determination to 'get your own way' cancel your future.

In old age it won't be the lost deals you will regret, but the things you should have said; the time you should have spent with those you love; the things you didn't do. To be alive, yet not to do—is that not a waste of life?

When the task is too big

Imagine having a dinner party for eight people. Everyone enjoyed it. You were a great success. However when the party was over you faced a small mountain of soiled plates, glasses, cutlery, pots, pans and casserole dishes. If you look at the task overall it feels natural to put off cleaning them.

Suppose you divided the load into segments (i.e. dishes, then cutlery, then pots, and so on). Suddenly you've broken down the 'huge' load into a series of smaller ones and the task does not seem so overwhelming. As Dr Robert Schuller says: 'Inch by inch, anything's a cinch.'

Rebellion

Have you ever tried to force someone into a task they didn't want to do? Were you surprised when they kept putting it off? Procrastination can be a form of passive rebellion.

If this sounds like you, remember it is often better to do the task straight away and get it off your back (if you have no choice). Otherwise be honest in the first place. Tell those concerned that you do not want to do it.

Sometimes rebellion results from 'conditioning drag'—that is, when what you have to do conflicts with your upbringing, way of thinking or with the way you see yourself. For example, if you have been conditioned into thinking that you could never rise above the level of a supervisor, any challenge to accept a higher position could generate negative feelings of inadequacy, self-doubt and discomfort. Whenever these feelings occur, they are the tethers of your conditioning dragging you back to your 'comfort zone'. Your desire to resist such challenges can manifest itself as rebellion.

Self-talk

The principles and effects of suggestion are well documented. Hypnosis would hardly be possible without it. However what might be lesser known are the effects of self-suggestion.

Self-hypnosis in one form or another is practised by millions of people. It is based on inducing a concentrated state of mind by self-suggestion. To a lesser extent we too condition our mind to believe things about ourselves. Our inner dialogues are almost ceaseless. What we say to ourselves affects our confidence, enthusiasm, self-esteem, happiness and general outlook on life.

When faced with a task we wish to postpone, we invariably open an inner dialogue with characters within us. It might go something like this:

Character 1: 'I should really do it.'

Character 2: 'Trouble is, I'm basically lazy.'

Character 3: 'I'll do it tomorrow.'

There we go again, telling ourselves we are lazy (tired, don't really feel like it, and so on) and playing the game of 'wooden leg'.

Positive self-talk keeps us from feeding negative self-images into our subconscious. Use it to paint a picture of a more determined, energetic you—of a reputation for getting the job done on time, cheerfully and well.

Fear of criticism/failure

This fear comes to the fore whenever we lack confidence in our ability to complete a task successfully. We think we'll get it wrong—that we might make a mistake, that we might fail. So what? How else can we gain the experience to succeed? The way to avoid mistakes is to avoid doing anything! To quit!

It takes single-mindedness and Self-leadership to stick to priorities, just as it takes Self-leadership and single-mindedness to achieve your Major Life Goal.

Author and motivator Tom Hopkins has an interesting definition of procrastination in his book *How to Master the Art of Selling*:

> *'Procrastination is the art of living in your yesterdays, avoiding your todays, and ruining your tomorrows.'*

Converting procrastination into a procedure

To beat procrastination recognise it as a challenge. Our system for meeting challenges is to convert them into a procedure. For example, ask yourself: What kinds of things do I usually put off? How do I justify putting them off?

Having listed those tasks and your excuses for procrastinating on them, design a procedure to get you going. The following system will help:

- If the task is too big, break it up into smaller, 'bite size' chunks.
- Prepare all the material and tools you will need to get the job done.
- If you don't know how to do the job, find out.
- List the 'bite size' chunks in priority order (you could use the Priority Planner at the end of Chapter 12).
- Set a time for the completion of each task.
- Prevent interruptions. (If your office is constantly badgered by drop-in time wasters, go to a separate office or to a place where you can't be disturbed. Take the phone off the hook. Advise everyone in your area that you won't be available. Whatever works for you will do. If the task is important enough, then it's important enough for you to get it done.)
- Don't give in to new excuses. A new distraction is a welcome visitor for the procrastinator. Don't think of reasons why a task should be put off. Get going.
- If you really don't want to do the job, consider getting rid of it or give it to someone else. Putting it off won't make it go away.
- When all else fails, 'plunge in'. It can 'kick-start' your engine much faster than could an eternity of thinking about it.

When Sir Walter Raleigh was asked how he got so many things done, he replied:

'When there is anything to do, I start it.'

Horace, the great Roman poet and philosopher, advised:

'Carpe Diem.' (Grasp at the present day.)

Indifference

Drifting through life, letting someone else take the initiative and allowing things to happen to you instead of designing a life worth living are the hallmarks of indifference—of living by the law of accident rather than by design. Without active involvement, a goal, a noble purpose, a sense of direction and the single-minded pursuit of holistic success, the price we pay for failure can be crushingly expensive. It is not a once-only payment. The terms extend over the rest of your life.

How long do you pay for leading an indifferent lifestyle if you wind up retiring broke? What about the anguish and debt burdens you could suffer in the meantime? Can you rely solely on government handouts when you retire? If you live in a place like City X, how will you survive retirement *without* government handouts?

Passivity

The national culture of the people of City X places great emphasis on achieving consensus. It would be wonderful if everyone agreed to every decision. However where consensus fails, someone has to make a decision. The result of this obsession with consensus in the country of which City X is the capital is that each decision is discussed with a large number of people—who rediscuss it and discuss it again. (I have sat in on meetings where the people involved in the discussions had no experience, background or expertise whatever in the matter under discussion. However consensus was still the aim.)

This drive for consensus, apart from dampening personal initiative and fostering a culture of procrastination, delays every project—even those that are urgent. Over the years the people as a whole, who are a friendly, warm hearted people, have developed a trait of passivity that still hinders the country's struggle out of poverty. Except for a few gifted individuals, most people wait to be led rather than take the lead.

To my mind consensus means reaching an agreement that nobody wants but are prepared to tolerate. At the personal level, trying to instil initiative and Self-leadership goes against the individual's whole upbringing. For the great majority of its citizens, the challenge of achieving personal success through Self-leadership and Personal Excellence in City X is formidable indeed.

However you don't have to go to City X to see people who are passive to the point of chronic procrastination. I am sure you can locate a few of this breed in your own workplace or community. Overall you might be fortunate enough to live in a nation where initiative is valued, encouraged and rewarded. And so Self-leadership should come to you far more easily than it would come to a citizen of City X.

See every challenge through the perspective of Self-leadership and reject passivity because people who have things done *for* them also have things done *to* them.

Decision paralysis

It's not the big decisions you take now and then that total success, but the little ones you take every day. Even this book had to be written a word at a time. However many people fear what might go wrong or worry about criticism so much they will avoid deciding even minor issues.

At restaurants they even ask others what they are having before deciding on a selection for themselves. Getting the 'I want to think about it' response from a client is one of the great demotivators of salespersons.

Dr Susan Jeffers writes in *Feel the Fear and Do It Anyway*:

'One of the biggest fears that keeps us from moving ahead with our lives is our difficulty in making decisions. As one of my students lamented: "Sometimes I feel like the proverbial donkey between two bales of hay—unable to decide which one I want, and, in the meantime, starving to death." The irony, of course, is that by not choosing, we are choosing—to starve.'

The key to understanding decision paralysis is to understand why people are reluctant to make decisions in the first place. In many cases it is simply confusion. People have not understood a proposal or its benefits. In City X, they know that their decision will be discussed in a group. So why bother?

A simple technique for making decisions is to divide a piece of paper with a vertical line down the centre. On one side of the line list the reasons 'for' the proposal, and on the other side list the reasons 'against'. The better course soon becomes obvious.

Another area of our personal life afflicted by decision paralysis is making up our minds what we want to be. Until we make this decision, progress becomes difficult because we can't know where we are going or if we are moving in the right direction. When you can't decide what you want, the following steps will help you beat decision paralysis:

- List what you don't want.
- List what you might like.
- List what you definitely would like, and choose from this list.

Decisiveness is one of the qualities of Self-leadership. Don't let fear of making a mistake inflict decision paralysis on you. It could ruin your present and cancel your future. Consider all the information, separate facts from information, list relevant facts, work out the 'for' and 'against' of the proposal, consider the consequences, then decide.

Worry

By his timely arrival the Austrian General, Boucher, saved Wellington at Waterloo and helped defeat Napoleon. Yet he worried all his life that he would give birth to an elephant!

Do you know anyone who is troubled by worry? Some people worry about everything. Half the world's heartaches are caused by worry over trifles. Of course we all worry to some extent. If you are in the path of an oncoming train it is wise to worry. This type of worry leads to action.

The great Tolstoy worried so much about hanging himself that he kept a piece of rope hidden from him. Dr Susan Jeffers says in *Feel the Fear and Do It Anyway*:

> 'It is reported that 90% of what we worry about never happens. That means that our negative worries have about a 10% chance of being correct. If this is so, isn't it possible that being positive is more realistic than being negative?'

Composer Leonard Bernstein was engaged in a concert tour of the Middle East. In Joan Peyser's *Leonard Bernstein*, he recalls a situation that would have been worrisome for most of us, and what people did about it:

'I gave a downbeat at this morning's rehearsal. It coincided with a perfectly timed explosion outside the hall.

'We picked ourselves up and calmly resumed our labours. We've had four incidents in two days: a kidnapping at this hotel, a train demolished, a police station blown up, a military truck bombed. But the cafe-sitters don't put down their newspapers, the children continue to jump rope. The Arab goatherd in the square adjusts another milking bag, and I give the next downbeat.'

The lesson I get from this story is not to empower worry (or circumstances) to deflect you from your mission. Here's a simple formula for handling worry. Write down your answers to the following questions:

■ What am I worrying about?
■ On the laws of probability, what are the chances of this happening to me?
■ If it does, what is the worst that can happen?

Once you have written down your answers:

■ Accept the worst as a possibility
■ Take steps to improve on the worst.

It is often better to accept things you can't change than to worry and stew because they aren't the way you feel they ought to be. Don't worry about your future: design it instead!

Pessimism

Before the motor car was invented Londoners were told that as traffic increased, within 100 years mountains of horse manure would make the city impassable. Naturally, the pessimists agreed. The optimistic thing about pessimists is they're seldom right.

It takes the same mental energy to develop the discipline of looking on the bright side of things as it does to look on the dark side. So why bother with pessimism? It feeds on negative self-talk.

It clouds our views on everything—including ourselves. Pessimism is a down-payment on a contract to fail.

Many people have burst through the pessimism barrier to achieve inspiring successes—people who could easily be forgiven if they held a very pessimistic view of their future.

People like B. P., who became a quadriplegic after a car accident, J. D., who was paralysed by Poliomyelitis, J. B., who was immobilised by severe arthritis, and G. B., who became a quadriplegic after a diving accident. All are among members of the Association of Mouth and Foot Paintings Artists, and developed their skills to the point where their work is sold nationally. Their aim (published in a leaflet promoting their work) is:

> '. . . to be financially independent—free from charity—and to lead useful, creative, normal lives.'

They and others in their group are people who have conquered pessimism and by doing so have achieved success through a high level of Self-leadership and Personal Excellence.

Martha Washington said:

> 'I am still determined to be cheerful and happy in whatever situation I may be, for I have also learned from experience that the greater part of our happiness or misery depends on our dispositions and not on our circumstances.'

Pessimistic people tend to be unhappy. (They might be happiest when their dire predictions occur. This justifies their continued self-flagellation.) They have mastered the mentality of the martyr. In many instances a pessimistic attitude can ensure its own fulfilment. If you think the world is bright and happy, it is. If you think it is dark and miserable, it is. How can it be otherwise? It's your world. You are creating it.

Remember that if you do what you have always done you will always get what you have always got (more worry).

Stubborness

Stubbornness is enacting the belief that if you don't give in, the world will mould itself into a shape pleasing to you. For example, if you are living in an environment marked by fast and frequent change, refusing to adapt won't stop change from occurring. Be flexible. Don't be afraid of new ideas. Be open to the possibility that others could be right, or at least partly right.

Stubbornness is a barrier. Eventually, barriers are removed. It should not be confused with single-mindedness. The single minded pursuit of your Major Life Goal requires you to be open to any change or idea that can help you attain it.

Stubbornness might be another manifestation of conditioning drag—an echo of the child who 'held its breath' until it got its own way. Aesop tells the story of two goats traversing a ravine and meeting on a log. Both insisted they had the right of way and were too stubborn to back off. Eventually they tried to push through and both fell into the ravine.

Henry S. Haskins warns us that:

'A stiff attitude is one of the phenomena of rigor mortis.'

Resistance to change

Resistance to change goes against our very nature because evolutionary survival depends on our ability to adapt. Therefore the ability to change is built into our very genes. Yet how many people fight against change, only to go under?

This resistance to new ways is so widespread that it not only affects individuals, but whole nations. For example, after the fall of the Berlin Wall a new world opened to East Berliners. West Berlin went to enormous lengths—and expenditure—to integrate the newly freed peoples of the former communist bloc. However the results have been mixed, and many would say, disappointing.

The changes brought high levels of unemployment and social disorder in the East, with many people openly saying they had it better under communism. Yet it wasn't the Western way that produced difficulties. The chief problem was the resistance of East Berliners to change the way they had been doing things, and so millions suffer the consequences.

Here is a case in point. Soon after the integration of Berlin a flood of East Berliners went to West Berlin looking for work and for a place to live. Agencies set up by West Berlin to assist these people were amazed at the expectations of the East Berliners, some of whom specified the type of house they wanted (one in particular specified a waterfront property), expecting that they be provided by the State.

The new arrivals found it bewildering that they had to find a place for themselves, had to find their own job, had to work to rules and be productive. Their conditioning drag had such a hold that automatically they assumed the State would provide for everything.

Before the situation can improve in East Berlin, its people's attitude needs to improve. This shows again that life will only get better when we get better. Those who have changed their attitudes and accepted change are prospering because they are helping to drive it.

Another case in point is 1994 Russia. Those who have changed their 'let the State take care of us' attitude are prospering, with millionaires emerging almost daily. A wealthier class is forming from Self-led entrepreneurs and business people who see opportunity where others see only difficulty and hard work. There too, the first priority is to change the attitude of the people. Primarily, to have them accept change, to work with it and to help to drive it, rather than let it overwhelm them.

Resistance to change is conditioning drag winning every round and cancelling people's future—both individually and by nations. It is a major attitude barrier for most of us and must be resisted with every means possible if we are to progress and prosper.

How about you? Can you remember instances where you resisted change simply because 'it made you uncomfortable'? If so, those were occasions when your conditioning drag won, and you lost. (However there will be many opportunities for you to win subsequent rounds.)

Failing to work your plan

How often have you spent hours creating a master plan only to follow it for a little while? Isn't it pointless to work out a plan that you do not intend to follow? Your plan should be your promise to yourself—a promise for your future. It is you designing the life you want to live—your own storyline.

You need to see the promise of your future clearly and want it earnestly or you will not make the sustained effort to achieve it. Fear of failure or, in some cases, fear of success, can be a major factor in preventing the execution of a plan. 'Plan your work and work your plan' and 'If you fail to plan you are planning to fail' may be cliches but they have withstood the test of time.

Low self-esteem

Swiss psychiatrist Alfred Adler coined the term 'inferiority complex' to explain our inborn determination to counter feelings of inferiority or of low self-esteem. As he put it: our urge to 'Turn our minus into a plus'.

For example, in 1994 accomplished actress and singer Barbra Streisand commanded a fee of $30 million for a two night appearance in Las Vegas. Although she has achieved extraordinary success in her work/business sphere of life she must constantly struggle against the low self-esteem inflicted by her cruel upbringing.

Her stepfather would taunt her about her appearance throughout her childhood, telling her how 'ugly' she was and comparing her to her 'more attractive' sister. On an outing he bought an ice cream for her sister but refused to buy one for her because, he told her, 'You're too ugly'.

While reportedly Barbra Streisand still dislikes appearing in public and feels uncomfortable with other people, she refuses to be dragged down by her conditioning. By converting low self-esteem into self-confidence, she triumphs.

Eleanor Roosevelt said:

'No one can make you feel inferior without your consent.'

We are genetically built for success. In the end how we feel about ourselves need not be influenced by our treatment at the hands of other people nor by what they think, but by ourselves.

Take a few minutes to complete the following suggestion. Divide a sheet of paper with a vertical line down the centre. Head the left section 'Things I like about myself' and the right section 'Things I don't like about myself'. Complete the lists. Which side has more entries? If the negative side has more, don't worry. All you have to do is to change one thing and you've already improved.

Master salesperson Tom Hopkins in *How to Master the Art of Selling* talks about self-acceptance as a motivation influence. He writes:

> 'Self-acceptance is the state of being your own person. You have arrived. Not where somebody else sent you, you have arrived exactly where you want to be.
>
> 'Self-acceptance marks the day when the opinions of other people don't control you any more. It's the day you start making yourself heard when you don't agree.
>
> 'It's the night you suddenly jump a jet to Europe for a vacation; it's the morning you stay in bed because you want to. It's the hour when you're all through with the games you don't want to play; through with the roles you don't want to live.
>
> 'It's the minute you finally unlock your potential, become you, know that you've become you, and know that you are completely and gloriously your own person.'

That could describe much of what it means to be a Self-leader. A poor self-esteem does not make for leadership. It even prevents people from becoming good followers.

Spiritual denial

So many people in our 'modern' world feel that to succeed they have to travel their road alone. No one can succeed by themselves because even at the basic level we need the co-operation of other people. However the conditioning drag transfer of people who are focused only on a material existence can influence us to deny deeper feelings about life's purpose. We can shut ourselves off from the broader essence of what it means to be human.

You might not feel a need to connect with this aspect of your success journey. However holistically successful people do not reject support from any source. Where they find their spiritual connection of great strength is in the way it balances what could easily become an obsession with material wealth.

If you feel there is a spiritual aspect to life that can help you, why place an attitude barrier in front of it?

Demolishing the barriers

Achieving holistic success means accepting that we are the architects and master builders of our own barriers. The good news is that as we built them, we can demolish them.

You will know of many cases where a positive attitude made all the difference to the outcome—disabled people who won't give up; sportspeople determined to win; and people from all walks of life who strive for and achieve success against incredible odds. They are strong leaders of self. All have developed an attitude that life *is* worth living, that success *is* worth attaining, and that they too are worthy of personal triumph.

Not for them the lethargy, pessimism and quitting attitude of the low achiever. They know that the key to winning is largely a state of mind. This state of mind—or attitude—can be developed until it becomes the way you live every day—bright, hopeful, energised, happy, successful.

KEY POINTS

- A *positive mental attitude* (PMA) can help you fail faster if you don't have the right blueprint for your success. Of itself, PMA can help you do things better than if you had a negative attitude; but it is not the only key to success.
- *Everything worthwhile takes effort.* There's no such thing as a free lunch, nor any 'free ride' to success.
- Become *a believer in yourself*, in your ability to grow, and to win. Become a Self-leader. Transcend belief and know you will succeed. Discard conditioning drag.
- Don't hand over control of any part of your life to *procrastination*. Be prepared for a task. Learn how to go about it. Be energetic. Foster a happy home and work environment. Focus on the prize, not on the task. Take the advice of a famous Roman and 'Carpe Diem' (grasp at the present day).
- If you don't care enough to try, you'll be part of someone else's success story.

■ Fear of what could go wrong or of criticism is unworthy of anyone serious about success. Consider all angles, work out the consequences, and then decide.

■ Don't worry! It doesn't help and in most cases 'it' probably won't happen. 'Worry' about positives instead of negatives. It's more productive.

■ You'll be happier, healthier and more successful if you develop the habit of looking on the bright side. Reject the mentality of martyrs.

■ Stubborness is the child in us determined to get its own way. It is a barrier to progress. Eventually barriers are removed.

■ Resistance to change is a triumph of conditioning drag that afflicts individuals and nations alike.

■ Fear of failure? Fear of success? Either will stop you from working your plan. If you don't work your plan, circumstances will work you.

■ If connecting with the spiritual aspect of life gives you strength and a sense of balance for your personal success journey, why deny it?

4

Success through personal growth

HAVE you ever attended a seminar in which key speakers outlined how they achieved their extraordinary success? You were full of admiration. Inspired. You might have thought: 'These people have it all—presence, speech, presentation, admiration, achievement.' Yet when you tried to do the things they do they probably didn't work quite as well for you.

More than likely the speakers were talking from a 10 or 15 year growth perspective while you might have been listening through a two or three year growth experience. It is almost certain that the way they went about their business when they had your experience level is markedly different from the way they do their work now. The difference between you and them was not one of ability, but of personal growth.

In his autobiography, Fred Hollows tells about the time he failed the same exam twice—six months apart. The reason? In his own words: 'I was a boy in a man's game.' He adds that he didn't know enough about ophthalmology, and so he decided to do as much practical work as possible to get the experience. He did this extra work for two years, 'working like a dog', then sat for and passed his exams. He said: 'I wasn't trusting to flair and a bit of luck, or blaming the system for anything. I'd grown up, I guess.'

In his experience—and achievement—Professor Hollows points the way. It is not enough to know success philosophy or to learn the 'book of success rules' by heart. We have to do; to learn and to apply skills; and to grow to the levels demanded by the success we want. There is no greater investment than in personal growth.

In Susan Mitchell's book *Tall Poppies Too*, Carmel Niland describes her 'personal growth':

> '*One of the things I've always wanted was to like myself. Clearly I never had. I always thought I had to save the world, but now I can like myself for who I am . . . At this stage of my life I feel a total connection with my past, present and future, and I have experienced a coming together of things, a wholeness. You could call it a spiritual reaffirmation. What drives me now is joy.*'

Personal growth begins from the moment we accept that we are accountable for our own future. Once this is accepted we can take stock of who we are and of how we can improve our knowledge, skills and attitudes to achieve success. It is the moment of self-acceptance and commitment to living our own storyline that gives us a first class ticket to our better future.

One of the world's great golfers, Greg Norman, spoke to John Garrity of *Time* magazine (November 1991) about personal growth. He said:

> '*I'm a country boy, really. I'm not a flamboyant individual. I was a very shy, introverted guy, and I had to change a lot to be successful.*'

In his life study of success Napoleon Hill found that some of the most successful people had to correct certain weaknesses in their personality, attitude and beliefs before they began to succeed.

You might need to change not only your thinking and attitudes, but any unproductive habits as well. The process may be stressful—even painful. The result can be stronger Self-leadership to wealth, health and happiness.

However all that is easier said than done. I know there are many flaws in my personality that I would love to change, and I can—temporarily. However in the heat of emotion—of pressure—it's difficult to respond other than through the drag of one's conditioning.

Conditioning drag works like gravity, exerting a weak but continuous attraction that keeps pulling us back to where we were. I believe it is one of the major reasons why so many people fail to achieve the success they want. Sooner or later, despite all the goal setting, positive mental attitude and effort, if we are not vigilant we can slide back to the patterns of our conditioning—and retreat to the 'safety' of our comfort zone.

The only way I know of overcoming conditioning drag is to set a specific Major Life Goal that you really want and that you have to work on every day. In other words, your daily activity must move you closer to your goal.

To remind me of my specific Major Life Goal every day, I wear a signet ring with the logo of The College for Success Studies. Its centrepiece is the directional star used on maps and navigational charts. It reminds me of my direction and helps to keep me on track.

This chapter offers ideas that will help you with your own personal growth.

Know who you are

It might sound like a cliche but knowing who you are is as essential to success and happiness as sunshine is to flowers. You need to know who you are to develop to the person you want to be.

Try writing down who you are. It will not be as easy as putting down a name and address. For example, what are your core values? What do you believe? How do you see the world around you? What are your attitudes to people? What is your personal totem? What is your philosophy?

Many tribal people embody 'who they are' by adopting a personal totem. This may be an eagle, lion, deer, wind, moon or sun. Each totem is perceived to have qualities such as strength, speed, courage and wisdom.

By adopting a personal totem the individual adopts its qualities, interprets the daily challenges of life through its paradigm and responds to them accordingly. In our case such qualities can be said to form our core values. These values must not only be adopted, but believed in and defended. For example, your totem could represent honesty, integrity, fair play, success only on a win–win basis (Personal Excellence) and so on. The point is that once you have adopted a totem it will enshrine your code of conduct.

Psychologist Dr Irene C. Kassorla believes honesty is a power tool. She writes in *Go For It*:

'You may never have thought of honesty as either a power or a

helpful tool, but it is. I believe that honesty is a symbol of strength. It demonstrates high self-esteem and inner feelings of security and dignity. Honesty is magnetic and will draw people to you. They may not be certain why they are attracted to you, but they will like you because honesty is so engaging ... In my therapy work, I have treated many corporate executives and leaders of Industry. It is interesting to note how many winning characteristics they have in common. Invariably, one of these traits is being honest.'

You have not begun to succeed holistically until you can define your personal totem—that set of core values that characterises you, and guides you on how you will live your life and how to achieve the level of personal success you want.

Your personality
Why is it that some people are extroverted and others introverted? Why are some people stable and others unstable? Why are some people tender minded and others tough minded?

Psychologists have concluded that a part of our personality is inherited through genes. However upbringing can influence how we turn out. Under pressure, this 'learned behaviour' can quickly yield to the character programmed by our genes. There are no right or wrong traits and we all have some of each. Your aim should be to discover your predominant trait and to take it into account in your dealings with other people.

A common factor of successful people is that they enjoy what they do, and so choosing the 'right' job or business can be a great start to your success. The wrong choice can lead to considerable financial loss and unhappiness. For example, an introvert could be unhappy in a position that demands constant exposure to people (such as in sales work).

Your conditioning drag
We are programmed by our genes, upbringing and environment to see ourselves in a certain way—to believe what we can and can't do; to limit our vision of how far we can climb; and so on.

This conditioning is a force that exerts its influence throughout our lives. It can only be defeated one success at a time; and even then it can drag us back to our 'comfort zone from time to time'. The point is that to know it is to recognise it when it arises and, by opposing it, dismiss it.

Your conditioning drag transfer

This can happen whenever our own conditioning drag defeats us and we stop trying to succeed, or to meet that challenge. How? By transferring our negativity onto other people.

You will recognise this phenomena every time someone is being negative, telling you that you can't do this or that or 'puking' their woes over you. Don't empower someone else's conditioning drag to cancel your day. Make an excuse to go to the bathroom. Anything. Just get out of there.

These three aspects of 'Who you are' are introduced here because our discussion on personal growth could not be complete without them. More on them later.

Look out by looking in

It is common to judge others by our own standards and experiences. When we are confronted by or introduced to someone we immediately invite them to view our travel snap shots, our family album or our 'travelogue'.

We project our ideas onto other people and criticise those corners, twists and bumps that don't fit into our picture. At the same time others have their own travelogue and project it onto us.

I can recall many instances where I projected my own standards onto others. An example was during the time I was an Air Force Officer and long hair for males was just coming into vogue. Given my own background and training, I looked down on men who chose to wear their hair long. I'm ashamed to admit that even years later as a civilian manager, I would turn down a long-haired male for a job in preference to someone who met my 'travelogue' by wearing his hair short.

What a preposterous world view I had—as if the length of hair was the mark of under-achievers or of males who simply didn't fit into 'the system'.

I've grown a lot since those early days, and the biggest lesson of that growth was that given the circumstances, I couldn't have grown any faster because personal growth takes time.

More recently my personal growth was tested when I spent four months consulting in City X. Customs eschewed in other countries are very much the order of the day. For example, many men wear their fingernails long, or at least one fingernail extra long. They eat with their hands—even rice dipped in sauce.

They think nothing of walking down the street with an arm around a friend of the same sex—males and females alike. Many people smoke while the person sitting with them is still eating. Some men have a number of wives and are legally married to them all. In Australia most people would probably regard some of these habits as unsociable or unacceptable. Customs aside, I found the people I met in City X are among the friendliest, genuinely warm people on Earth who openly show their affection for friends and for each other.

The true test of my personal growth came when I had to hire and train 50 new staff. My only interests were their personality, presentation, education, experience and abilities and I appointed them only on that basis.

I am pleased to say that, as a result, we established a happy and close-knit team that worked together as a family. The project was successful and pioneered a new industry in City X and in that country.

So at least in the aspect of perception, I am happy to report that I have grown and have been enriched immeasurably by it. I've since discarded my 'travelogue'.

But individuals are not alone in projecting their travelogue onto others. Nations do the same thing to other nations! They project their version of history, their set of values and their culture onto their neighbours.

Instead of valuing differences it seems to be a human trait to beat others into conforming with the travelogue we project upon them. We expect people to dress as we do, speak with our accent, enjoy the same music, sport and food. If they don't, many judge them inferior, discriminate against them or abuse them. Millions of immigrants, including myself, can vouch for that through our experiences at the hands of some ignorant residents whose forebears had arrived earlier than we had.

In developed countries we tend to be smug about our material progress and it is easy for us to remember how thin is the veneer of civilisation. Who would have believed that in 1993 Germany Neo-Nazi 'skinheads' would set fire to hostels housing Turkish workers and causing many deaths? The reasons for the attack? The victims were Turkish!

Bosnia Herzegovena has suffered one of the most brutal wars of the twentieth century. It has endured atrocities not seen in Europe since the Third Reich. The reasons? Certainly historical, but even the historical factors are based on the fact that Serbs, Croats and Bosnian Muslims see themselves as 'different'.

The most obvious fact about individuality is that if there were no differences, none of us would be special, nor unique, nor simply... who we are. A mark of personal growth is the ability to value and celebrate differences—to acknowledge that it is the differences that make us special to each other. By looking within ourselves before looking at others we might avoid projecting our travelogue and achieve a most blessed release—a release that comes when we stop judging and accept people as being pretty much like us.

The fear of success

If you are anything like me, initially you will be puzzled that any person would be afraid of success. Yet this fear is one of the major causes of holding back—of being a follower rather than a Self-leader.

Zig Ziglar tells the story of a small elephant tied to a post. It cannot break free because the rope is too strong. However when the elephant grows to maturity it could easily break the rope but doesn't try because it has been conditioned to believe it doesn't have the strength.

Our conditioning affects us too. If a person grows within a poor family they might see themselves as belonging to that level of society. They might think and act as do the people of their group. Social pressures to conform will further entrench them with that socio-economic grouping. They might develop a self-identity as a 'worker', 'battler' or as someone who does not 'belong' in any other group.

There's an old saying that 'no man is a hero to his valet'. I learned the truth of this wisdom indirectly as a drummer in a band. The band was popular and we were engaged for many 'upper crust' functions. I was able to observe society's intoxicated luminaries behaving pretty much like other drunks. I thought that if those were our success stories, captains of industry and political masters, no one need doubt their own ability to reach and surpass their station.

This was reinforced in my transition from sergeant to commissioned rank. Beforehand I held commissioned officers in awe. When I became one, I was disappointed. They were just like anyone else. My disappointment was so complete that four years later I resigned my commission and ended my Air Force career.

The biggest hurdle you have to jump in overcoming the fear of success is to accept that changing any pattern or routine can, initially, be uncomfortable. Leaving who you are or what you are doing (comfort zone and part of self-identity) to change, or to do something else, can be risky as well. However fear of risk can also be an echo of conditioning drag, of living a storyline written by others.

The second biggest hurdle in defeating fear of success is that you have to make a firm resolution to live your own life. I don't mean just in the philosophical sense. I mean it literally. You have to be the master of your fate and accept the responsibility for how your life turns out.

Do you remember the true story of Terry White who changed his job as a sheet-metal worker, became an insurance salesperson, succeeded beyond his dreams but tried to take his life? Had he found the move away from his conditioned 'self' as a sheet-metal worker too distressing? Too fearful? Was he totally overpowered by conditioning drag?

We are conditioned to be afraid almost from the time we can walk—and often by well-meaning parents and friends (e.g. 'be careful,' 'the world is full of sleazy people,' 'you could be mugged/killed,' 'you'll lose all your money,' and so on). Consequently many people sabotage their own success. Not to the extreme that Terry White tried to do, but through excuses, procrastination, 'puking', half-hearted effort, passivity, absenteeism and so on. Extraordinary as it might seem they do these things to keep themselves within the known and familiar—within their comfort zone.

Others are too afraid even to try for success. They have been conditioned to think they can't or shouldn't achieve it or are awed by the perception they have of 'successful people'—as was I, until I grew wiser. They have been shackled to the post as surely as was the baby elephant in Zig Ziglar's story. But as you have decided to design you own life and to embrace a totem geared to achieving wealth, health and happiness, you are empowered by a noble purpose. That power will enable you to lead yourself out of fear-conditioning and into new possibilities for a bright and successful future.

Self-confidence

Many people who lack self-confidence worry more about what others think of them than what they think about themselves.

The fashion industry makes a fortune by exploiting this fear. How many women would be happy going to an important function in last year's fashions?

Whatever causes a lack of self-confidence—past ridicule, upbringing, fear of criticism, conditioning drag—the reality is that few people will pay much attention to you if you don't have confidence in yourself.

To boost your self-confidence concentrate on what lies ahead. Gather all your experiences and invest them in future successes. Here are some helpful hints:

■ *Planning.* Among the worst eroders of self-confidence is lack of planning. If you know you will face a tense situation (e.g. giving a talk to a group) plan for it. Know what you are going to do and say.

■ *Be prepared.* You have already recognised the value of preparation or you would not be reading this book. Researching a topic or problem gives knowledge. The motto of the Royal Australian Air Force's School of Parachuting is 'Knowledge Dispels Fear'.

In many cases what unsettles us is fear of the unknown. This generates negative feelings of doubt and worry. The result? Loss of confidence! Planning and preparation provide this knowledge and give us a feeling of control and of confidence!

■ *Group activity.* By this I mean the time tested confidence-builders such as cross-country hiking, camping, team sports and so on. These can strengthen us physically, socially and spiritually. For example, my son Paul and daughter Kerrie train regularly at a Karate club. The club, developed by a young man named Stuart Butterworth and styled 'Shin Yu Kai', emphasises tradition, self-discipline, persistence, mutual support and encouragement, and cheerfulness. It teaches members to avoid violence, to use their skills only in self-defence and then only as a last resort.

Through the exercises, club responsibilities, camaraderie and outings that are a strong feature of their club, Paul and Kerrie can attest to the increase not only in their own self-confidence, but in the self-confidence of many other people who have joined their club.

As the leader and founder of this Karate style, Stuart Butterworth encourages confidence-building by allocating responsibilities and providing tangible recognition for effort through awards, trophies and by expressing honest and sincere appreciation.

■   *Understanding mistakes.* A missile 'learns' by registering successes. The only way it can do this is by experiencing mistakes (i.e. veering off-course). The corrections (decisions) it makes to stay on-course are its responses to these 'mistakes' and lead it to its goal.

Greg Norman in his interview with John Garrity in the November 1991 issue of *Time* says of mistakes:

'Whether I've played exceptionally well or poorly, I've always been able to proceed as if nothing had happened. What's the point of crying over spilt milk? It's just going to create more anguish between your ears.'

Mistakes are never a sign for us to quit, but a time to gather what we have learned from experience and invest it into our next attempt.

Buck Duke, founder of Duke University and a chain of retail stores, said:

'A mistake? I've made mistakes all my life. And if there is one thing that's helped me, it's the fact that when I make a mistake I never stop to talk about it. I just go ahead and make some more!'

The person who never makes mistakes usually doesn't make anything.

Self-assertiveness

You probably know of people who always wind up with the routine jobs and miss out on fun and life because they are too timid to assert their 'rights'. These people are not uncommon. Courses are devoted to help them through assertiveness training. An essential problem for them is that they equate being assertive with being 'pushy', being a bully or simply with being aggressive.

Self-assertiveness is a manifestation of self-confidence. It is not aggressiveness, shouting, threatening or any other discredited tactic of the bully. Self-assertiveness simply means that you present your arguments, ideas or wishes with honesty and directness. You do it in a manner that does not offend, ridicule or humiliate other people.

Just because you have the ability to assert yourself does not mean you have to do it every time or that you have to 'make a stand' on every minor issue. Assertiveness is a method you need to apply only when:

- Your own interests, welfare or safety are being threatened.
- You are in a group and are not being given an opportunity to express your views fairly.
- Your views are being disregarded out of hand without due consideration.
- You know you are right but someone else is trying to change the way you think or wants you to do something about which you disagree.

If you are reluctant to assert yourself or your position, why not use our formula for meeting a challenge? Simply convert it into a procedure. For example:

- Adopt a polite but firm manner from the start.
- Introduce your position clearly, and early. Indicate your strong belief in your position, and that you intend to pursue it.
- Be persistent. Restate your view whenever you feel the meeting is moving in a different direction, that someone is hijacking it or that you are being ignored.
- Give credit where it is due. If someone makes a good point, accept it even if it is critical of your position, but show how and why it will not affect your stand.
- Listen. If there is a contrary view, criticise it objectively and calmly. Reinforce the benefits of your own position.
- Where someone else's view is equally valid, search for a compromise if that will achieve your objective.
- Don't get involved in character assassination or in personal attacks. If others attack you personally it weakens their position. Simply restate your case in a calm but direct way, pointing out the reasons why you feel strongly about it.
- If you feel the meeting is becoming 'overheated' with emotion, ask for another time to discuss your position after the emotion has cooled and everyone has had more time to think about the issues.

In the meantime, remember that:

- There is a difference between assertiveness and stubbornness, and between assertiveness and aggressiveness.
- It is the result that counts. If you can achieve the same result by adopting a compromise solution you have asserted yourself in a way that will have created a win–win outcome in the process.

The power within you

The power of the human mind is awesome. Jack Canfield, President of Self-Esteem Seminars, developed an interesting demonstration of the power of a positive mental attitude. Dr Susan Jeffers relates it in her book *Feel the Fear and Do It Anyway*. She writes:

> 'I ask someone to come up and stand facing the rest of the class. After making sure the person has no problems with his or her arms, I ask my volunteers to make a fist and extend either arm out to the side. I then tell them to resist, with as much strength as they can muster as I stand facing them (attempting) to push their arm down with my outstretched hand. Not once have I succeeded in pushing their arm down on my initial trial.'

Dr Jeffers then asks the volunteers to put their arm down, close their eyes and repeat 10 times: 'I am a weak and unworthy person.' She repeats the arm experiment and is able to bring the volunteers' arms down immediately.

Dr Jeffers asks the volunteers to close their eyes again and repeat 10 times: 'I am a strong and worthy person.' To everyone's amazement, she cannot lower the volunteers' arms again.

I have carried out the same experiment many times in Australia and abroad, and it has always worked. It demonstrates the awesome power we hold within our mind to influence our abilities and actions. That means we can empower those things that are positive and helpful to our Major Life Goal, and refuse to empower those things that are negative and harmful.

While it is difficult to choose a calm response, and to ignore and therefore not to empower a situation to hurt us when emotions are involved, it can be done. We might not be able to change how we feel but we are empowered to change what we do about it. This power is not in mere words or events, but within ourselves. We're in charge.

Read the books

I love good books. One of my treasured possessions is a personal library of some 1000 quality books collected over 25 years. I decided very early in my working life that the best schooling I could get would be the education I could give to myself—and this wouldn't include memorising the annual rainfall of Peru, drawing maps of the British Isles or the study of any subject that did not interest me.

I was interested in people, in what made so many of them extraordinary and in how I could pass on their secrets to those who wanted to achieve personal success based on Self-leadership and Personal Excellence.

Through my self-education program I learned that success leaves clues, and so I decided to learn from the experiences of those who had 'made it'.

Others who came to the same decision include Henry Ford, Thomas Edison who said 'I devoted every cent, regardless of future needs, to scientific books and materials for experiments', Simon Lake (developer of the submarine), Dwight D. Eisenhower (Supreme Commander of Allied Forces in World War II and later president of the United States), Robert E. Peary (discoverer of the North Pole) and novelist Rudyard Kipling.

There are many more people inspired towards their goal by a single book. Novelist Edgar Wallace read the dictionary from cover to cover, as did Millard Fillmore (president of the United States), playwright Laurence Bassett, British prime minister William Pitt, writer O. Henry and many other noted achievers. Their command of words made them outstanding communicators.

Even King Solomon advised: 'Buy learning, and wisdom, and understanding.' Self-leaders must have read King Solomon's advice too, because almost invariably, they are readers.

Humour yourself

Most people equate humour with the telling of jokes. However that is not what I mean by 'humouring oneself'. In my definition, maintaining a sense of humour means taking our work seriously, but ourselves lightly.

The ability to take ourselves lightly can preserve our reason in the most tense situations. For example, on being deposed from his throne King Farouk of Egypt said: 'There will soon be only five kings left; the king of England, Diamonds, Hearts, Spades and Clubs.'

Playwright Oscar Wilde, handcuffed and standing in pouring rain on the way to prison, took himself lightly when he told his guard: 'If this is the way Queen Victoria treats her prisoners, she doesn't deserve to have any!'

Humouring ourselves means the ability to look at life in perspective, not over-reacting at every trifle, and seeing humour in the things we and others do—including our folly. It can save our life. The following verse from a poem by Ella Wheeler Wilcox makes a point worth remembering:

> *T'is easy enough to be pleasant*
> *When life flows by like a song*
> *But the person worthwhile*
> *Is the one with a smile*
> *When everything goes dead wrong*

Your list of required success skills

In addition to what has already been covered, most successful people have skills in:

- developing success in human relations
- influencing others—winning co-operation
- influencing themselves—self-motivation
- dealing with their 'moments of truth'
- developing their instinct to win–win
- negotiating to win–win

■ speaking in public
■ managing time and work flow
■ managing money and making it grow
■ designing business plans/personal goal plans (a Life Blueprint)
■ tapping into their spirituality.

The remainder of this book for your success deals with each of these vital success skills.

If the journey of personal success is beginning to sound as if it needs too much effort—too much Self-leadership—a Bohemian proverb might help to focus your thoughts:

> *'The time will soon come when winter will ask us: "What were you doing all summer?"'*

For me, winter will be old age—that time when we've used up all our second chances; when we mostly live in our memories. That winter will ask: 'What did you do with your life?'

I don't want to reply: 'If only . . .' or 'I could have been . . .' I want to be able to look life in the mirror and say: 'I scripted the life I wanted, and then lived it.'

How about you?

KEY POINTS

■ Personal growth begins from the moment we accept that we alone are responsible for our future. This acknowledges that we must lead ourselves to the success we want, and not wait for someone else to lead us.

■ Adopt a personal totem. It will give you a place to stand—a way to interpret and meet daily challenges.

■ Knowing your own personality is important for success in human relations.

■ We often project our own travelogue onto other people. This is a great mistake. Value differences. Look out by looking in.

■ Some people fear success. This is because of conditioning. Live your own storyline, and not one written by others. Be a strong leader of self. Resist conditioning drag.

■ Self-confidence is vital. Bolster it through preparation, planning and activity. Learn from mistakes; don't fear them.

■ Self-assertiveness is a manifestation of self-confidence and indispensable to any leader. However it is not aggression or bullying. It is simply stating our case directly, calmly, consistently and in a persistent way.

■ We all have the ability to empower events or remarks to hurt us. Give power only to positive things.

■ Study is vital for achieving and maintaining success. Read the 'books'. One good book can save you many years.

■ A sense of humour is vital to happiness and well-being. It also helps us keep perspective. Take your work seriously, but yourself lightly.

Part 2

Developing your personal success skills

5

Developing your success in human relations

IN City X there is an entrepreneur who had achieved enormous success in his financial sphere of life. He owned one of the largest and most modern shopping centres in an upper class suburb, a very successful land development and housing estate and a variety of business enterprises. Yet he lost nearly all of it during a game of golf because of an abject failure in human relations.

He was following an elderly man who was playing golf some distance down the fairway. Although the elderly man was retired, he was still one of the most influential people in the country and carried a lot of clout. The entrepreneur knew who the elderly person was, but was irritated at his slow rate of play, and so he sent his caddy to ask the elderly man to step aside.

The elderly man politely sent a message that he wanted to play a relaxed game of golf, and would the entrepreneur please be patient. The entrepreneur sent his caddy back demanding the elderly man step aside, added a curt message to the effect that old pensioners shouldn't be allowed on the golf course, and that he was hitting through anyway.

In City X, few people get to such positions of wealth as did the entrepreneur without some sort of 'involvement' with people in government. At the end of the game the elderly person telephoned all his contacts in government and by the next day the 'government' and the entrepreneur's financial supporters withdrew from his projects. The result? The entrepreneur had just finished the most expensive game of golf in history. Overnight he was almost bankrupted and lost many millions of dollars.

This is, of course, an extreme case because the elderly person had the power to retaliate. But how many people facing 'insulting' situations would retaliate if they could? Many 'wounded' people may not retaliate instantly; they may not even get angry. They wait for a chance to get even.

Yet if you were to ask some arrogant people whether or not they were successful at human relations, my guess is that almost all would reply positively. If so, how would the majority of 'normal' people—people like you and me—reply? Here's an indication.

A US study by Tom Peters and Robert Waterman (from *In Search of Excellence*) asked 100 males selected at random to rate themselves on their ability to get along with other people. All of them rated themselves in the top 50 per cent; 60 per cent of them rated their abilities in the top 10 per cent and one in four placed themselves in the top 1 per cent.

Most of us like to think ourselves successful in our relationships with others. And if we are not so successful in this area, does it really matter? I believe it matters a great deal because human issues aside, we succeed best when we are able to get other people's best. That happens when people want to do the things we ask of them, not when they have to do them.

Most successful people regard their ability to get along with others as one of their chief assets. Some say it is their chief asset. They put a major effort into enhancing human relations in their business. For them, good human relations is a philosophy, not a tactic.

In the words of a great philosopher, Immanuel Kant:

> *'Every man is to be respected as an absolute end in himself and it is a crime against the dignity that belongs to him as a human being to use him as a mere means for some external purpose.'*

If we are to achieve holistic success we need to appreciate the value of other people, their contribution to our mutual success and their right to grow with us.

Yet a great many people who in a moment of reflection might agree with these principles, abandon them utterly when dealing with their employees, customers or with the community at large. Why not prove it for yourself? It would be a safe bet that if you were to ask 100 people whether they believed in 'respect for the individual', at least 99 of them would say 'yes'. So why do so many people say one thing yet do something else?

Many colleges teach people to be financial controllers, accountants, engineers—but how many teach human relations? Are people only 'consumers'? My own research indicates that how well you get on with other people depends largely on how you perceive them in relation to how you see yourself. That's where it all seems to start.

America's pilgrim fathers perceived the American Indians as savages who failed to make proper use of their land. Thus they justified taking it from them. (Of course, historical hindsight shows that the Indians were excellent managers of the land, creating open spaces so that game would proliferate. When the pilgrims saw that these spaces had no crops they were aghast. They judged the Indians from the perspective of European farmers.)

When the British claimed Australia they conveniently ignored the Aborigines who had lived there for the preceding 60,000 years, by declaring the continent, 'Terra Nullis' ('no-one's land'). They perceived the Aborigines as 'non-existent'—or as fauna. Only after 200 years of white settlement did the High Court of Australia acknowledge the lie and recognised native title under what has become known as the 'Mabo' legislation. How could those early settlers—most of them churchgoers who perceived themselves as good Christian folk—have failed so miserably in human relations on such a large scale?

In many countries corruption is so rife that any chance of improving the standard of living of their peoples is severely impaired. For example, in December 1993 a United Nations representative claimed that the factor most responsible for holding back the progress of Vietnam is its ubiquitous corruption. How must Vietnam's corrupt officials perceive their people to fail them so badly?

One major lesson I have learned in my travels is that different parts of the world progress at a different pace. It is easy for those of us who live in developed countries to look at the whole world through materially privileged eyes. But the world is not homogeneous. It's more like a patchwork quilt of different stages of development. Even within the United States different states live in different 'times'. New York, Los Angeles and Hawaii are not representative of all the United States.

If you want to travel back in time you don't need a time machine to do it. There are many countries where social, agricultural and industrial development is still centuries behind developed countries.

How do these differences play themselves out? Often, in global misunderstanding, suspicion and conflict. For example, two long-running tragedies of mutual fear and mistrust have played themselves out over many years. The uprising of the Palestinians against Israel is a particularly moving tragedy. Dispossessed of their land

and homes the Palestinians had been living under a harsh and often brutal Israeli occupation. This led to an uprising on the West Bank of the Jordan River. But Israeli soldiers had tanks and rifles. The Palestinians did not even have the sympathy of the world.

Yet they took a desperate stand year after year, meeting soldiers, tanks and bullets with stones. Many men, women and children died in the struggle. In effect the Palestinians were saying to the Israelis 'Kill us or free us,' using the only weapons they had— their hearts and stones.

The Jews who were brutalised by Hitler did not become gentle occupiers because of their own experiences. Much like brutalised children, they were transformed into particularly harsh bullies and oppressors.

Another example is the war of terrorism waged by the Catholic and Protestant people of Ireland. However both examples are national issues. What about at local level? How do people within a city see themselves? Consider the following, untypical example.

The November 1993 issue of Australia's *Who Weekly* reported that in Rio De Janeiro off-duty police officers patrol the streets at night and kill street kids for profit. In 1992, 1500 youths, most of them street kids, were killed in Brazil—more than four per day. In July, 52 adolescents were killed in Rio and by November of the same year 100 more deaths were added to the barbarity. Why?

Shopkeepers pay these off-duty police officers to kill the children because they fear being robbed. Authorities seem to turn away. But how do the citizens of Rio view this atrocity?

Opinion polls showed that 16 per cent of the people in Rio approved the killings. They think those police officers are just doing their job. To approve of the killings, how must those citizens see the children?

To quote Rio sociologist Herbert de Souza:

'Society sees these children as dangerous animals and that's why they want to eliminate them.'

In Bolivia many children live in sewers to escape similar death squads. Apart from the atrocities themselves, to my mind, when a society starts killing its children it must rank as the ultimate failure of human relations. (It must be acknowledged that many citizens of Rio and of Bolivia are just as appalled as are you and me.)

In 1994 Rwanda whole villages were incited to slaughter the people of neighbouring villages—men, women and children. It is estimated that over 500,000 people were murdered in this way. Why? In support of one side of a power struggle between two leaders and to grab the land of murdered people.

So here we are, in our 'modern day and age' and with the benefit of historical hindsight, witnessing the repetition of human relations fe ..ures that have plagued humankind for thousands of years. Why do people behave towards each other in this way? Part of the answer could lie in a game we all tend to play: the game of labelling.

The game of labelling

Generals label soldiers 'military assets', 'casualties', 'personnel' or 'infantry'. Labelling others masks their humanity and enables our conscience to cope with the injustices we inflict on each other. Why don't newscasters report the 'people toll'? Instead, they use the term 'road toll'. But it is people who are injured or who die.

Ellis Island was the gateway to 'the tired, the poor, the huddled masses yearning to breathe free' who emigrated to America. How did some Americans perceive the new arrivals? They met them as they came ashore and exchanged their European money—their life savings—for counterfeit American dollars! The victims weren't people; they were immigrants! That label helped make the difference.

The device of labelling is also used to help make actions more acceptable. For example, the Bosnian Serbs justified bombing their Muslim minority out of their homes in Bosnia Herzegovena through a label they called 'ethnic cleansing'. Perceptions guide—and help to mask—actions.

The year 1994 also spawned unscrupulous 'business people' who contracted would-be emigrants into what was little more than modern-day 'bonded labour'. By finding desperate people in China they entered into a contract with them to smuggle them illegally into the United States. Of course, the victims could not afford to pay the $30,000 fee, and so were contracted to many years of unpaid labour in the United States until the 'fee' was repaid. These 'business people' who traffic in human cargo perceive other people as products, not as human beings.

To succeed in human relations we need to have a human perception of ourselves, and to see our own needs, feelings and humanity in others—to see past the labels.

Succeeding in human relations through holistic success principles might not be essential to making money, but it is vital to happiness—to living a satisfying and fulfilling life. We are gregarious creatures. Few of us can be content in a life of social or physical solitude. To be truly happy we need companionship. We tend to enjoy beautiful things when we have someone to whom we can say: 'Isn't that something?'

Sharing ourselves, our feelings and achievements seems to be a fundamental need of the human psyche. So if to be happy we need each other, doesn't it make sense to learn how to get along? How to help one another? To do this we need a good understanding of how people think and behave.

How do you see other people?

As general manager of a large holiday resort complex one of my tasks was to hold monthly meetings that involved about 100 staff. In the weeks before each meeting I would analyse progress to date and identify any issues to be resolved. Before the meeting I would have all the answers with plans to implement them.

I couldn't understand why many of the staff didn't appreciate my efforts. After all, I always considered their welfare. Had I not done them a favour by saving them the effort of having to work things out for themselves? Hadn't I put in 12 to 14 hour days preparing all the material for them? Why weren't they more appreciative?

One day I read Dale Carnegie's book *How to Win Friends and Influence People*. What a revelation! It wasn't that I had ungrateful staff; the problem was me. Unwittingly, I perceived my staff as incapable, unable to solve problems or to contribute. Worse, I must have signalled inadvertently that I didn't appreciate or value them.

The way I perceived them triggered my response which to their ears must have sounded like 'I have no confidence in you. You couldn't solve even minor problems so I have done it all for you. This is how you will do it.'

What an oaf! My good intentions did not mitigate my actions at all! If I had grown enough to realise this (or had I read Dale Carnegie's book sooner) I would not have caused myself so much anguish. I would have benefited from the talents of my staff and the place would have enjoyed a happier environment producing even better results. To this day I feel ashamed when I think how blind I was, and how patronising my management style had been.

Consider the view of television advertisers. Do they see people as humans or as consumers? How do advertisements talk to you? Do you deserve to be congratulated because you buy a specific brand of margarine? Are you clever because you use a specific laundry detergent? Do you win sex with beautiful people if you drink 'Superfizz'?

How do others see people? Salespeople might see them as prospects. The police might see them as suspects. Shopkeepers might see them as customers. Airline workers might see them as passengers. Industrialists might see them as labourers. Politicians might see them as voters. Does that sound far fetched? Let's see.

In 1991 there was a severe drought in Queensland, Australia. The capital, Brisbane, recorded its longest period without rain. However this four month bounty of clear skies did not please all residents. When I took my car to a panel beater I asked him how things were going. 'Terrible,' he sighed. 'No rain—fewer accidents—bad for business. I hope we get rain real soon!'

To that panel beater, people were only customers. Never mind about injury, shattered families and trauma. Of course, not all panel beaters take such a selfish view. All I am saying is that it is too easy to see others through the looking glass of our own travelogue and to label them accordingly. Shouldn't we see each other for what we all are—as people much like ourselves?

Having travelled throughout Asia, Europe and the United States, the things that all people have in common stand out so vividly that it becomes virtually impossible for me to see other people as races apart.

By this I mean that if you observe people's daily routine of getting up, dressing, rushing to work, eating, working, worrying about our children, talking about the future, gossiping, fussing over appearance, enjoying music, films, and so on, we have infinitely more in common than we have differences.

Global travellers will tell you how small the world becomes. Within a few hours you can be on a different continent. The airport frenzy, the delays, the tiredness, the anxiety—all are the same for everyone.

Yet, inconceivably, someone somewhere is dropping a bomb upon someone else because they see their 'enemy' as 'different' from themselves. To world travellers that is not only an atrocity, but an anachronism; it is an irrelevancy to the real needs of the world and a discredited form of conflict resolution.

I am convinced that future generations will be amazed that we chose to create new problems of mutual destruction, atrocity and the propagation of human misery as the most appropriate means of solving our other problems.

In City X, respect for others is built into the very language. There are respectful terms of address even for the most lowly employee. At the popular level the culture is one of enjoying friendship, food and each other. But at the political level, the system is rife with corruption. One bank manager demanded (and received) a house valued at US$450,000 before he approved a commercial loan (at a more favourable rate of interest). At lower levels, everything has a kick-back. Police corruption is commonplace.

In the end, all these extra costs are borne by the poverty-stricken majority of the population through increased prices, further entrenching the poverty they desperately want to escape.

Recently their president appealed to all citizens to stop bribing police. He also appealed to businesses to increase wages five-fold in the next 10 years, and for people to cut down the high road toll—as if simply issuing a statement would bring these changes into effect. Most people in City X know that corruption, bribes and kick-backs reach up to the highest levels of government, and joke about it.

A short time ago the United States threatened to stop its humanitarian aid if the country did not improve the conditions of its workers.

Knowing the obstacles that face them and the system that suppresses them, it is a sobering sight to see uniformed school children marching with flags unfurled and with eyes filled with aspiration for the future. Yet outwardly the centre of City X looks like a modern metropolis with many high rise towers, hotels and some of the biggest monuments I have ever seen. So how do those in power see the people of City X? Generally speaking, people anywhere tend to get the government they deserve or the one they are willing to accept for the time being. (I do not want to give you the impression that all the people of City X are passive about the needs of their country and of their people. Many of them practise Personal Excellence and even more of them see the urgent need for change.)

In the end, a nation is made up of individuals, and if enough individuals want change for the better, sooner or later that change must occur. (At the time of writing these words there were three secessionist movements operating in the country of City X.)

In our journey we are seeking a change within ourselves—namely, an increase in our personal, holistic success. Unless we also succeed in human relations, we can't achieve that.

And while we strive for ourselves we can also influence others in our community to do the same by drawing their attention to these precepts. In doing so we can be instrumental in bringing about positive change. That way our whole community, including ourselves and our families, will benefit.

Holistic success requires that we treat others with the same consideration and human dignity with which we want them to treat us—that we seek to value the positive qualities of a person's character rather than to colour them with our own travelogue then gripe about the parts that don't fit, and that we seek to understand rather than to judge. That's Personal Excellence.

How do other people see themselves?

Most people are annoyed when others dump litter onto the roadside, start their lawn mower at 7 a.m. on Sunday, damage property and so on. They ask 'How can they do these things? Don't they have a conscience?' Well, yes and no.

Nearly everyone regards themselves as basically good. If you were to criticise most people for something they had done they would either suggest where you should go, or they would rationalise their action.

They had to start the mower at 7 a.m. because they would be going out for the day; they had to dump that litter on the side of the road because they didn't know the location of the nearest bin; or they had to rob that bank, sell that drug, beat that person.

The more you criticise people, the more they defend their position. Consequently it's almost useless criticising anyone for anything because it is unlikely to change a person's behaviour for very long and can breed resentment for a lifetime.

Seldom do we blame ourselves for anything and we certainly detest uninvited criticism from others. The fact is that most of us feel superior to others in some way.

If we teach ourselves to listen with the intent to understand rather than with the intent to reply, we might discover the other person's viewpoint. At that moment progress becomes possible. At that moment Personal Excellence is achievable.

How well do you like people?

Generally, if you are really interested in people they will like you. They will also be more co-operative and willing to 'buy' what you have to 'sell'. The question is: How can you like others if you simply . . . don't? It's dangerous to fake interest in others to win their favour. Such tactics transform genuine human interest into a device for our own ends. When placed under pressure our true nature breaks out for all to see and we are found out.

One of my favourite sayings is 'God invented people because He liked to listen to stories'. The seed of developing a sincere liking for your fellow humans could lie within that saying. Talk to people. Listen with empathy. Ask questions about things that interest them. You will soon realise that even the 'dull and ignorant' have their story and, more often than not, it is a very good one.

Before you can like others you need to like yourself. To like yourself you will need to base your life on core values of integrity, fair dealing and honesty—on Personal Excellence.

Give others a good feeling

One of the marvellous things about dogs is they live for affection. Regardless of what sort of day you've had at work your dog will always be glad to see you—eager to give and receive affection.

The other great thing about dogs is they give affection without a 'catch'. They are not trying to sell you anything or to flatter you to get their own way. It's little wonder that dogs have earned the reputation as 'man's best friend'. We can learn a lot about getting on with people from dogs—namely, be glad to see people. Treat people you meet as if they were guests in your home. Make them feel important. Isn't that the way you would like to be treated? If so, remember that most of us are just like you!

Learn the vital art of communication

When you go to a social gathering, what type of people do you find boring or irritating? Aren't they those who spend all evening talking about themselves? What they did, what they want, what they think? They don't give us a chance to talk about what we did, what we want, what we think.

If only conversations were like speech in books—one talks, the other listens, then replies. It's very orderly. Everyone has a turn. But in reality, life happens. Often two or three people have parallel conversations, talking about different things at the same time. For example, Parent A talks about Johnny's excellent efforts at football on the weekend, while Parent B listens, then replies with a statement about young Mary's tennis match. Parent A retorts with another salvo about Johnny while Parent B replies with a rejoinder about Mary. It's all smooth, conversational, friendly and all smiles. Yet the two parents are talking with—not to—each other.

Many people listen with the intent to reply or for words that enable them to steer the conversation in the direction they want. For those people, smooth and relaxed conversations elude them. It's because empathic listening is so rare that we enjoy a sense of importance when others really want to listen to what we have to say.

Is there a method for achieving effective person-to-person communication? For relaxing people at the outset? For getting them to talk? For being a good conversationalist? The answer is 'yes', but as for anything else, the art of good conversation takes effort and practice to master. Note the following discourse overheard at a party:

He: 'Did you watch the football yesterday?'

She: 'No'

He: 'Aren't you interested in football?'

She: 'No.'

He: (changing subject) 'Have you known [the hosts] long?

She: 'No.'

He: 'I've known them for years. In fact, I first met them . . .' (and off he went talking about himself).

There are several problems with the structure of this type of conversation. He was on the right track by asking questions. However they were 'closed' questions—the kind that can be answered with a 'yes' or 'no'.

So the conversation was awkward, stilted and uncomfortable. He then changed the subject to himself hoping the conversation might go more smoothly. The overall problem was that he talked about his interests rather than about the things she preferred.

Asking questions and listening with empathy are the two most vital keys to effective person-to-person communication. However to generate conversation that is relaxed, smooth and flowing we need to ask open questions. Those are questions that encourage a fluent response— questions that start with what, where, how, when, why or who (the six dialogue starters).

The previous conversation might have progressed in the following way if 'he' had used any one of those open 'question starters':

He: 'What did you think of the football yesterday?'

She: 'I didn't watch it, really.'

He: 'Oh? That's a pity. It was a great game. How often do you get to see the home matches?'

She: 'I don't. I'm afraid football doesn't really interest me.'

He: 'Oh? What sports interest you?'

This is not a 'great' conversation by any means but it flows easily and both people feel relaxed. At least he is trying to find out her interests.

Why not try it? Use any of the six 'open' dialogue starters. Be sincere in your interest. People will see you as charming and as good company provided you listen with empathy to their answers. But you too must play your part. If you don't understand a point, do not be too embarrassed to ask for further explanation.

One of my greatest periods of frustration occurred when I was training a new sales team in City X. The culture of the people is one of politeness and respect. When they don't understand your point, often they will smile and nod rather than ask you for more clarification. Even when I pleaded 'Please, if I am not making myself clear, say so. I won't be offended,' they would smile as if they understood. Most of them did not understand at all and even with the help of an interpreter, training was extended an extra week.

At work there might be an additional factor that can block good person-to-person communication—low morale. In those circumstances hardly any communication can take place because one party (staff) doesn't really want to listen. They don't even want to be there! In those cases morale needs to improve before effective communication can take place.

Avoid arguments

The best way to win an argument is to avoid it. Even if you prove your point correct, when you win an argument you lose. That's because when you win you've struck a body blow at the other person's ego—a blow that will not be forgiven easily.

You can't change people's opinions. They need to change them for themselves. Time shows again and again that the way to help others see your point of view is to show a sympathetic grasp of their point of view first. Saying to someone, 'You're wrong!' or insulting them by calling them names is not likely to influence their opinion one bit—quite the reverse. They will become defensive and resent you. Consider the following example of this principle at work.

In December 1993, Paul Keating, prime minister of Australia, publicly called Dr Mahathir, the prime minister of Malaysia, a 're-calcitrant' for not attending an APEC conference in Seattle. Did Dr Mahathir change his views? Here is what happened.

Within 24 hours of the statement an international row resounded in the corridors of Canberra and Kuala Lumpur. The media in both countries picked up the story and fanned the flames until it loomed bigger by the day. For two weeks statements and counter-statements darted across the Equator leading to threats of a trade war unless Mr Keating publicly apologised to Dr Mahathir.

In a poll taken in Australia during the height of the row, 75 per cent of respondents said that the Australian prime minister should apologise. The Australian Liberal Party (the opposition) had a field day in both houses of parliament.

Business people pleaded that hundreds of millions of dollars in trade were at risk. In the end, Mr Keating sent a letter to Dr Mahathir expressing 'his regrets'. However in the interim a lot of parliamentary time was wasted and much ill feeling was caused in both countries.

This incident eloquently makes the point that you can't change a person's views or make them want to co-operate by calling that person names—even at prime ministerial level.

In many cases it is our own attitude that leads to arguments. Instead of valuing differences we try to stifle them. Fear of differences can lead to extremes such as the Inquisition, the Holocaust, the poisoning of Aboriginal water holes in Australia, the murder of over 24,000 Polish officers and intellectuals by the Soviets at Katyn and at some NKVD offices in Poland, the gassing of Kurdish civilians by the Iraqis, the 'ethnic cleansing' of Bosnian Muslims by Bosnian Serbs, the massacres in Rwanda, and so it goes on.

Perhaps we can improve international behaviour by firstly improving the way we behave within our own community? (It might have been in recognition of such a proposition that Buddha centred his teachings on self-enlightenment and self-improvement.)

Jesus recognised this approach and focused on encouraging people to improve their own behaviour rather than on calling for political change. But many of us find that changing ourselves is extraordinarily difficult. If this were not so, when we have a personal disagreement why is it so hard to say in a warm and sincere manner: 'You have a different view? Great! Help me to understand how you see it.'

Given the previous example of Mr Keating's gaffe, would not this approach have produced a more acceptable reaction?

I hope we will always have differences of opinion. They are the spice of our intellectual life. The problem is not that differences of opinion exist. Mostly differences are converted into problems by the way some people express them and how others react to that expression. Given that we will always face these differences it is important to know how to respond in a win–win way. An effective start is by beginning in a friendly tone.

For example:

'I see your point. In many cases I think that would be quite right. But on this occasion it seems to me that . . .'

Or:

'I could be wrong. Let's look at the facts together so I can get it right.'

Isn't that much better than:

'I disagree! How can you have the gall to say that when you know . . .'

Or:

'You are a recalcitrant because you don't agree with me.'

Often we might argue over a statement that, in itself, may not be the issue in contention. What we might be objecting to may be the tone in which it was said or the manner in which it was conveyed.

Nevertheless in our day-to-day dealing with other people we are likely to encounter some who either don't know much about fostering good human relations, or who do not care. Like it or not, that is the reality.

They might want to argue with us and sometimes 'they' can be our boss. They could be someone who has the power to reward or to hurt us. Personal Excellence demands that even in these situations we must strive for a win–win outcome.

You can ensure a win–win result by converting the challenge into a procedure. For example, when you are summoned to a meeting that you know is likely to lead to an argument or confrontation:

■ Prepare yourself. Get all the background information you can on the issue. Make sure you understand the central issue itself and try to analyse it from the other person's point of view.
■ Make a list of important dates, communications on the matter with others, and so on.
■ List the main points of the issue in order of importance.
■ Be your own 'devil's advocate'. Think of the points and counter points the other party will make.
■ Develop answers to those points.

At the meeting:

■ Apply your empathic listening skills. Hear the other party out— totally. Let them make their case fully. Before you answer, take a few moments to consider what they have said. This shows you are not taking their view lightly.
■ When you reply, start in a calm, friendly tone.
■ Present your information and opinions tactfully and calmly. Don't lose your composure. Let the facts do the 'shouting' for you. Be persuasive but empathic.

- If the issue is important enough, 'bring on your witnesses'. That is, if you know of people who can clarify any point of misunderstanding or who can support your case, consider asking them to attend the meeting.
- Remember to create a win–win outcome by letting the other party 'save face'. You can achieve this with a simple concluding statement like:

'It seems that you weren't given all the information on this issue. Under those circumstances I can see how you reached the conclusions that you did, and without all the facts I would probably have reached the same conclusions myself . . .'

However there are times when you are caught in a heated meeting or argument for which you have had no opportunity to prepare. In that type of challenge the following process will help enormously:

- At all times bear in mind that many arguments can be diffused or avoided by good manners and gentle words. (This philosophy alone can convert what could seem like a heated argument into a valuable and calm discussion where everyone gets to understand how the issue looks from the other party's point of view.)
- Start friendly.
- Listen with empathy with the intent to understand and not with the intent to reply.
- If you are wrong or have made a mistake, admit it with good grace. You will be respected for it, and your Personal Excellence will be strengthened.

Avoid arrogance and rudeness

Again, how we respond to people comes down to the way we perceive them in relation to ourselves. You might have seen examples of people who are charming and polite to a boss, but quite rude to the secretaries or office clerks. Their perception is that secretaries and clerks aren't important. Not only is rudeness counter-productive, it is utterly unnecessary and reflects sadly on the person dispensing it.

Arrogance, on the other hand, comes from a feeling of superiority over others. Philosophers can fall for this trap too, as the great Immanuel Kant pointed out (from *100 Great Thinkers* by Bromberg and others):

> 'I am myself by inclination a seeker after truth. I feel a consuming thirst for knowledge and a restless passion to advance in it ... There was a time when I thought this alone could constitute the honour of mankind, and I despised the common man who knows nothing.
>
> 'Rousseau set me right ... I learned to respect human nature, and I should consider myself far more useless than the ordinary workingman if I did not believe that this view (respect for the individual) could give worth to all others to establish the rights of man.'

The story of the visit to Papua New Guinea by the Leahy brothers includes an encounter with 'hidden' tribes. The natives were amazed at how the brothers survived. After all they neither hunted nor fished. Over time the natives began to see the Leahy brothers as 'gods' or as 'spirits of their dead ancestors'.

One day their perception changed. The chief, with his most respected warriors secretly followed the Leahy brothers and observed them defecating. Afterwards the chief and his entourage went to inspect the excrement. At once the chief observed: 'It smells just like ours!'

I hope you will forgive this crude, but true example. It does make the point that arrogance has no place in human relations.

Build your human relations trust account

Stephen R. Covey's view expressed in his book *The Seven Habits of Highly Effective People* is that we build 'trust' accounts. In other words, my friendship and prior interaction with you has won trust and confidence. Every time I do something that builds on that, I deposit more trust into my account with you. Whenever I do something that asks you to accept it on trust, you make a withdrawal from my account.

Your account might have healthy trust deposits with family and friends, but what about with your work colleagues? How does your human relations balance look with employees, associates and other people in business?

Consider the situation where a person is falsely accused of a misdemeanour at work. If the balance in that person's human relations trust account is high, would not the company stand firmly by that person? What if the account were bankrupt?

Develop employee human relations

How we treat employees is determined by our perception of them. For example, if our emphasis is on the financial sphere of life we could regard them as 'labour' to do our bidding—another label masking their humanity!

I know an entrepreneur in City X who employs 2000 people. Although financially successful, he is not very successful with employee human relations. Staff turnover is high, initiative and morale low, and most employees put in the minimum effort required to keep their job. Why? Because the entrepreneur forgets that other people have families. He often calls very late meetings without notice and arrives one or two hours late for them.

He frequently asks key employees to work through the night to meet a deadline. They are not given additional rewards, are rarely consulted in a genuine way, and if anyone dares to question the entrepreneur's thinking, that person is embarrassed in front of his or her peers. Their pay, even by the standards of City X, is low.

Yet the entrepreneur asks for initiative, berates the employees for not 'using their heads', encourages them to do more, and often wonders why they do not perform efficiently nor show him any loyalty. He does not understand that people 'volunteer' to work with us; that we do not own them; and that if we treat them as volunteers, they will volunteer their best efforts in return.

Whether at work or at home, the value we place on human relations is a reflection of our own self-value and of our general set of values. The City X entrepreneur's chief value is money (self-confessed), which means that, to him, people must come in at second place. His philosophy is reflected daily in the way he manages his employee human relations trust account.

To fulfil our human needs people are all we have—so why not give them honest and sincere appreciation? We're sure to get it right back.

But of course, there is the constant pull of conditioning drag, of which I too am a victim from time to time. For example, I had a neighbour who was a builder. I needed an expensive extension for my house. Because he was a next door neighbour and short of work I didn't bother getting quotes. I gave him the job and all progress payments with alacrity.

When the work was done he had overcharged me by $1200 for bricks that were neither delivered nor laid. Naturally, I assumed this to be a simple error and using my best human relations approach talked it over with him, being sure to leave him a face-saving 'out'.

But he refused to check the work. I tried again, calmly and in a friendly manner, saying that I would be happy to pay him the extra if he insisted, provided he would first see if an honest error had been made. Many groans. Total intransigence.

To my discredit I threw away everything I knew of good human relations, influencing people and so on, and told him that if he didn't come over to see for himself, I could only assume that he deliberately cheated me—his own next-door neighbour.

He retorted that I was trying to cheat him, and we both lost our cool. I paid him the total amount, less a compromise of $800, with a note telling him that as soon as he could show me the extra bricks, I would pay him the balance and take him and his wife out to dinner at my expense. The result? A neighbour with whom we didn't talk.

The fault? Mine. I could have handled it better. I could have 'walked my talk'. I could have appealed to his sense of honour. The problem was that I hadn't yet reached a sufficient level of personal growth. And even then I suspect we won't win them all. Why? Because the other party's level of personal growth and conditioning drag also influences the outcome. The important thing is that by doing our best we'll win far more than we lose and reinforce our Personal Excellence in the process.

KEY POINTS

■ We succeed best when we are able to get other people's best. This happens when people want to do the things we ask of them, not when they have to do them.

■ How well you get on with people depends largely on how you see them in relation to how you see yourself. That's where human relations start.

■ We all tend to play the game of 'labelling', when we give people tags such as 'emigrants', 'foreigners' or 'labourers'. Labelling masks humanity. To succeed in human relations we need to have a human perception of ourselves, then lead ourselves to see our humanity in others—to see past the labels. That's Personal Excellence.

■ People centre their lives on different core values. They have their own personal totem. If we listen with intent to understand rather than with intent to reply, we might discover the other person's viewpoint.

■ It is not uncommon for success-driven individuals to look down on others who seem to have little ambition or drive. We should not project our own travelogue onto others and expect them to fit into the picture we have projected.

■ Give others a good feeling about themselves. Building their self-respect is the best way to win loyalty.

■ We all enjoy a sense of importance. Ask open questions about their interests, then listen with empathy to the answers. Let them do most of the talking.

■ If you win an argument, you lose. The only way to win arguments is to avoid them. If they can't be avoided, prepare for them, stay calm, listen with the intent to understand, not with the intent to reply, present your facts in an empathic way, and aim for a win–win outcome by allowing the other party to save face. If you are wrong or have made a mistake, admit it clearly and honestly. You will be respected for it.

■ There is no place for arrogance or rudeness in human relations. They are a weak person's imitation of strength and a block to learning.

■ Keep your human relations trust account balance high. You never know when others need to make withdrawals.

■ If we treat employees as volunteers—as we want them to treat our best customers, as if they are people with needs and dreams just like us—our human relations trust account balance will be high. Such high balances have saved companies.

6

Influencing others—winning co-operation

DUBBED 'The Queen of Sleaze' by some of the world's media, the undisputed pop queen of the 1990s, Madonna, toured her sell-out show in cities across Australia. It would have been easy to gain the impression that she organised it all herself. The truth is that she required the help of a small army of people on the ground and $25 million to put on her 'one star show'.

Sir Edmund Hillary and Tensing were the first people to climb Mount Everest. But to achieve their historic feat of endurance, courage and perseverance they needed the co-operation of 40 Sherpa guides and 700 porters.

Cigarette companies are experts at influencing people. They have raised smoking to celebrity status. Indeed, cigarettes have been called the world's cheapest status symbol. By linking cigarettes to 'beautiful people', the outdoors, film stars and sports events, they fool countless people—particularly the young—to equate smoking with status and an exciting lifestyle.

Pierre Cardin made his fortune by creating designer clothes for the affluent and famous then promoting his label around the world. The result? He sold 'celebrity-hood'. When people buy the Pierre Cardin label they buy status. They want others to be impressed with their purchase.

To achieve almost anything, including wealth, we need the ability to work with others—to influence them and to win their co-operation. Working with others is not like driving a bus where you are behind the steering wheel and everyone gets to where you steer. It's more like being in a vehicle that has lots of steering wheels—but only one belongs to you. The object is to get everyone to want to steer in the same direction.

So how do you influence people to want to do something you want done and have them like it? The key lies in the ability to influence and lead ourselves. It comes back to looking out by looking in—to Self-leadership and Personal Excellence.

It is through these skills that some people evoke deep feelings of loyalty in their employees. They influence them to perform unpleasant tasks and to work long hours willingly. Here are two examples.

Australian Airlines (now Qantas) is a carrier that at one time had captured a relatively minor share of the business market. Through an imaginative advertising campaign based on the friendliness and co-operation of their staff they reversed their plight to become the market leader in Australia within a very short time.

According to its chief executive, James Strong, over 150 staff volunteered to take part in taping a television commercial. With takes and re-takes they remained on the cold tarmac until 3 a.m., with no pay, no complaint and only an airline meal as recompense. Wives and husbands had also been waiting to take their spouses home, but all remained to help the company build its image.

Another airline, Compass, had launched its career based on cut-rate fares but unfortunately did not survive. However as directors were frantically trying to establish a line of credit so the airline could keep going, staff appealed to the public for donations. They used their imagination, gave freely of their weekends and nights, and in a short while had collected over $3 million.

These things were not achieved through 'manipulation' or cajolery but through a basis for more satisfying human interaction—through a philosophy, not a tactic. This means we need to lead others to co-operate by creating win–win situations. A 'win' for the other person is one that reinforces their sense of self-esteem, recognises their humanity, enhances their feeling of being appreciated or benefits them materially. The win–win philosophy is far more effective than are fear or threats.

While in most cases it is true that if you threaten to dismiss an employee the task will get done, it will be done in a grudging, resentful way. The result? Staff who aim to do only the minimum, who usually need further threats to motivate them and who will have little or no loyalty to you or to your business. That style of 'influencing' creates a dispirited and unhappy atmosphere. Often the solution employed by senior management is to dismiss the manager.

In an age where people tend to be loyal to their profession rather than to their company, developing the skill to win co-operation is even more important. To earn co-operation we need to co-operate. We might have to meet others half-way, give in to a minor point to win a major one, or compromise. Why? Because there is only one way to get other people to do something well, quickly and cheerfully—they must want to do it. There is no other way.

Many successful men and women will tell you that one of their most important assets is their ability to influence others. You too have that ability. If you develop it you will be promoted more quickly and succeed to a greater extent. Here are some effective methods that have worked well for countless leaders.

Use the sweetest sound

The most important thing to us, is us! Our ears tune in whenever we hear our name. It has a sweet sound that we value above music. It is ours. It *is* us. Morning, noon and night, we love the sound of our name.

Roger Viard, director of the famous French restaurant, Maxims, addressed clients by name, knew their special demands and where they liked to be seated.

When our name is called we listen attentively to the sentence that follows it. Professional salespeople use it just before making an important point. Teachers use it to get our attention. Good conversationalists use our name often to stroke our ego. We lap it up. So if you want to influence people and win their co-operation one of the very basic requirements is to use their name.

That is not always easy. Our natural inclination to evaluate each other when first introduced means that most of us forget the person's name immediately. So we cop out by pleading 'I'm terrible with names.' The truth is there is no such thing as a bad memory—only a lack of Self-leadership. For salespeople, remembering and using names is a vital element of sales success. Here's the 'IRA' formula for improving your name-memory:

■ *Impression*. When you first meet someone, get a clear impression of their face and name. Link the two together in your mind. If it's appropriate, ask them to repeat it or to spell it.
■ *Repetition*. Repeat their name to yourself (and use it) at short intervals.

- *Association.* Associate their name and face with a mental picture, preferably a moving picture. (The more ridiculous the association, the easier it is to remember it.)

So the first rule of influencing people and winning co-operation is to make a practice of remembering and using names. (Jot them down. Ask people to spell them so you can form a stronger impression. Use the names often so they will be imprinted in your mind. Use your imagination to link their name with their most prominent feature.) If we can't remember the other person's name how can we expect them to remember us?

My entrepreneur friend in City X takes a shortcut to winning co-operation. Whenever he visits an executive of a large company he takes an a small sum of money and leaves it as a 'thank you' for the executive's secretary. He might not remember the secretary's name, but he or she will remember his (and be more willing to put him through on the phone or to make a future appointment).

Smile

Have you heard of the man who fell in love with a smile and wound up marrying the whole woman? It may be a humorous extreme, but it illustrates a smile's powerful influence on the person receiving it.

Research shows that people who smile often tend to lead fuller, happier lives, raise happier children and, for salespeople, sell more. When we smile we signal to others that we are friendly and glad to see them. Smiles are free! They make it almost impossible to be angry while smiling in a heartfelt way. So when you meet someone who's run out of smiles, why not give them one of yours? (They'll give it straight back!)

Appeal to people's sense of honour

We often do things to live up to other people's faith in us. Sometimes appealing to one's honour can influence the most unco-operative individual. Consider the following conversation:

Manager: 'John, the company's doing it tough. But we can pull out of it by working together.'

Supervisor: 'What do you mean?'

Manager: 'You're in charge of a good team, John. But the results they're bringing in are lower than those of other teams—and they've got fewer people. We need increased productivity from everybody.'

Supervisor: 'I don't know who you've been talking to, but I can tell you we're all working our tails off.'

Manager: 'I'm not saying you're not working hard. What we've got to do is to work smart.'

Supervisor: 'What are you getting at?'

Manager: 'John, I know you'll do whatever it takes to help. If you have to get new staff, I'll back your judgment. Meanwhile take a look at how you can improve your team's work practices. Talk to other team leaders. Find out what they're doing. I know I can rely on you.'

There's nothing wrong with trying to influence an outcome by appealing to a person's honour. It has the added benefits of building their self-image and reinforcing positive values. Appealing to honour, coupled with a demonstration of faith in the person, is far more effective than using fear tactics. It creates an environment of approval, acceptance, co-operation and goodwill.

To inspire an otherwise passively conditioned group into becoming a top sales team in City X, I appealed to their sense of pride and commitment to their family. In their culture people will more often be motivated and influenced by what they can do for their family or by what their family will think of them, than by the prospect of personal gain.

I asked the team to reflect on the fact that they were introducing a new industry to their country, generating wealth, creating jobs for others and helping their community.

I suggested their job would give them an opportunity to achieve their personal goals, help the company grow and to win the respect of their families. Everything I said was true. I had faith in them.

They could see it and they responded. Did it work? Yes! In a short time they achieved results that even surprised me.

Faith in the individual's ability to perform well is the other magic ingredient for winning co-operation. Many leaders find this a difficult thing to do because for it to work they have to risk that people will make mistakes. So they seldom let go. But by not letting go they rarely get optimum results.

At the conclusion of the American Civil War, victorious general Ulysses S. Grant told president Abraham Lincoln: 'I was successful because you had faith in me.'

Appeal to people's imagination

Have you ever presented what you knew was a great idea but failed to excite anyone into backing it? To win others to our way of thinking we need to appeal to their imagination. We need to impress our idea so it will not be forgotten or buried with others vying for attention.

For example, imagine you were selling a new seat belt on the basis of its great strength. How effective would it be to table a list of specifications including stress tests, material specifications, comparisons, and so on? It might gain you sales, but how long would it take for your competitor to win business away from you or for your product to be forgotten?

Why not appeal to imagination? Why not have a helicopter lift a car by a single seat belt? You won't need statistics to convince anyone of your product's strength. More importantly, they would remember the image you created for a very long time. The publicity would be an added plus. Appealing to imagination is stock in trade for advertisers, film directors and entertainers, and it could work for you too.

Author Colleen McCullough discovered that back in 1972 Random House received 7000 unsolicited manuscripts each week. When she wanted to publish her first novel *Tim* she decided to go through a literary agent. However most literary agents are not usually interested in unpublished authors. Rather than post yet another unsolicited manuscript, Colleen McCullough decided to send the best letter an agent had ever seen, on the theory she would consent to read the manuscript 'only if my letter showed her what a terrific writer I was'. The subject of her letter was 'How I hated cleaning the stove.' It worked!

So when next you are presenting an idea, use flair! Don't say your idea will sell 20 more cakes for every two sold now; take 22 cakes to your sales presentation. Place two on one side of the table and 20 on the other.

Recently this principle worked even for a marriage proposal. Faced with his loved one's indecisiveness, an enterprising young man took her to a restaurant for what she thought would be a dinner date. She had no idea what was in store even when the television cameras arrived.

At the right moment, the curtains opened. In the garden outside their window, fireworks slowly and magnificently lighted the words: 'Shirley, will you marry me?' She accepted.

Find the reward

WIIFM? (What's in it for me?) is alive and well in all of us. Reward need not be monetary. It could take the form of recognition, appreciation, esteem or satisfaction. We do things because we get something out of it. We give money to charity for a feeling of unselfishness. (Sometimes we do it to prevent a feeling of embarrassment.) Whatever we do, we do it because of WIIFM?

If we know that people crave appreciation and reward, doesn't it make sense to provide it?

Thomas J. Watson, founder of IBM, believed that the way to win people's loyalty was by bolstering their self-respect. His son, Thomas J. Watson Jr, later to become chairman of IBM, learned the importance of bolstering self-respect when he saw how his lack of self-confidence was transformed by his Air Force manager General Bradley.

In his book, *Father, Son and Co.*, he writes:

'On [my] reports General Bradley would often scrawl: "Thank you very much", and sometimes "Excellent" or even "Splendid"—small compliments that drove me to do an even better and more vigorous job. My months with Bradley were among the most important of my life because he showed me I had an

*orderly mind and an unusual ability to focus on what was
important and put it across to others.'*

For many years Christian Dior was the world's guru of fashion. He
made a special point of giving credit to others such as his head tailor, a young man named Pierre Cardin. He said to Pierre publicly:
'Take up the torch. It can be yours.'

Another of Christian Dior's talented staff was a young man
named Yves Saint Laurent. Christian Dior made sure the fashion
world recognised the talent of his gifted employees. Passing credit
to others is a great reward for the giver and the receiver.

When other people reward us with faith and confidence we
tend to rise to meet their expectations. Rewarding each success—no
matter how small—is an effective way to reinforce co-operation. It
also provides a good feeling and a sense of achievement for the person
rewarded. It builds success patterns.

Next time you want to influence someone to co-operate, ask
yourself: WIIFH? (What's in it for him or her?) Credit? Appreciation? Recognition? Importance? Material gain? If there are none of
those, they might not be influenced to co-operate at all.

Give people a challenge

Sometimes we try our best to influence others but to no avail. Why
not give them a challenge? Why not appeal to their ego?

In meeting a challenge the rewards are self-esteem, self-confidence, recognition and achievement. (Often it helps to have a material reward as well.) Competitions are largely based on this principle
just as 'bonuses' are given for achieving work quotas. (Even bonuses
work better if there is an element of competition involved.)

A manager might post a junior officer to a more senior position.
The challenge is for that officer to handle the job successfully. In the
meantime the manager makes it clear that if the junior succeeds, a
promotion could result.

Individuals who say they can't be bothered with a challenge
are probably afraid of failure and are making excuses ahead of time.
They are simply making a 'wooden leg' to strap on later as their 'cop
out'. They have surrendered to conditioning drag.

Give people a good reputation

Wild Bill Hickock was given a reputation he had to live up to—or risk being shot dead. During a gunfight he killed two men—in self-defence. The story found willing ears in the sensation-hungry West of America's new frontier. It grew so much that as people repeated it the number of men Wild Bill was supposed to have killed single-handedly grew to ten. Armed only with a pistol and a hunting knife, he was supposed to have sent all of them to 'boot hill'.

He strenuously denied the story, but people thought he was being modest. He became the target of any young thug out to build a reputation. To stay alive he had to practise using his pistol for hours every day just so he could 'live up to his reputation'—and stay alive.

You might have seen the principle of influencing a person to 'live up to' a reputation at work. A president or secretary in charge of a meeting will thank 'Mr Jones' for his outstanding contribution to a particular effort and might add: 'He always produces outstanding results.'

It follows that, more often than not, Mr Jones will try to live up to his reputation because we all want to enjoy respect and admiration. You could use the same principle. If you have an important task to be done but feel you won't be overwhelmed with volunteers, you could try the following approach:

> *'[Jane] I need someone who can be relied on to get things done. I know you're very busy, but I couldn't trust this job to someone less able.'*

Giving people a good reputation to live up to builds their self-esteem and lets them know their skills are recognised and appreciated. Everybody wins when you take that approach.

Learn the art of counselling

In City X I witnessed two outbursts by a chief executive of a large company. In the first instance he lost his temper in a management meeting. He castigated and ridiculed a manager in front of her peers and her superior. He accused her of incompetence and within a short time she left the room—and the company.

Had she been incompetent? No. The fault lay in the chief executive's usual failure to communicate. The company lost an effective office manager and it took weeks to find another half as good. On the second occasion he called to task a senior officer in front of a group of executives (as the corporation's consultant, I happened to be there too). Virtually yelling at her, he continued to berate her even though he had already made his point.

I stopped it by reminding him that if he didn't leave for the airport right then, he would miss his flight to New York. It worked.

But the officer walked out of the office and out of the company, leaving a pile of important tasks unfinished. Only she had the knowledge to complete them.

That was not counselling. That was bullying.

Counselling others, drawing attention to their mistakes indirectly and admonishing in a supportive, constructive way in private while letting them retain their dignity is the hallmark of Personal Excellence.

When we are counselled we expose our ego. We become emotionally vulnerable. In those sensitive circumstances everyone feels uncomfortable. Here are some suggestions to lessen the discomfort of counselling, to preserve dignity and to win co-operation:

- Find something you can praise about the person. Express your appreciation for their efforts. Be specific. Mention instances.
- Discuss the problem area. Listen with empathy to their point of view. Make the problem appear easy to fix. Preferably, ask for their suggestions. If necessary, help them find ways to fix it.
- Praise their good points again and encourage them to keep up their good work. Let them know you're pleased they're in your team and that you have confidence in their ability to fix the problem.

If you want to modify a person's behaviour you'll succeed only if they want to modify it. (Because of conditioning drag, it's difficult enough to achieve behaviour modification even when people want it.) The challenge is to lead them to want to change, otherwise there can be no prospect of lasting success.

Clear co-operation barriers

Sometimes people want to co-operate but have so many 'feelings' and 'things to moan about' that these factors form a barrier to effective win–win behaviour. I learned this point when, as a newly appointed sales manager for a large insurance company, I could not get the sales team enthused about my ideas. I knew the ideas were sound because they had worked very well for me elsewhere. The problem was that the team was so full of gripes about what the company had 'done to them' that they simply were not motivated to put in any 'extra effort'. Taking my own advice I converted the challenge into a procedure by doing the following:

■   I called a meeting and explained my feelings of frustration at the lack of enthusiasm.
■   As we had to work together, I asked them to help me find a way through the impasse.
■   Using a whiteboard I listed all the things they felt were preventing them from co-operating and from working together as a team. As the answers came in—slowly at first—I listed them on the whiteboard. My empathic approach encouraged others to put their views and before long we had identified a range of co-operation barriers.
■   I divided the list into the following issues:
    —   those about which we could do nothing
    —   those that were established company policy but about which we felt we should fire a 'rocket' at head office through a letter (on those issues we agreed not to expect any positive action and not to let any lack of reply prevent us from striving to achieve our goals)
    —   those that we had the power to control.

In the end we decided to ignore the first two groupings and discussed ideas on how best to deal with the items within our control. We prepared a plan of action and set time limits for its achievement.

Having given the team an opportunity to vent their feelings and to let me know how, in their perception, they were treated unjustly by the company, we emerged from the meeting in a co-operative frame of mind. Looking back to that day I regard it as the moment when the staff and I became one team. We went on to win awards.

Avoid giving orders

It is helpful to remember that leaders get to the top largely on the efforts of those below them. So if you do not like taking orders from your superiors it should come as no surprise that most people are just like you.

When people choose to invest a third or more of their life in working with us it does not follow that we own them. We 'buy' their labour. We don't 'buy' them.

So whether we are a senior or junior executive or a worker at the bottom of the line, we all prefer being asked to being ordered. We gain much more from the efforts of our employees by winning their loyalty, by making them want to co-operate and by treating them as volunteers. Instead of barking 'Do this!' or 'Do that!', why not try something like: 'Could you please . . .', and add 'Thanks'.

Truly successful people don't give orders. They suggest. For example: 'Could you give some thought to how we might . . .' and 'Do you think . . . could be more effective?' or 'What's your recommendation?' That approach avoids resentment and grudging acceptance. It treats people with dignity and creates a happier work environment.

General Ike Eisenhower, commander in chief of the Allies during World War II and later president of the United States, had all the authority anyone could ask. Did he go around ordering people?

According to Stephen E. Ambrose: 'Eisenhower's method was to lead through persuasion and hints, rather than through direct action.' The man who could order, preferred to ask, hint and suggest.

Aesop wrote a fable that I believe encapsulates the essence of effective human interaction.

Here's a paraphrase:

'The wind saw a man in an overcoat walking along a dusty road and said to the sun: "I bet I can force that man to take off his coat!" So he blew and blew and created a mighty wind. But the stronger the wind, the more tightly the man held onto his coat.

'Finally it was the sun's turn. With a smile he increased the warmth of the air. Feeling the kindly warmth the man gladly removed his coat.'

Brainstorm instead

Many managers call staff together, present a new system or change as a fait accompli and then expect unswerving commitment and co-operation. I have fallen into the same trap many times in the past, but have since found that you can win more co-operation by involving staff and by giving them an opportunity to contribute their own ideas.

Brainstorming can be a great way of getting solutions to challenges—solutions that might never occur to you. Done well, it not only strengthens co-operation but builds morale and staff confidence. It can also help to relieve stress and can be a lot of fun. Here's the procedure:

■ Outline the challenge (e.g. how to increase 'widget' production).
■ Explain that as they have the 'hands on' experience (or as they will be implementing the new system), you need their ideas on the best way to achieve the goal.
■ Explain the 'brainstorming' process. Ensure they understand that you want all their ideas—no matter how 'silly' they might appear to them at first.
■ Ask them to withhold judgment on any idea until the end of the process. Your primary aim is to list as many ideas as possible.
■ Conduct a practice run. (The one I use is to invite ideas for using a paper clip. Some groups come up with 50 uses or more. It's fun, familiarises them with the procedure, and relaxes them.)
■ Delegate someone to list the ideas on a whiteboard.
■ Again outline the challenge to be solved. Write it as a heading on the whiteboard. Ensure everyone understands the issue.
■ List as many ideas as possible.
■ When the group has run out of ideas, ask them to identify those ideas that are similar and which should be deleted, and those that are impractical, unlikely to succeed or plainly impossible.

■ Work on the ideas that are possible.
■ Select a final list. Place the ideas into priority order.
■ Thank everyone for their contribution.
■ Consider the issue. Develop a strategy to meet the challenge.
■ Have the final list and your proposed solution typed.
■ Convene another meeting of those involved and outline your solution.
■ Ask for comments.
■ Implement.

This procedure wins co-operation because those affected were consulted and involved. They have part ownership of the process and of the solution. Their co-operation was not taken for granted 'yet again'.

Value the input of others

Do you call a meeting to find out what others think, or to tell them what to think? Is the following example something like the meetings you have opened?

> *'Thanks for coming to today's meeting. As you know, our target for this quarter is less than half way to being met and we only have three weeks to do something about it! So what you will do is this, that and the other . . .'*

Or is it reminiscent of meetings you have attended? I'm ashamed to say those are like the meetings I used to run! That approach leads to some of the key failures of meetings. That is:

■ 'Group think' where no one will air doubts or say anything that could threaten the harmony of the group.
■ 'Silence equals agreement' where you assume that because no one raised any objections or aired concerns they must be in agreement.

I've found this approach is far better:

> *'Thanks for coming along to today's meeting. As you know,*

our target for this quarter is less than half way to being met
and we only have three weeks to do something about it.

'If we put our heads together we can use our combined
experience to work out an effective plan of attack.

'I'd like to hear from each of you. I want to hear what you
have to say. In your opinion what can we do starting right
now that can get us back on track?'

I would list their suggestions for all to see, give credit and encouragement to those making them, weigh up each suggestion and after adding my own expertise devise a plan that would recognise achievement and provide reward.

Too many leaders think that because they are the managers they have to think up strategies all by themselves. That is a great mistake. It shows a misunderstanding of effective management.

No one has a monopoly on good ideas. By excluding input from others you deprive yourself of their resourcefulness and experience. I know, because earlier in my management career that was one of my major failings.

A successful technique for ensuring that doubts and differing views are aired is to appoint a 'devil's advocate' whose job is to argue against the motion. This would lead to discussion and avoid another common weakness of meetings—letting a few do all the talking.

The role of good leaders is to point the way, and then use every resource to co-ordinate the efforts of those in their charge to achieve a desired goal. The challenge is to lead others to lead themselves. To do this we need co-operation. However the 'boss' also needs to co-operate.

If that thought makes you feel insecure, it shouldn't, because far more is achieved in a spirit of harmony and co-operation than in an atmosphere of disapproval or autocracy. Not the least of those achievements are a far happier staff—and manager.

Win co-operation for change

One of the greatest challenges in winning co-operation is leading others to accept change and to work with it rather than against it. The truth is we all tend to resist change that:

- ■ is going to cause us inconvenience or discomfort
- ■ will cost us money
- ■ will decrease our perceived position on the corporate totem pole or will diminish our perceived 'seniority'
- ■ will force us to change the way we do things
- ■ resists our conditioning drag.

Resistance to change can cost companies billions of dollars. For example, IBM invented the technology for personal computers. Although managers down the line saw the potential of the new product, senior managers resisted the change away from mainframe computers—IBM's traditional product. Consequently companies in Japan, Europe, Taiwan and South Korea were able to become the new market leaders, costing IBM its leadership and many billions of dollars.

General Motors spent US$77 billion to 'robotise' its manufacturing plant—all to resist change. Up to then they had dictated what type of car people would buy. Their new plant would produce cars more efficiently, but only one model at a time—the model GM decided to produce. They left out the flexibility to respond to market demand and lost billions in sales.

At a personal level many of us have idiosyncratic reasons for resisting the challenge of the new. Again, an effective method for meeting any challenge, including resistance to change, is to convert the challenge into a procedure. Namely:

- ■ Get people involved early in the planning stages. Help them to suggest areas for change, solutions, and so on. Give them some ownership of the process. That way they won't be 'ambushed' by a fait accompli.
- ■ Identify those in the group who have the respect of others. Bring them on board and win their support for the change. They are opinion leaders and will influence positively the other people in the team.
- ■ Initially, work on and with those who are happy for things to change. They will form a platform upon which you can build.
- ■ Analyse the change itself. Who will be most affected? Interview those people separately and provide them with assurance and support. Promote the positives to counterbalance any negatives of the change.
- ■ Show leadership by formulating a 'plan of action' for implementing the change. Ensure it clearly identifies possible problems

and offers solutions. This will build confidence in you as their leader and will help to allay any fear of 'what could go wrong'.

∎ Be enthusiastic about the change. Outline the benefits change will bring, especially to those affected by its implementation.

∎ Work out a timetable to implement the change a step at a time, w...a a minimum of disruption.

∎ Be empathic. Show consideration for the fears and feelings of those subjected to the change and who are not responding as well as are others.

∎ Be responsive to the human needs for assurance, respect and recognition.

Leave people a face-saving exit

Avoiding embarrassment and humiliation is everyone's goal. We smart at anything or anyone who inflicts blows on our perceived dignity. More often than not, such wounding leads to long-term rancour and even violence.

In Asia, avoiding such injury to ego is termed 'saving face'. This need is alive and well in Western countries too but is not given the same emphasis. Nevertheless we ignore the fragility of the human ego at our cost.

You may have witnessed examples where a manager rebuked an employee in front of his or her peers. How did the employee feel? Even at home, one family member may embarrass another in front of guests. What is the result?

If the people who were humiliated did 'co-operate', was it in a grudging, resentful way? Did it bring about lasting co-operation? Or were they simply waiting for a chance to get even?

The following true story is a marvellous example of winning co-operation by leaving a face-saving exit.

Bruce, a do-it-yourself handyman, installed a ceiling light in his house. He basked in the extra light and warmth it provided during the daytime and the soft moon glow that washed his lounge room at night.

Reclining in his armchair and contemplating the pleasures of his work he heard the rattling noise of what he thought were rocks being thrown onto his roof. Quickly looking up he saw a crack that ran down the protective exterior of his ceiling light. Rushing outside he caught a glimpse of two boys running away from his house, and recognised them.

The next day Bruce patiently climbed onto the roof, temporarily repaired the ceiling light and retrieved the 'rocks'. Only, to his surprise, they were potatoes. His next step was to consider what should be done about the situation to avoid further damage.

If you are like me and most other people you probably would have talked to the boys' parents, explained what had happened and sought replacement of the cracked glass. But Bruce didn't think that would work. It might have replaced the broken glass, but the boys would have been humiliated in front of their parents and in revenge could wreak more damage.

Instead, Bruce washed and peeled the potatoes, made a tasty potato soup, filled a bowl and took it to the boys with a note that read: 'Boys, this is another use for potatoes.'

The result? The boys ate the soup, returned the washed plate and apologised. (As it happened, Bruce was also an avid model train collector, and while they were in his home the boys were allowed to play with the trains. A friendship developed.)

By not reacting angrily to the situation as most people probably would, Bruce had the broken ceiling light replaced by the boys' parents, he ensured no further damage would be done to his house by the boys, won their friendship, and everyone 'saved face'. That's Personal Excellence.

To avoid causing loss of face in your dealings with people, why not develop the habit of considering, before you act, whether or not your decision, action or statement could cause the other person embarrassment?

Develop genuine empathy

The principles we have discussed will help you achieve co-operation. However there is one ingredient that you and you alone can add—a genuine empathy for the needs and aspirations of those working with and around you. People will recognise the person who has a sincere regard for their welfare and who promotes a win–win outcome.

If you only remember one aspect of this chapter let it be this—before you act, put yourself in the minds of those you want to influence and ask yourself: 'How would I feel? How would I react? How would I like to be approached?' That's Personal Excellence—the foundation of the holistic success formula.

Personal success formula refresher

$$S = \frac{Asl^2}{PE}$$

Success equals Attitude times Self-leadership squared over Personal Excellence.

KEY POINTS

- To attain your specific Major Life Goal you need the co-operation of others.
- To influence co-operation convert the challenge into a procedure. Use people's names. Smile. Appeal to their sense of honour.
- We all love ideas. To impress your ideas, appeal to the imagination.
- Nothing succeeds like reward. Recognition, appreciation and a feeling of importance are the most sought-after rewards.
- In some cases winning co-operation might be as simple as providing a challenge.
- Most of us try to live up to a reputation. You can influence some people by 'creating' a reputation for them. This builds their Self-leadership.
- Counselling is behaviour modification. Let the other person retain his or her dignity. Encourage. Praise specific achievements. Use your qualities of Personal Excellence.
- Brainstorm instead. When you face a challenge that relies on the co-operation of your staff to succeed, there is no need to think of all the solutions yourself. Why not involve them early in a brainstorming session? Get their ideas. Give them ownership of the issue and of the solution. Often you will uncover great ideas that might not otherwise have occurred to you. Everyone wins.

■   Don't give orders. Ask. Thank. Lead others to want to co-operate.

■   Call a meeting to find our what others think, not to tell them what to think.

■   To win co-operation for change you need to be sensitive to the human needs of others. Identify who will be affected and give them assurance and support. Get people involved early. Design a change action plan. Be enthusiastic about the change. Win over opinion leaders in the group. Be empathic and show consideration for the feelings of others.

■   Remember to leave others a face-saving way out. Striking a blow to their sense of dignity or embarrassing them will not win you their co-operation. Before you act, develop the habit of asking yourself: 'How would I feel? How would I react? How would I like to be approached?' Then proceed accordingly.

7

Influencing yourself—self-motivation

IN October 1993 a plant operator clearing fire breaks lay injured for hours when his dozer rolled sideways up a steep incline. His leg was trapped. He couldn't move. He was too isolated for anyone to hear his cries for help. He had to make a gruesome decision: either lay there and bleed to death; or cut off his leg, crawl to his car and phone for help. He chose to cut off his leg with his pocket knife, and was rescued. (He had worked as an ambulance driver and so had some medical knowledge.)

He took the action that he did because his reasons were sufficiently compelling. He wanted to live. Despite the terrible choice, he was able to reach within himself for extra strength. Through the power of self-motivation he created an urge to act in a way that saved his life

Although his case is unusual, many other people have to motivate themselves to make life or death decisions every day. How? Ask any doctor and they will tell you that modern medicine is almost powerless to cure a patient who does not want to be cured. Even though a course of treatment might be successful of itself, the patient who is unmotivated to live will seldom recover.

Conversely, patients with a motivated, positive outlook on life recover more quickly, more often, and tend to stay well. In many cases, the patients' self-motivation has beaten diseases otherwise considered fatal.

Those are matters of record. They demonstrate the awesome power of self-motivation—a power we can tap into every day to energise us for our personal success journey.

But self-motivation is not something you can switch on and off like a light bulb. It is a way of living, an outlook, and an ability to draw out what is best in you and lead yourself into positive action.

Yet millions of people are still waiting 'to write that book', 'paint that canvas', 'do that course' or 'get a better job'. Either they are waiting for something external to motivate them, or they can't want to do those things badly enough.

Do you remember the story of the mother whose face was terribly disfigured by fire after she had rescued her daughter? She was self-motivated to risk her life because her reasons to succeed were also sufficiently compelling. She didn't wait for someone to suggest what she should do.

Achievers seldom wait for external events, threats of losing their job or for anything else to motivate them. They motivate themselves. They know that external motivation is only temporary—that it doesn't last because our external environment is always changing.

The keys to sustained self-motivation are a specific Major Life Goal, compelling reasons to achieve it and a definite plan for that achievement. With such a track to run on what could derail you? And even if you are derailed from time to time, wouldn't it be much easier to get back on track?

What demotivates you?

The last decade of the twentieth century must surely go down as one of the most volatile and uncertain in history. Mass movements of people (up to 100 million were on the move between 1990 and 1994) and the construction of a global economy were major features. These and other factors created mass unemployment, particularly in developed countries.

A sinister feature of that unemployment was that it took some people a very long time to find another job. The phrase 'long-term unemployed' became established in our lexicon.

Needless to say, millions were in a constant state of 'demotivation'. They reacted, rather than responded, to the situation. In turn, their demotivation made it even harder for them to find another job.

So if you're like everyone else on Earth, you too will experience life's lows as well as its highs. A self-motivated lifestyle can't prevent the lows from visiting you. But just as physical fitness can help you recover quickly, self-motivation can get you back on your feet and moving forward much faster. For example, even during periods of high unemployment many self-motivated people flourish. They find new and better jobs and make more money than ever before.

Some people see an opportunity and start profitable businesses. Others form self-help groups and get busy with social programs and fund-raising, learning new skills in the process. Many study and improve their skills. I guess some people even manage to write 'that book' or to paint 'that canvas'.

The point is that if job loss is a key demotivator for you (as it would be for the majority of people), and you know it will take you some time to locate another job, the motivational way out is to design a program of skill improvement, job hunting, perhaps a physical fitness program and to make a start on those projects you may have been putting off. At least that would be responding and getting better, not reacting and getting worse.

If you know of a better alternative, great. But if it could take you a year or more to find another job and you can't change that, think of what you can do in the meantime to turn the period of enforced inactivity into an opportunity for self-improvement. Exercising opportunity thinking is the way of a Self-leader. It's fuel for self-motivation.

Another demotivator is being stuck in a job you don't like. Self-leaders equip themselves to do something else, even if it takes time.

Consider how more fortunate you may be compared to your brothers and sisters in City X and the many cities like it around the world. Even with the best self-motivation they have to battle a system of entrenched corruption, third world working conditions, no social security benefits and very low pay.

How can we squander the opportunities that, through an accident of birth, have been given to us and denied to them? By deciding that you will live a motivated lifestyle and enjoy the many personal, health and financial benefits that flow from it, you are recognising both your privilege and your duty.

A good way to begin is by listing those things that demotivate you, especially those things that are demotivating you at present (if any). Then write your own storyline by developing a Self-leader's plan to break through the shackles.

What motivates you?

Have you ever wondered, deep down, what motivates you? Why not take time to list those things that really get you going (e.g. recognition, prestige, family life, pressure, challenge, self-improvement, financial security, leisure time or personal growth). Once you know your motivators you could use that knowledge to:

- increase your success
- increase your happiness
- enjoy your work more
- win more respect
- like yourself and others even better.

If that sounds like promising a miracle, it is! You are empowered to work miracles in your life. All you need are an understanding and acceptance of the self-motivation keys. So why not absorb the principles and apply them until they become a part of the way you live and work? Self-motivation is money-making good. It's healthy. It's happy. It's you.

Maintain a positive mental attitude

Often we cannot see what is right in front of our eyes because our attitude prevents it. Consider the following encounter between two new arrivals in town and an old man:

John: (To the old man) 'We plan on stayin' for a while. Look for work. What are people like 'round here?'

Old man: 'What are the people like where you're from?'

John: 'Most unfriendly, cold, forbidding people I ever saw.'

Old man: 'People around here are no different,' he replied. Noting the flash of disappointment in Ted's eyes he asked him 'What are the people like in your home town?'

Ted: 'Great! Warm, friendly, always speak kindly to strangers.'

Old man: 'People around here are no different!'

If we go through life seeking negatives we find them in abundance. When we look for positives we find them in abundance too. But can you find positives even in the bleakest circumstances? Let's see.

A doctor in the Johns Hopkins Medical College in the United States was treating a woman who was in her mid-thirties and who had contracted AIDS through a self-administered injection. My first thoughts of the woman were: 'There's someone who, sadly, had made a mess of her life.' But the doctor's comments set me straight.

The way she saw it, the woman was successful. Considering an upbringing of deprivation, alcoholism, violence and drugs, her patient had succeeded in surviving, albeit in her own way. The doctor saw her as successful within the context of the woman's circumstances. I saw all the negatives. But because the doctor had looked for the positives, she found them.

Again I learned that by projecting our own travelogue we'll find the inevitable—that most people simply don't fit into the picture we create for them. So why not seek the good? The positive? The motivational? They will help you to achieve your specific Major Life Goal, to lead a healthy and happy life and to strengthen your Personal Excellence.

Do you see traffic lights as 'stop lights' or 'go lights?' Is a day partly cloudy, or partly sunny? It's all in how you see things. Maintain a positive attitude and everything around you becomes positive too.

Few would say they engage a personal interpreter, yet everybody has one. When you have a positive mental attitude it acts as a wonderful interpreter. For example, during the early days of World War I, Ferdinand Foch, Marshal of France, was asked how things were going on his 'front'. He replied:

> '*My right wing is in retreat. My left wing is withdrawing. My centre is disintegrating. Situation excellent. I am attacking!*'

Your interpreter will tell you that cost is investment; a problem is a challenge; a mistake is a chance to try again more intelligently; a setback is a road sign to be read before proceeding; 'failure' is success deferred, not denied; 'no' is an answer, not a decision.

A positive mental attitude creates a bright atmosphere of hope. It connects you to the success wavelength. It interprets everyday occurrences into a sparkling language that transforms personal defeat into victory. Don't leave home without it.

An urge to act; to draw from within; to lead yourself

Years ago a man was so sick of shaving with the old-fashioned cut-throat razor that he decided to do something about it. He hit on the idea of designing a blade that had the sharpest edge possible and that could be held by two clamps. He set to work. However it took repeated efforts over an eight year period before he developed a successful model for the safety razor. His name? King Gillette.

Have your ever promised yourself 'I'll really do something about (X),' but never got around to it? Perhaps you have had many great ideas and years later saw someone else develop and market them? Many people have good ideas. But the ones who profit are those with the Self-leadership to realise them. They take Horace's advice: 'Carpe Diem' (grasp at the present day). They draw energy from within; they lead themselves to act.

I suspect we might be blamed in the end more for the things we haven't done rather than for those things we have done. In the words of psychologist Dr Susan Jeffers in *Feel the Fear and Do It Anyway*:

> *'Most of us do not "sculpt" our lives. We accept what comes our way . . . then we gripe about it. Many of us spend our lives waiting—waiting for the perfect mate, waiting for the perfect job, waiting for perfect friends to come along. There is no need to wait for anyone to give you anything in your life. You have the power to create what you need. Given commitment, clear goals and action, it's just a matter of time.'*

What often stops people from doing what they really want is the initial discomfort. Many of us are conditioned to relinquish a long-term gain for an immediate reward. But then you might ask: Is anyone who is not prepared to back his or her own abilities by accepting risk, worthy of reward? Whatever your answer, self-motivation depends on the storyline you have written for yourself, and on your ability to draw out what is best in you.

Self-motivation is self-leadership

Self-leadership has six key disciplines:

■ motivation
■ preparation
■ organisation
■ application
■ setting and working to specific goals
■ maintaining energy and momentum.

To succeed in Self-leadership you need to be an activationist. An activationist does things. To become an activationist, practise your skills. Organise your day, week, month, and year—your future. Keep busy.

Set goals good enough to excite you. Build a reputation for energy—for getting things done. Put in that extra effort. Life itself is action—movement. Encourage yourself. Guide yourself. Praise yourself. Reinforce your positives. Focus on the reward not on the task. 'Do it now!' is the motto of the self-motivated.

Personal success formula refresher

$$S = \frac{AsI^2}{PE}$$

Success equals Attitude times Self-leadership squared over Personal Excellence.

We get 27,375 chances to win

Every day we get another chance to try again. For a person who lives to age 75, life will grant him or her some 27,375 chances. Every day Life says: 'Here's another 24 hours. Try again.' Then:

Me: 'But I've blown it. I've messed it up!'

Life: 'Don't worry. Here's another 24 hours. Try again.'

Me: 'Sorry. I've goofed again.'

Life: 'That's OK. Here's another 24 hours. Take another shot. You can do it. Be a Self-leader.'

For most of us life does this day in, day out, 27,375 times. Isn't that wonderful?

Past mistakes don't count so long as you keep trying! Doesn't the very thought of it motivate you?

If you are hurting from memories of the past, put them behind you because your future is in your tomorrows. Thankfully, we are given a new tomorrow every day. And just as thankfully, we are given our future one day at a time.

Where's the benefit in being negative?

Being negative is obstacle thinking, not opportunity thinking. It is also far less practical. Research shows that only about 10 per cent of what we worry about actually happens. So benefits aside, isn't being positive 90 per cent more practical?

Negativity distorts our view of others, of ourselves and of the world around us. Why empower negative people, events or circumstances to drag us down? To throw rocks into our pond? Why cultivate a martyr mentality? Martyrs die. In *Super Leadership* Dr Charles C. Manz and Professor Henry P. Sims report:

> *'Research shows that individuals' expectations become selffulfilling prophecies; that is, positive expectations enhance the probability of actually doing it. Conversely, negative expectations decrease the probability. The state of mind about oneself has a clear impact on ultimate performance.'*

Recently I met an old acquaintance who was window shopping. He was in his fifties, serene and very happy. This itself is not unusual. However I discovered that he suffered from an enzyme deficiency that caused his lungs to shrink. He was given eight years to live. I couldn't work out how he could be so happy! But as he saw it, some people had only eight days.

Negativity is a disease fatal to success, but the cure is readily available. When we know that we are heading in the direction that we have planned for ourselves, with a positive mental attitude, we get better straight away! And everyone else gets better after we do.

You might be thinking: 'But I've got problems!' I would say: 'Congratulations! That's great! Life is about solving problems.' The only people without problems are dead. A problem is an invitation to grow—to succeed. Problems themselves cannot beat us without our consent. It is the way we see them and what we do about them that counts. See them as a challenge and meet it by converting the challenge into a procedure.

Negativity never solved a problem but created many! If you say you have enough problems why create more by being negative? Consider the following true story.

A minister of the church was struggling to write his sermon because Tim, his nine year old son, kept interrupting. Finally he hit on an idea. He remembered seeing a map of the world printed on a travel brochure he kept in his drawer. He quickly tore the page into two dozen pieces and promised Tim that if he could put all the pieces back in the right order, he would buy him all the ice cream he could eat. The minister was certain Tim would be kept busy for hours, but to his dismay, not 20 minutes had elapsed before Tim completed the puzzle. 'How did you do it?' asked the minister, dumbfounded.

Tim replied; 'There is a picture of a person on the back. I knew that if I got the person right, the world would be right.'

Convert dissatisfaction into motivation

There are two types of dissatisfaction—proactive and reactive. You can recognise reactive dissatisfaction whenever you hear people whine or complain yet do nothing. Those people love misery and want to share it with everyone. They have the mentality of the martyr. For example, one group of young people sees a person driving by in the latest Mercedes Benz Sports Coupe. They react by hissing: 'Rich bastards! Who do they think they are? Parading their wealth around!'

Conversely, proactive dissatisfaction is a force for good. It is powerful. It creates energy, enthusiasm and motivation. It gives a sense of direction and achievement. It's money-making good.

Another group of young people sees the same rich person driving by in the latest Mercedes Benz Sports Coupe and responds by promising: 'I'll be driving around in one of those!' See the difference?

Proactive dissatisfaction works for children too. This true story of a 12 year old boy's experience illustrates the point.

David O'Connell lived in a country town of about 50,000 people in Queensland, Australia. For a whole year he worked after school at odd jobs and saved every cent until he had the money he needed to buy his very own bicycle.

The Saturday before Christmas was the most important day of his life. David gave the money to his father who promised to buy the bicycle and to bring it home. The bicycle never arrived. David's father had called in to a hotel and spent the money on drink. His father was an alcoholic.

David had enough reactive dissatisfaction to last a lifetime. But he was too bright and proud to let a temporary setback rob him of his dream. For a month he let proactive dissatisfaction work for him. He led himself to the local tip and found a bicycle frame in good repair. He scrounged or borrowed a wheel here, a handle-bar there and every part he needed to build his own bicycle.

David is a successful financial planner. His eyes still sparkle when he tells the story of how at the age of 12 he built his own bicycle: 'The best and fastest in town.'

Recognising proactive dissatisfaction is simple. It embodies a specific promise to solve the problem, such as:

> *'I'm fed up with being broke! I'm sick and tired of not being able to provide the lifestyle my family deserves. Starting right now, I'm going to strive for success. I'm going to learn all there is about succeeding. I'm going to succeed if it takes every ounce of my strength and I'm going to do it with integrity.'*

See the difference? Proactive dissatisfaction becomes a catalyst for action. It is the power behind humankind's great achievements. Many of the discoveries of medical science had their origins in proactive dissatisfaction with suffering and disease. Proactive dissatisfaction is your subconscious telling you that you can do better.

Keep a bank of positive thoughts

How often do we read a phrase that 'speaks to us', then forget it? Why not keep a notebook indexed A to Z. Whenever you read a quote, phrase or idea that is meaningful for you, jot it down. It also works as an energy charger for self-motivation.

By reading through your notes from time to time you will refresh your spirit, redirect your thinking and put that spring back into your step.

Motivate someone else every day

When given with sincere appreciation, a phone call, card, letter, flower or other thought can really brighten someone's day.

Here again, the law of increasing returns applies. By giving motivation to others you'll get it back a hundredfold. You will receive motivation in return plus the pleasure of knowing you have brightened someone's day. Does it really work? Let's see.

In a recent position I had three secretaries working with me. Sometimes the pressure of their work increased tension in the office. I was always amazed how a little thought or gesture of appreciation swept away days of friction.

The thought? I would buy each of them a small chocolate, or a cake for morning coffee, or take them out for a cappuccino. Nothing elaborate, just some little thing to show them they were appreciated and that I valued them as people as well as employees.

This worked even by remote control. A humorous card or phone call would often do the trick. I did this even for some of our head office staff.

One time I sent a bouquet of flowers to three sections with a message of appreciation for all their past work. The reaction was electric. No one had done that before.

The notes of thanks, phone calls, handshakes and kisses I received were far more gratifying than my small gesture merited. From that day, any work sent to head office from my region was processed swiftly, efficiently and cheerfully.

And the result in my own region? Dedication and loyalty. Many extra hours were worked without reward and without having to be asked.

Why did I do it? Pure selfishness! It gave me a great feeling to see the appreciation in their eyes.

I enjoyed making people feel good about themselves and I wanted more of it because it motivated me more than it did them.

If you can't change it, cool it

The spectacle of an impatient, fuming driver stuck in a traffic jam is a common example of mild dementia. How does it help to get out and shout: 'Come on! Move it!'? What is the point of raising your stress level if the event has already happened and you can't do anything about it? Surely only fools worry about what they can't change or control? After all, events are of three kinds: those that concern you and that you can influence, those that concern you but that you can't influence and those that don't concern you at all.

Why empower events that are outside your control to drag you down? Of themselves they are merely events. It is you who chooses to give them power to hurt you. So the next time someone does something to displease you, remember that it has already been done. You can't rearrange it so it didn't really happen.

The best advice I know on 'cooling it' is this: 'If you can change it, go ahead. If you can't change it, all the worry and fuss in the world won't make the slightest difference.'

Even for those who have achieved outstanding success, neither people nor life were prepared to fit precisely with their plans. Yet they succeeded in crying 'Enough!'; in changing their life forever; and in success through Self-leadership and Personal Excellence.

Why empower other people or events to cancel your day; your week; your future? It's not your fault that God didn't see fit to distribute intelligence in equal measure.

You can curse those who frustrate you all you like, but they probably don't even know you exist.

Happiness is in the way you think

You might recall the Hindu story about the creation of happiness. Here's a brief paraphrase. Apparently one day God decided to create happiness. When they saw how wonderful it was, several of his 'angels' decided that happiness was too precious a gift to give to mortals. So they decided to hide it.

The first angel suggested they hide happiness in the mountains. But the second angel thought humans could find it there, and so suggested they hide it in the depths of the ocean. But that too, was thought too easy. Eventually they decided to hide happiness in the human heart, because they felt that very few people would ever think to look for it there.

George Bernard Shaw had a marvellous way of looking at happiness. He wrote in *Dramatic Opinions and Essays*:

> *'This is the true joy in life—that of being used for a purpose recognised by yourself as a mighty one; being a force of nature, instead of a feverish, selfish little clod of ailments and grievances complaining that the world will not devote itself to making you happy.*
>
> *'I am of the opinion that my life belongs to the whole community and as long as I live it is my privilege to do for it whatever I can. I want to be thoroughly used up when I die. For the harder I work the more I live. I rejoice in life for its own sake.'*

Happiness or unhappiness is largely a state of mind. This is not surprising when you consider that life itself is mostly thought, not form. You can test this easily. Stretch out your hand and snatch a moment of life. Now open your hand. How many moments did you catch? Zip? Just like the rest of us!

That's because in the same instant that things happen, they pass into time. Think of an event that happened last week. Where is it now? Does it exist? Viewed correctly this is a most wonderful discovery for happiness. If life is mostly thought, we can be as happy as we make up our minds to be because we control our thoughts!

We need not wait until we win the lottery, drive the latest sports car or live in a bigger house by a lake. Those are form, not thought. Every piece of form we own will be serving someone else a few years from now! Neither do we need to wait until we find the 'perfect' partner. Let other people play 'Who's got the biggest house?' and 'Who drives the most expensive car?' games. Choose not to join them.

To be happy is a matter of choice too because lasting happiness comes from within ourselves. To quote Stephen R. Covey from *The Seven Habits of Highly Effective People*:

> *'I have had the opportunity to work with many people—wonderful people, talented people who want to achieve happiness and success, people who are searching, people who are hurting.*
>
> *'I've worked with business executives, college students, church and civic groups, families and marriage partners. And*

in all my experience, I have never seen lasting solutions to problems, lasting happiness and success, that came from the outside in.'

Rinse your brain

Have you ever met 'pukeaholics'? They are the masters of 'stinkin' thinkin'"—of striving to be average, of living life by the Law of Accident. Pukeaholics are people who can't resist 'throwing up' their woes all over you. Ask them how they are—and they'll tell you! They'll add the traffic jam on the way to work, the row with their partner, the high cost of living, difficult customers, ingrown toenails—the lot. Suddenly, puke! puke! puke! Who needs it? Pukeaholics can't break free from their conditioning drag.

They are people in the process of becoming 'If only's', or 'I could have beens'. They apply 'conditioning drag transfer'. That is, they smear their negativity all over you. The thing about puking problems onto other people is that half of them don't care that you have them, and the other half are glad that you do!

Get excited about your Major Life Goal

One of the greatest self-motivators is to recommit yourself frequently to achieving your Major Life Goal. That's why it's vital to write it down. Without the sense of purpose and direction provided by a specific Major Life Goal and the solid foundation of integrity embodied in your personal totem, it is almost certain you can't live a happy, motivated and holistically successful life.

You will, of course, be motivated by external events from time to time. But these 'highs' serve only to punctuate the despair of your 'lows'. Once the high is gone you start to wander again, blown adrift by every wind of change. There are few feelings as motivating as those that help you see you're going where you want to go.

Inoculate against 'excusitis'

Every low achiever has this disease in its advanced form. People afflicted with 'excusitis' can give you a litany of excuses. They all have a 'wooden leg' and seldom list themselves as the chief reason for their woes. They invent more excuses than they need in case they don't have a strong enough case to fail.

George Bernard Shaw hated excuses. He said:

> *'People are always blaming their circumstances for what they are. I don't believe in circumstances. The people who get on in this world are the people who get up and look for the circumstances they want, and, if they can't find them, make them.'*

Defeat fear

Many people are conditioned into fear from a very early age. It's part of their upbringing and will drag them back. To achieve sustained success they will have to resist it.

However in its biological sense fear is an urge for survival. It prepares us to run or fight. If you choose fear (to run) it will obey you by generating negative feelings.

If you choose to fight (persistence) your subconscious helps you by generating positive feelings. Then you look for ways to win! The answer lies in the choice you make. Substitute feelings of fear with positive expectations by keeping your mind on future successes—on the things you want and off the things you don't want.

Aim high

Life is an obedient employer. It will pay only the wages you demand of it. The higher you aim the more you will achieve. Satisfied needs don't motivate. You won't achieve Personal Excellence by aiming at mediocrity.

Be enthusiastic

Enthusiasm without action has only amusement value. It's a bit like saying: 'I don't know what I'm going to do, but I'm sure as hell going to do it!' Combined with a plan and correct action enthusiasm alone can double your success. If you're not enthused about yourself, your company, your job or your product, why are you there?

The great John Wesley, founder of the Methodist Church, was forbidden to preach in the churches of his day. He had to preach in the street or in fields. Despite this he attracted thousands of people to his sermons while mainstream churches were relatively empty. Asked how he could draw so many people he replied: 'I set John Wesley on fire, and they come to watch me burn.' When was the last time you 'set yourself on fire' with enthusiasm?

When my enthusiasm is running low I take a few days off and step back to see the wider picture. As part of this strategy I might visit a resort or affluent tourist area and enjoy the view of expensive yachts bobbing up and down on a glassy marina; the multimillion dollar homes; the sculptured lawns and gardens; the private clubs; the up-market boutiques, restaurants, cafes, and so on.

I find that surrounding myself with those visual promises has a positive effect on my motivation. It reminds me that it is all possible—that people do have an opportunity to live with whatever level of comfort and dignity they want if they are willing to prepare, work and strive to achieve their dream.

It is not the display of wealth that I find motivating. It is the tangible evidence that a life of dignity, of freedom from want, puts us up where we all belong.

KEY POINTS

- What demotivates or motivates you? Find out what your motivation influencers are and use them to power your success journey. Self-motivation is a way of living. It's the ability to influence and lead ourselves—to draw out what is best in us. Get high on your specific Major Life Goal.
- A positive mental attitude is the switch that allows positive energy into the mind. Keep it switched on.
- A problem is an invitation for us to grow—to succeed. Convert dissatisfaction into motivation. Turn reactive into proactive dissatisfaction.
- Motivate someone else every day. To do this you will have to motivate yourself first.
- If you can't change things, cool it. Don't raise your stress level. Work around it.
- Happiness lives in the way you think. It comes from within and starts when you decide to be happy.
- Defeat fear. Aim high. The higher you aim, the more you'll achieve.

8

Dealing with your moments of truth

D URING China's Tiananmen Square uprising the budding democracy movement was brutally crushed by 'The People's Army'. Of the many acts of bravery by the demonstrators there is one that stands above the rest. A young man, armed only with courage and a yearning for freedom, faced an urgent moment of truth. Would he make a stand, or run?

When a column of tanks rumbled towards him he too cried: 'Enough!' By standing his ground he brought the entire armoured column to a halt. His act captured the imagination—and sympathy—of the whole world. Although the bid for freedom was put down he had faced his moment of truth, and triumphed.

In 1993 India, an older woman faced a moment of truth that would impoverish her. Her daughter, with a daughter of her own, returned after having been kicked out of her home by her husband because she had not brought enough dowry (even though it included a new car and the equivalent of 15 years' pay).

The daughter's life was effectively over in that no one else would marry her (her parents were too poor to pay another dowry). Yet the mother defied the ire of the other villagers and instead of shunning her daughter she took her in and with it, responsibility to support, raise and save a dowry for her grand-daughter.

To those of us in developed countries this may not seem such a terrible moment of truth. But in a country where over one million infant girls are murdered by their parents each year just because they are female (principally because the dowries required can impoverish the family) it represents enormous courage and sacrifice on the woman's part. Yet she faced her moment of truth, and she too triumphed: over custom; over indignation; over fear.

Down the street from me lives an older couple who are raising a healthy seven year old boy. Neither the boy's father nor mother wanted him, so the couple, who are the boy's grandparents, had to face a moment of truth. At a time when most people their age look forward to their independence this couple decided to accept the responsibility that the boy's own parents had rejected. To my mind they too have triumphed over their moment of truth and achieved a high standard of Personal Excellence.

Most of us are lucky enough not to be challenged in major ways. Yet we all face moments of truth of one sort or another every day.

Elvis Presley had to decide whether he really wanted to be a singer when after his first concert he was told he should consider becoming a truck driver. Composers Handel, Schumann, Bernstein, Varese and Boulez had fathers who were strongly against their chosen vocation, yet they persisted. (Varese's father locked the piano, covered it with a shroud and threw away the key.)

When leading fashion designer Elsa Schiaparelli looked for design work she was told she would be better off planting potatoes!

Those are moments of truth that test our resolve—our Self-leadership. They test our effectiveness through the way we respond to people and to our job.

Leonard Bernstein faced his moment of truth when Bruno Zirato phoned him in the dark morning hours and said (from Joan Peyser's *Leornard Bernstein*):

> '*Well, this is it. You have to conduct at 3 p.m. this afternoon. No chance for a rehearsal. There is no way to get the orchestra together and you will report at a quarter to three backstage at Carnegie Hall and conduct this afternoon.*'

This was the first time he was to conduct a major philharmonic orchestra. What did he do in his moment of truth? In his own words:

> '*So there I am, standing in the wings. All atremble . . . listening to Bruno Zirato who had come out on stage to address the audience and tell them the unhappy news that they would not be hearing Bruno Walter that day.*
>
> '*Many groans. But instead they would be hearing a young conductor called Leonard Bernstein, the assistant conductor of the Philharmonic, and on I had to come . . . I strode out and that's the last thing I remember until the end of the*

concert when I saw the entire audience there, standing and cheering and screaming.'

Leonard Bernstein faced his moment of truth, triumphed, and a brilliant career was launched.

It's all very well to base your success journey on a road of integrity and principle (Personal Excellence). But how do you respond when your principles are challenged? I have a friend in City X who prays regularly and observes Friday as his main prayer day. Despite being a chief executive of a large group of companies he will take all Friday afternoon off just to observe his Friday prayer rituals. If you were to ask him whether or not he were a devout believer, he would undoubtedly reply that he was.

His holy book extols integrity, honesty and the other virtues endorsed by all major religions. Yet when my friend is faced with this moment of truth he will think nothing of bribing an official to get a deal through, to keeping mistresses, or to submitting 'mickey mouse reports' to his bankers so they will advance extra funds. (Of course, his behaviour applies to many other people and, to be fair, the system in City X is so corrupt that if he did not provide 'incentives' to officials, he would probably not get very far.)

Nevertheless it still comes down to our personal totem. When faced with a moment of truth if we do not uphold what we believe, we erode our self-esteem and diminish our Personal Excellence.

Here are some examples. What would you have done if you were the advertising executive who was instructed to create a campaign that would hook adolescents onto smoking? Thinking of his own children, that executive wept but did it anyway.

If you could make money out of a 'slightly shady' deal and knew you wouldn't get caught, would you do it? Would you overlook the transgressions of a key employee if he or she were a valued performer?

When general manager of a large holiday resort development I had to dismiss my sales manager and another key employee. It was a decision that really hurt because, their value as employees aside, I was particularly fond of the sales manager and regarded him as a friend.

Unfortunately he was engaged in an affair with one of his staff and the situation was undermining the morale of the team. Accusations of favouritism, gossip, loss of respect—especially as it broke up his marriage—had eroded the goodwill his team had for him.

Initially I didn't want to believe it was happening—hoping it would abate. But eventually I had to make a move, and did. I must say the organisation was better for the example, although even years later I still wish there had been some way of keeping him and retaining our friendship.

Success through Personal Excellence also requires us to be consistent. That can only come through preparation and practice. Of course, we must be honest with ourselves and recognise our own limitations. As a wise man once put it: 'I'm smart in spots so I stay around those spots.'

We can study a dozen success courses, nod wisely, and become enthused only to let it unravel as soon as we are faced with the principal requirement—effort. (For example, have you written your personal totem as suggested earlier? Have you determined your core values? Have you decided on the success you want for each sphere of life?) Your answers to those questions might help you see the truth in the holistic success formula.

Personal success formula refresher

$$S = \frac{Asl^2}{PE}$$

Success equals Attitude times Self-leadership squared over Personal Excellence.

Australian swimming coach Laurie Lawrence demonstrated his commitment in a startling way. When a swimmer complained of pain in pushing himself for one more lap of the pool Laurie scraped his own clenched fist against a rough-brick wall and holding up his bleeding knuckles exclaimed: 'This is pain! Now get on with your training!' Is it any wonder he trains Olympic champions?

I faced a personal moment of truth when operating my own public relations and marketing consultancy. The business was in its infancy and I needed all the clients I could get. Two lucrative offers came my way. The first was a promotion account with a major cigarette company, and the other was a similar account with a leading brewery. The money I could have made would have saved me several years of struggle. However I had to face my own principles, which are that I will not help promote any tobacco products, nor will I help promote alcohol, because invariably both affect children's conditioning, safety and welfare. Of course, someone else filled the gap. But it wasn't me. (I don't want to stop people having a social drink. I simply will not do anything to encourage anyone to drink more than they do already, nor to harm their health—and that of others—by smoking, because to promote these products is to glamorise them.)

In the long run the decision freed up time for me to accept a consultancy with the government of Western Australia, and another to promote a state-wide festival for a community-based group. Those appointments gave me far more credibility than I would have gained and led to many other offers.

I faced another moment of truth when operating a travel agency and travel club. My partner was, at that time, the second largest travel wholesaler in Australia with offices in several countries. Through my travel club we provided passengers for package holidays. However six months later my partner was placed in receivership, leaving many travellers with worthless tickets.

The moment of truth was: Do I walk away from those passengers and suggest they put their loss down to experience? (I had no legal obligation to refund their money.) Or: Do I make good their loss through personal savings because there was a moral principle involved?

I chose the latter, and although it sapped me of all my financial resources, years later I am still convinced it was one of the best decisions I've made. Those were moments of truth challenging my personal totem. There are many other kinds.

Here are two interesting examples. St Francis of Assisi was so saintly as to be called the second Christ. Yet he was born the son of a wealthy cloth merchant, was raised with the best that life could offer him and was the envy of nearly every youth in his town. Suddenly he decided to turn his back on his good fortune in favour of a life of poverty and service to others.

His first moment of truth was in facing the violent rage of his father. But there was a more telling moment of truth to come. Until that time he feared and avoided lepers. When he comforted and embraced a leper he faced his ultimate moment of truth, and won. From that moment he knew he could devote his life to God's work.

Another type of moment of truth is being able to withstand professional criticism and ridicule when you know you are right. For example, a Sydney architect designed a university without pathways. Derision followed. Pressure was applied for him to put in the paths but he resisted. He knew that the best places to build the footpaths would be shown to him by the students themselves through the tracks they would wear into the grass. He was right, and built the paths accordingly.

We all have individual moments of truth but the following are common nearly to everyone.

How much effort is required?

It hardly occurs to most people that the polished performances of the athletes, artists, dancers and sports people they admire require endless effort and practice. For example, *A Chorus Line* is one of the great musical productions. Begun in 1974 it is still delighting audiences across the world. Yet how many people would realise that the daily routine for every dancer in the show includes six hours of practice, six days per week?

The show is their work. Their polished performances are the result of the effort they are willing to put in to achieve Personal Excellence in their work sphere of life. As a result they earn—and deserve—admiration, recognition, personal satisfaction and reward. How do you measure up to the same moment of truth?

- Write down the amount of effort you are putting into your work (e.g. 25 per cent, 50 per cent, 75 per cent). _____
- Write down the yearly income this amount of effort is producing (e.g. 50 per cent effort = $X per year). $ _____
- Consider this formula carefully. Say you could give 50 per cent more effort, to what extent would giving it:
  — increase your income? by $ _____
  — increase your chances for promotion (out of 100 per cent)? _____ per cent
  — build your business (out of 100 per cent)? _____ per cent

If by increasing your effort you will improve in any of those areas, write down your answer to the following three questions:
  — Do you want to earn more income?

— Will using the energy you are holding back help do that for you?
— What is stopping you?

If you want 100 per cent success it will demand 100 per cent effort. Is there such a thing as 50 per cent success? Few have succeeded on 50 per cent effort and of successful people fewer still would agree there is such a thing as half success. How do I know? Consider the following example.

Christian Dior was a task master who often made impossible demands on staff. Yet even after working 18 hour days for weeks, an exhausted young tailor was always first to volunteer for extra duties. His name? Pierre Cardin.

Most people who give 100 per cent effort usually love what they do. Those who hold back on giving their 'all' might do so because they are perpetual 'grazers'. If you have interviewed people for senior positions you will have seen many resumes. You will have noticed many talented people who have achieved responsible positions in a variety of industries.

Moving from industry to industry can be a good thing for variety and experience. However the point has to come when success-minded achievers have to stop 'grazing' if they are to attain their specific Major Life Goal. You need to reach the point where you can say:

'This is me. I'm a banker. I'm a travel agent. I'm a salesperson. I will stop grazing and build my success here. I will resist any side-ways movement away from my chosen field. Here is where I will make my fortune. Here I stand.'

Until this point is reached, it is unlikely you will give 100 per cent of your talent and abilities. How can you? You're still looking around in case you might miss something.

If you are giving less than 100 per cent to your occupation perhaps you don't love what you do? If you are going to share eight to ten hours of your day five or six days per week with an employer or in a business doing something you don't love, what's the point of doing it at all?

If you do not love what you do for a living, decide what it is you really want, then do it. Make sure it will move you closer to your specific Major Life Goal. If you can do that, you can stop grazing.

To achieve your specific Major Life Goal might require a change of job or profession. But you might not be able to change jobs straight away. You might need the work. That's now. What you can do is decide what it is you really want and prepare for a change, even if that change lies in the future.

Facing your moments of truth is not always a pleasant task. For example, how do you face up to these?

■ Is it your style to run away from difficult situations or do you stick it out until they are resolved?
■ Do you think of quitting your job every time something doesn't go your way? (I did, sometimes. But I learned to resist it.)
■ Can you organise and run an effective meeting?
■ Can you manage people in a spirit of co-operation and harmony?

Before you can increase your personal success you might need to change the ways you get things done. For many of us change is not pleasant because it involves modification of ingrained behaviour. It takes us out of our comfort zone and we feel the discomfort of resisting our conditioning drag.

But life will only change for us when we change. So the sooner we make a start, the sooner we will achieve greater recognition, success and reward.

Do you have the right skills?

What is your level of skill in areas critical to your personal success? Can you write a clear, concise letter? Do you manage the family budget so money is set aside to meet regular bills such as rates, phone and electricity, or do you panic every time you receive an account?

How good are you at problem solving? Do you decide through intuition, go on instinct or do you follow a procedure that helps take the emotion and irrationality out of tense situations? If you don't have such a procedure, why not adopt this one?

■ Ask: What is the problem? Write it down. What's happening or not happening?

■ List the possible reasons for it. Are there facts to support your conclusions? Do you need more information before you can act?

■ Whom do you need to consult? Can you involve others in framing the best solution?

■ List possible solutions. Take people issues, risks, timing and economy of effort into account.

■ Decide on the best solution and on methods for its application. Apply your solution. Evaluate its effectiveness.

Throughout this procedure, keep restating the problem. (You'll be surprised how often you catch yourself in trying to solve the wrong problem!) Sometimes the way we see the problem is the problem.

Do you insist on quality in all that you do?

The father of mass production was Eli Whitney (inventor of the cotton gin and the mass-produced rifle). He staggered competitors by producing low-cost, high-quality armaments. His secret lay in using a line of workers each of whom was responsible for manufacturing a specific piece of a rifle. Until then, each rifle was made completely by one person.

Everything depended on quality because each piece had to be made with a high degree of precision so it would fit into another piece made by someone else. Henry Ford used this principle in manufacturing his Model T.

Mass production (speed) is made possible by ensuring precision in each step of the process. It depends on quality work. Quality control in manufacturing checks not only the quality of materials used but the manufacturing process itself, including product testing.

If you were to break your job down to a series of steps and someone checked each step randomly, would you be happy with what they would find?

We are paid for quality time—for the results we bring to an organisation. Was your answer on the amount of effort you are putting into your work 100 per cent? (If it was only 50 per cent you could owe your organisation half your wages!) But as for almost anything else the challenge of producing quality can be met with our formula for turning challenges into achievement—namely, by converting them into a procedure. For example:

- Divide your work into steps and apply your own quality control.
- Check each step to ensure it is done as well as you are able.
- Take another look.

Don't be afraid to change procedures even if they have been followed for many years. (Your aim is quality work, not the preservation of traditional systems that probably can stand improvement.)

If you feel that will take too much effort, check that you are not succumbing to conditioning drag. Determine to resist it. Insist on quality in all you do as your trade mark—as your conquest of a cardinal moment of truth.

Self-led is much more effective than externally led quality control because, in the former method, Self-leadership is involved. Believe in quality; push for quality; achieve quality.

Traditional Japanese see inanimate objects almost as if they have an inherent life or soul. Japanese craftspeople and workers take great pride in what they produce.

Thomas J. Peters and Robert H. Waterman Jr, in their work *In Search of Excellence* tell the story of a Honda employee who on his way home would straighten the wiper blades on any Honda he would see parked nearby. He could not bear to see a flaw in something he had made.

To get a feeling for this philosophy of pride, why not try an experiment? Pick up any manufactured item and focus on it. Imagine it is a thing of great inherent value, but not yet perfect. How could it be improved? What changes would you recommend? What flaws does it have that you could put right?

The beginning of increased success can be found in the place where you are now. You can:

- Do your work much better.
- Do it fantastically better.
- Build a reputation for energy, skill, co-operation, honour and quality! Do your job so well they couldn't bear to see you go.
- Take charge. Be a strong leader of self.

Even if you plan to leave your job later, become outstanding in it now. Leave it from a position of success—of strength and Personal

Excellence, not of weakness. Let every company you ever work for be sorry to lose you. (Later you might want to buy the company!)

Are you a morale saboteur?

Morale saboteurs are captives of conditioning drag. Many don't even know it. You can test yourself against this moment of truth with your answers to the following questions:

- Do you like to air all your company's shortcomings?
- Whenever you don't agree with an issue, do you like to tell everyone about it?
- Do you like to huff and puff about people you don't like?

If so, the answer is simple. Whenever you feel like talking to so and so about him or her—don't! If you don't like the company's decisions, don't puke all over others; leave the company or work your way up to a level where you can make the decisions you prefer.

Conditioning drag transfer (you doing the puking) is another version of playing 'wooden leg'. The only thing it achieves is to make others happier when the people doing it are not around.

Conditioning drag receiving (you doing the listening) weakens your resolve. Don't listen. Get out of there. Fast.

Do you save and invest?

It is the money you save (and invest) that makes you wealthy, not the money you earn. For example:

- Can you write a cheque for $20,000 and honour it?
- If you had saved 20 per cent of what you have earned to date, would that make a difference to your circumstances now?

(This area is so vital to personal success that it forms a separate chapter—see Chapter 13. It is listed as a moment of truth because we face it every pay-day.)

Health matters

Many people are successful high fliers, chief executives, wealthy entrepreneurs or successful artists. They are often very successful in their business/work sphere of life but can be abject failures in managing themselves as a human being with intellectual, emotional, spiritual and physical needs.

The idea of obtaining wealth is to help enjoy life! Where is the joy of wealth without health? Here are moments of truth in five key areas of self-management.

Diet and exercise

There's no need to run a marathon or pump weights. A moderate exercise program—even as little as 30 minutes three times per week—can keep you healthy.

For what it's worth, I try to build some exercise into my daily routine. For example, I park as far as I can from where I want to go to force me to walk. I go on a brisk walk every day. I walk up stairs wherever possible. Those are only little things, but they add up.

Your moment of truth is: Write down what you definitely will do about it starting today.

Regardless of your age, use it or lose it is the principle most apt to exercise. It's not good enough to 'conquer the great indoors'. You've got to move too. Research in England found 90 year olds who do aerobics. Within a few weeks they increase their muscle tone and strength by a third. People are abandoning their wheelchairs and putting away their walking sticks.

As for diet, one of the great crimes of Western society is to spend billions of dollars convincing women they are the wrong shape. Why? So merchants can sell clothes, diets, fads, gym membership, diet books and so on.

All the promoters of 'the diet message' have achieved is to make many people unhappy with themselves, increase disorders such as anorexia nervosa and bulimia—and to make vendors and publishers wealthier in the process.

To see the nonsense in their 'message' all it takes is a good look at any mixed group of people. Do you see the variety of shapes that makes up the human race? Those are real people. They are not air-brushed or stretched photographs of lanky 13 to 14 year olds destined to appear as older people in fashion magazines.

And what started this unnatural fuss? To the best of my knowledge it was to please couturiers who decided their creations looked better on taller, slimmer people. So they put in their order for people who, by an accident of birth, were shaped to suit their fashions. Ironically, the same shapes that are touted as 'ideal' today would be considered freakish only a few decades ago.

The price many women have had to pay for this artificially created 'standard of beauty' is lower self-esteem, a lifetime of 'watching their figure', spinal problems due to wearing high heels, and general dissatisfaction with who they are. So when I mention diet, I am not talking of crash-diets, slimming diets or any other sure-fire weight loss program. I mention it in the context of a balanced, nutritious intake of food designed to give you energy and enjoyment, not to take it from you. But does not being on a 'diet' really work? Let's see.

In City X the great majority of people are slim. During a four month consulting assignment there I saw very few 'fat' people. That is not because the people didn't have enough to eat. I am talking of people who have good jobs and can afford to buy all the 'junk food' they like. Yet they are slim.

That is even more surprising when one considers the great emphasis their national culture places on food. It is the focus at get-togethers and many functions are judged on the quality and quantity of the food served. Often you will hear people ask: 'Have you eaten yet?' almost as if it were a casual greeting. For them, food is not only essential to survival, but one of the great joys of life. For them, food is not 'the enemy'.

The mid-day meal is considered their main meal, and most people have a generous portion of everything. The key to their slimness lay in the combination of the foods they eat—not on the quantity.

An interesting thing about people in City X is that if they do not have rice with their meal, they don't consider they have eaten. So every meal includes a generous helping of cooked rice, usually with vegetables. Even when ordering fast food such as KFC they order a side helping of cooked rice. They manage what they eat, enjoy it to the fullest and, with it, each others' company.

Self-leadership also means self-management in diet and in regular, moderate exercise. It will not change your basic shape. If you are an older person, it will not make you 18 years old again. But it can make you healthier, give you more energy and increase your self-acceptance. It will also help you to manage stress.

Managing stress

Laughter and sex are the two greatest stress relievers we know. However as the director of the Coolum Hyatt Resort, Dr John Tickell, says: 'If they come together you know you're getting old.'

Externally what we encounter is pressure, not stress. Stress is something we create internally. It can be a good or bad thing, depending on how you see it and on what you do about it. If you like the stress of a challenge and you use it to achieve a good result, that's great! That's very good for you.

But if you see stressful situations as suffocating, you will have a negative reaction to stress and could weaken your immune system. If the latter is your constant reaction to stress, in the long term you could develop problems ranging from itching to heart disease.

People with a positive mental attitude see challenging situations as opportunities. That is an excellent use of stress because in that case stress is actually a tool to aid achievement. Achieving and winning are good for us. They have physical and psychological benefits. Creating positive stress can motivate us to do our very best. However we need to build in safety valves. We need to unwind regularly—to get out of the 'pressure-cooker' from time to time. We can do that through regular, moderate exercise, mini-vacations and a balanced but nutritious intake of food.

Above all, we can help any stressful situation by maintaining a positive and cheerful outlook on life. (Imagine tackling a problem after a belly laugh or joyful experience. Would not your approach change? Would you take yourself so seriously? Probably you would solve 'the problem' more fairly and with much less 'bad' stress.)

Why not develop a de-stressing routine to practise before and after a tense 'moment of truth'? This could be as simple as a three-minute relaxation exercise or a brisk walk.

Humour

The impact humour makes on our health is well documented. As has been said, happy, smiling people tend to be healthier, live longer, are more successful at life and raise happier children. This is not a 'modern' secret. Proverb 17.22 of *The Jerusalem Bible* teaches that:

> 'A glad heart is as an excellent medicine. A depressed spirit wastes the bones away.'

A sense of humour is that ability to take our work seriously but ourselves lightly. It gives us perspective. It enables us to respond calmly and clearly in crises. Sadly, as we grow older many of us lose our sense of humour—our sense of joy in living. C. W. Metcalf, a brilliant presenter, actor, mime and humorist, cautions us not to develop a case of 'terminal professionalism'.

We don't have to be serious all the time. There is really nothing 'wrong' with people who are jovial, even at the office. Having a good sense of humour does not make them 'air heads'.

The ability to laugh and to take ourselves lightly boosts our immune system. Those who lose that ability suffer more than those who retain it.

C. W. Metcalf suggests the more 'humourless' among us should visit a private photo booth and take some pictures of ourselves pulling the funniest, most ridiculous face we know. When next we confront a tense situation we can take one of these photos out of our wallet and look at it! Does that sound foolish? It could be.

However fear of 'foolishness' can prevent you from being spontaneous, happy, relaxed and joyful about living. Perhaps it is more foolish not to be a little 'foolish'?

Be unaffected; discard hang ups. Accept yourself! Reward yourself! Enjoy life! As long as it doesn't hurt others, why not be a little 'foolish'?

Smoking

It is not my wish to offend smokers. However as achieving and maintaining good health is a vital part of the holistic success formula it would be unthinkable for me not to discuss it. (If you are a smoker, please bear with me. My comments are aimed at the habit of smoking, not at people who smoke.)

It has already been mentioned that cigarettes are the world's cheapest status symbol. In the words of a teenager:

> 'When you go to a club or hotel, the first thing people want is to see you with a drink in one hand and a smoke in the other. It's as if having these things makes you a complete person.'

In a tragic irony, the man who helped create the image of 'freshness, outdoors, etc.' by riding a horse through streams and open fields for cigarette advertisements died from lung cancer caused by smoking. Before his death he had become an ardent anti-smoking campaigner.

Did the cigarette companies get the message? Sadly, no. As smoking is declining in developed countries they have taken their wares to underdeveloped nations where strict advertising and other restrictions don't apply.

The people in City X, being so trusting and, relatively speaking, some years behind the West in community medical education, are a case in point. There smoking is on the increase, particularly among adolescents. To their credit, many smokers do not like to see this happen. They know how difficult smoking can be to give up and hate to see their children take up the habit.

If you are a smoker, have you questioned why you are injuring your own health and the health of others while swelling the coffers of multinational cigarette companies in the process? Smoking is definitely an obstacle to achieving and maintaining good health. Your moment of truth is: Give it up. Do it now. (Your health and wealth will improve straight away!)

Excessive intake of alcohol

What is excessive? For some people it is difficult for them to drink moderately (a glass of wine with dinner, for example). That's partly because of societal pressure that encourages drinkers to see themselves as 'macho', or as 'celebrities enjoying the good life' if they drink to excess.

In Australia, beer drinking is the national pastime for many men. Their ability to drink is equated to their degree of 'manhood'. Beer companies hire sporting heroes to extol the virtue of drinking beer and pay them handsomely for it.

Yet over 50 per cent of all road fatalities and injuries are attributed to alcohol, as is most of the domestic violence and child abuse that so plague an otherwise beautiful country.

However as education is increasing, attitudes are slowly changing. For example, when I was 18 years of age I enlisted in the Air Force. I didn't like beer very much as in my home the tradition was to drink a glass of wine with the day's main meal. (Although, my uncle having got me extremely drunk when I was seven years old ensured I would not like the taste of wine very much.) When I went to the Airmen's Club on a hot day and asked for a lemon squash I was refused service because, as the bartender rudely informed me, 'We don't serve any girls' drinks here!' Nowadays such a reaction would be rare.

Nearly 2000 years ago, one of the great founders of the Christian Church, St Paul, advised: 'Drink a little wine for thy stomach's sake.' Since then tests have shown that a glass of wine with a meal is actually good for you. The French habit of drinking wine with their meals may be responsible for 'The French Paradox'. That is, despite the French penchant for eating 'almost all the wrong foods' laced with oil, cream, butter, sugar and fat, they enjoy the second lowest rate of cardiovascular disease in the world (next to Japan).

So I am not suggesting that people should not drink any alcohol at all. However, if you do not have a physical predisposition to alcoholism and provided you do not react violently or drive under the influence of too much drink, then why not exercise Self-leadership and drink moderately?

Drinking to excess is the antithesis of Personal Excellence. You cannot be serious about holistic success by saying: 'I'll achieve wealth but won't worry about health or Personal Excellence.' Almost everyone is a role model to someone else and children are expert mimics of adults who are influential in their lives.

Do you have more than two alcoholic drinks every day? Why not consider having at least three alcohol-free days per week? If you are unable to achieve that, could it be that alcohol might have control of you rather than the other way around?

Do you keep your cool?

When we are confronted by an angry client or abrasive colleague the emotion welling inside us tests our self-control. Those are moments of truth when, should we fail, we could say or do something in haste that we will regret at leisure.

I have to say that from time to time I fail the test. My usual reaction is to cut the other person down to size with a barrage of facts or to humiliate them by showing the silliness of their statements. Groan. Immediately I do it, I regret it. So I try again. I remind myself that this challenge can be met by converting it into a procedure. For example:

■ Realise that when something has angered you it is almost impossible to hide it because, even though you don't say a word, you body language gives you away. So you may as well speak your mind, but in a calm and tactful way.

- If you feel you are about to do something really silly or to say something you will regret for a very long time, get out of there. Make an excuse. Visit the bathroom. Take a break for a few minutes. Enjoy a few deep breaths and a cup of coffee or tea. Give yourself some space and time to calm down.
- Remember that what you haven't said can be said any time. So you won't lose anything by reserving that cutting barb.
- Often it is not what is happening that angers us, but the way it is happening (e.g. you may not have been consulted on a major decision affecting your area and suddenly you learn of the decision in front of your peers at a meeting). In those cases, ask if you can have time to consider the implications.
- If the process itself is getting under your skin, ask if a different approach can be taken because you don't feel comfortable with the way things are proceeding.
- Acknowledge that the other party could be right, or at least partly right.
- If you can't resolve the issue, try to agree on involving a mediator whom both parties will trust.

If none of this works for you try to remember that losing your cool and howling abuse at someone has never solved a problem. Rather, it has enlarged many and created new problems in the process.

You listen, but do you hear?

Almost everyone would say they want to avoid mistakes, delays, arguments, ill feeling, misunderstanding or bad communication. Yet few take time to develop the skill that accounts for 50 per cent of communication: listening; empathetic listening; and listening with the intent to understand, not with the intent to reply.

For many of us, including me, listening with empathy is a difficult discipline to maintain. Conditioning drag can seep in and we either listen without hearing, do most of the talking or let our mind drift. The moment of truth for people like myself is to face up to this weakness as a challenge. To admit it. To do something positive about it. Fortunately, as for any challenge the key to meeting it successfully is to convert it into a procedure:

- Wherever you are, be there. Don't drift. Focus on the speakers and concentrate on hearing every word they are saying. Resist thinking about what you want to say.
- Listen with empathy—with the intent to understand, not with the intent to reply.
- Face each speaker squarely and maintain eye contact. This is vital because 50 per cent of what people really say is communicated by their body language.
- By nodding, repeating a key phrase or asking an open-ended question (questions that start with what, where, who, when, how and why), encourage the speaker to talk. This shows you are interested in what they have to say.
- Show you understand and empathise by encouraging the speaker to talk freely. Don't question their motives or judgments.
- Test your understanding of what is being said by summarising key points or by asking for clarification.
- Focus on the issue, not on the personality. This is important where you might dislike the person or where their dress, manner, attitude or opinions annoy you. Leave emotion out of the conversation and keep your cool.
- 'Read between the lines' to get to the heart of the issue because people will seldom speak the whole truth directly and plainly. However test your assumptions with summaries or with open-ended questions.
- If the discussion is important, take notes of key points, facts, etc.

Listening and hearing with empathy takes great effort, discipline and practice. It is a moment of truth many of us must face and conquer if we are to succeed at being effective communicators and avoid terrible mistakes.

Are you really an effective leader?

Many people are appointed to positions of leadership by their company without leadership training to support them. They can get by because of their technical knowledge and because they have been empowered to reward or hurt (promote or fire) their staff.

Fear of dismissal, especially in times of high unemployment, keep staff 'towing the company line'. But working at the minimum level required hardly produces high morale and good productivity, let alone a win–win situation.

We have already discussed effective human relations and the skills required to win co-operation. Your moment of truth is: Are you really an effective leader? Here's a test:

■ Do you have staff working in their position of highest and best use (i.e. utilising their strengths and skills to best advantage by matching them to the demands of the jobs that require those strengths and skills)?

■ Do you involve staff when making decisions on matters affecting them or their area.

■ Do you lay down a set of rules 'cast in concrete' or do you encourage staff to use initiative and creativity?

■ Is their workplace comfortable, safe, bright and as aesthetically pleasing as possible given the nature of their work?

■ Do you encourage and support the formation of a staff social club for out of work get togethers?

■ Do you give your team a reputation to live up to? Even a name with which they can identify as belonging to that group?

■ Does your team know they can come to you for advice and assistance without fear of rebuke or ridicule?

■ Do you give your top performers honest and sincere appreciation?

■ Do you make each individual feel as if they are an important part of the team and that you are glad to have them working with you?

■ Do you ensure your staff have all the tools, resources and information they need to do their job well?

■ Is your communication two-way, or from you downwards only?

■ Are you fair in your reprimands? And do you reprimand staff in private?

■ Do you lead by example?

■ Do you ensure all staff are treated with respect?

If your answers to most of those questions are positive then you will have conquered an important moment of truth. You are an effective leader who promotes co-operation through a win–win outcome. Congratulations.

If your answers are mostly negative, then this moment of truth is facing you right now. Answer it by identifying your problem areas, by acquiring the knowledge to fix them and by applying that knowledge in an understanding, empathic way.

Are you a Monday morning martyr?

We have all met them—the Monday morning martyrs. After each weekend they show up at work as if they need a place to recover. Yet Monday morning is the starter engine for the whole week. If you are a leader, what you do on Monday morning can set the tone for what happens in the days ahead. Monday-itis could be another moment of truth if it affects you. If it does, or if you know someone else whom it affects, why not convert that challenge into a procedure and conquer it too? Namely:

- On Fridays, use your Priority Planner (see the end of Chapter 12) to list, categorise and prioritise all the jobs you have on hand.
- Complete as many of the jobs as possible on Friday, but, if you can, leave the most interesting job either unstarted or unfinished until Monday morning. This will give you something to which you can look forward.
- If you have a week of meetings or appointments coming up, schedule the most stimulating of these for Monday morning.
- Remember that you need to lead by example, and so arrive at work early and fully energised. Perhaps some early morning exercise will help put some spring in your step?
- Avoid having a late night on Sunday.
- If you have a big job to do, try not to start it on Monday morning or it can seem a little daunting, thus draining your motivation. Instead, spread the job over the week.
- Before you leave work each Friday, put everything on your desk away so on Monday you are greeted with a clean, clear desk.
- If you are a salesperson, schedule at least two sales presentations for Monday morning. If you have a sale to conclude and money to pick up, schedule it for Monday morning. This way you will be off to a great start for the week.
- Follow that procedure each Friday before you leave work.

Do you need to improve your general knowledge?

In a recent television interview a brothel keeper in Bangkok was asked about the spread of AIDS. She replied: 'My girls okay. Very clean. They take bath two times day.'

It has been reported that up to 75 per cent of the people in northern Thailand are infected with the HIV virus. (According to the United Nations, they will number 6 million by the year 2000.) In Africa, entire communities are infected. In 1994, the United Nations estimated there were 20 million HIV infected people in the world.

I mention this point because health is vital to holistic success, and a lack of general medical knowledge can have disastrous personal consequences (e.g. not knowing how to prevent contracting the HIV virus).

In the financial, business and work sphere of life we need general knowledge of another kind. What do you know about economics? Recessions? Inflation? Interest rates? You need not be an economist to succeed. However a general understanding of economic cycles and trends would help.

To illustrate, if the economic indicators are trending towards a deep recession you would be very cautious about the investments you make or the business you start. If you don't have the knowledge, find out. Talk to experts. Read financial journals. Research before you act.

Do you need to face up to letting go?

Every good organiser knows the importance of delegating. Yet many people can't face up to letting go. They want to do everything themselves, and that is impossible.

Is a reluctance to delegate a moment of truth for you? If so it is a challenge that can be met by converting it into a procedure. For example, examine the reasons for your reluctance to delegate, and then test your findings against the following:

■　*You lack faith in the ability of your staff to get the job done, to get it done well and to get it done on time.* The answer here is to

know their individual strengths and weaknesses and to delegate
accordingly. If they lack knowledge, train them.

■ *You don't want to miss out on the kudos for getting the job done.*
Invest the kudos and credit in your staff instead. It will pay
handsome dividends. You will get more than enough kudos by
being seen as an effective leader.

■ *You want to show you can handle any job without help.* We all
need help. Even Christ, Mohammad and Buddha needed help-
ers. Relax. We're all pretty much like you. By asking for help
you are also helping those who give it by enriching their work
and increasing their skills. Getting help is win–win.

■ *You don't want to upset your staff by giving them more work.* If
you are in charge of people you should not be trying to win a
popularity contest. Try winning their respect instead. It works
far better and is far easier on your nerves. Staff will tell you if
they already have too much on their plate. Simply ask. You
don't have to 'order'.

■ *You fear a disaster.* Why? You can check the progress of the
task as it is being done and build in time to assist and to
intervene.

■ *You think no one can do the job as well as you can do it.* You
might be right. But how will others approach your level of skill
without practice? Help them to help you or they won't be able
to learn how best to assist you. Delegate, then check progress.

Delegation is a tool to help you and your team get the job done in the
best and most cost effective way. And who will get most of the credit
when that is achieved? You—their leader. Why? Because you dele-
gated effectively and blended the skill of others with your own skills
to ensure a win–win outcome for everyone.

Do you need to tap your spiritual strength?

Why is this a moment of truth? Because many people feel a sense of
spirituality yet deny this part of their life because in the 'modern
world', spirituality can be regarded by some people as irrelevant.
They succumb to the conditioning drag transfer of others.

If reconnecting with your spiritual dimension will give you
strength, purpose and a more fulfilling life, why turn away from it?

The storyline for your life needs to be written by your own hand, not by the hand of others. Your spiritual moment of truth is to follow your own intuition and to resist the conditioning drag transfer of people who might not be as sensitive to the deeper meaning of life.

Because so many holistically successful people are also deeply spiritual, Chapter 15 is dedicated to 'Tapping into your spirituality'. It is a personal note.

Have you developed the right filters?

Other moments of truth face us whenever we need to solve a problem, make a decision, feel dispirited or lose our focus on where we are heading and why we want to get there (when we relinquish Self-leadership and idle along without direction—simply allowing things to happen to us).

You won't be able to face your moments of truth consistently well if you do not have a clear idea of who you are, what you stand for, where you want to go and why you need to get there. This knowledge is a filter for handling challenges. It helps you see what falls within your mission and what will lure you away from your specific Major Life Goal.

For example, not too long ago I faced a moment of truth that will determine the outcome of the rest of my life. It was this: Do I believe in my ability, in what I can contribute and achieve, or do I simply mouth platitudes and interesting stories from the comfort and security of a highly paid executive position?

If I believed in myself and in my message then I shouldn't hesitate to throw in the job, the plush office, the company car with unlimited petrol, the bonuses and retirement package. I shouldn't equivocate about devoting the rest of my working life to practising what I preach—to helping others achieve holistic success through Self-leadership and Personal Excellence.

The down side was my increasing age, as highlighted by my mother-in-law with the time worn 'You're not getting any younger.' (I was only 45, but to be fair to her it's an age that begins to make applicants less attractive to many employers.) We were also in the middle of Australia's worst ever recession.

Having faced this moment of truth the decision was simple: the storyline I wanted to live was the one I would write for myself. This book is one product of that commitment.

I could not have decided which way to go if I did not have a clear idea of what I wanted, where I wanted to go and why I wanted to get there. Did the decision work out? You be the judge.

Within 12 months of making that decision my new venture earned over $100,000. The sell-out first edition of *The Personal Success Handbook* was published.

In the next six months I was a guest speaker at an international convention in Bangkok, experienced new cultures, consulted for companies in six Asian countries and opened doors into a future that would not otherwise have been possible. In the succeeding six months my wife and I toured Europe and the United States.

If facing moments of truth may lead to change, then I say so be it. I have found that as one door closes, another opens. What you will find on the other side of the opening door will depend on how well you have prepared for success and in how much you believe in yourself.

I discovered a long time ago that to achieve holistic success it's never enough to talk. One must also walk that talk.

Legendary prima ballerina Anna Pavlova said:

'To pursue, without halt, a single goal. That is the secret of Success.'

KEY POINTS

- We all face moments of truth every day. How we deal with our moments of truth will determine how successful we become.
- There are many common moments of truth. For example, what amount of effort are you putting into your work? Is it 50 per cent? What is stopping you from putting in 100 per cent?
- Do you have the right skills to achieve the success you want?
- Do you believe in quality in all that you do. Push for quality. Achieve quality.
- Are you a morale saboteur? Don't puke on others and do not let others puke on you. By doing either you automatically become part of the problem and not part of the solution; you become a morale saboteur—a victim of conditioning drag.
- Do you save and invest? It is what you save and invest, not what you earn, that makes you wealthy. Develop the habit of saving and investing.

■ How healthy are you? Consider your diet, exercise and alcohol intake. If you smoke, why would you want to damage your health and make others wealthy in the process? Develop a de-stressing routine.

■ Do you have a sense of humour? Take your work seriously but yourself lightly. Be a little 'foolish'.

■ Can you keep your cool? It's a vital part of self-management. In confrontations stay calm, state your views directly and give the other party a chance to save face.

■ Do you listen, but not hear? Listen with empathy—with the intent to understand, not with the intent to reply. Focus on the issue, not on the speaker. Keep emotion out of the discussion. Maintain eye contact; half of the message is delivered through body language.

■ Are you an effective leader? If so you involve staff in decision making, encourage them to use initiative and creativity, give them a comfortable place in which to work, give honest and sincere appreciation and make sure all staff feel appreciated and valued. Lead by example.

■ Are you a Monday morning martyr? Monday morning martyrs can be transformed. Turn the challenge into a procedure. Finish as many tasks as possible on Fridays. Leave the most exciting work or meeting for Monday morning to give yourself something to which you can look forward.

■ Do you need to improve your general knowledge?

■ Do you need to delegate more?

■ Have you developed the right filters to enable you to deal with your moments of truth? Do you have a clear idea of who you are, what you stand for, where you want to go and why you need to get there?

■ Do you need to tap your spiritual strength? Holistically successful people are also deeply spiritual. Consider reconnecting to this timeless source of strength to help you on your life's success journey.

9

Developing your instinct to win–win

O NE book that has gained a reputation as one of the most infamous literary works in history is *The Prince* by Nicolo Machiavelli. Its author has been compared with the devil. His very name has entered our lexicon as a term describing sinister plots. Yet Machiavelli only sought to write a factual account of the realities of survival in the sixteenth century. He was telling his prince:

> *'This is the set up. You don't have to like it or follow it, but if you want to survive at least you'd better know it.'*

Machiavelli's point was that a fundamental of developing your instinct to win–win is to look at life as it is. This is not as easy as it might seem, especially if you have people around you who tell you about things as they would like you to see them.

While we can strive for Personal Excellence by adopting a totem of honour and integrity it would be sheer folly to assume others will operate in the same way. The realities are that most people in business are constantly trying to gain an advantage by undermining their competitors. Advertising does it every day by trying to convince you that brand X is better than brand Y.

But do we really need to snatch our living from another person's throat? Do we need to become 'Machiavellian'? Is there reward for the businessperson of character—of integrity? Perhaps surprisingly, the answer is a resounding 'yes!'

Many of the world's great corporations were built on integrity. Nevertheless they hired lawyers to look over any contract before they signed it! In the words of former US president, Ronald Reagan, we need to: 'Trust, but verify.' Let that be a major article of policy in developing your instinct to win–win.

To anyone who has been in work even for a short time it soon becomes obvious that hard work alone does not guarantee success. If you doubt it, consider the following example.

In City X I saw a number of ragged men building a large waterway. In developed countries it would be unthinkable that such a large task would be undertaken by men using only picks, shovels and cane baskets. Yet by hard work they dug a channel at least six metres high and 250 metres long, lined it with a stone wall and finished the job professionally.

Day in and day out they laboured in humid tropical heat, relentlessly swinging their short-handled picks and shovels. They carried rock in wooden barrows for considerable distances—one man pulling while the other pushed. The work was back-breaking. Yet they persisted.

My admiration for their achievement was tempered by the knowledge that they were paid a mere pittance (about US$25 per week). This was evidence indeed of the principle that hard work, of itself, will not guarantee the level of personal success that will secure a lifestyle of comfort and dignity.

The same principle will apply in a modern corporation. Working diligently as one cog in a corporate wheel and hoping you'll be 'discovered' is not a particularly successful tactic. The chances are that if your area is working smoothly (even if thanks to you), there is no fuss and you tow the company line, you probably won't even be noticed by those who count.

No one ever said we live in a fair and just world. Honesty and good are not always rewarded; neither is deceit and evil always punished. We might not like this reality but we have to know it.

The main thing is to live up to the core values embodied in your personal totem, and to keep striving for holistic success through Self-leadership and Personal Excellence. We need to observe this principle regardless of what others do. Be content in the knowledge that the wonderful thing about winning is that, after winning, there comes more winning.

To enjoy our share of the good things we need to eschew conditioning drag; to trust but verify; to develop success behaviour patterns and ingrain them into our psyche—into our daily routine. These include the following win–win fundamentals.

Treat business as business

Emotion is a poor basis for committing to a new business venture or for signing a contract. When you are in love with an idea, under pressure to grab that opportunity before it's too late or when people urge you to sign, that is a time to think, not rush.

In between jobs I was tempted to start a business with a partner who had a knack for promising much but delivering little. Nevertheless I had known him for many years and our dealings had always been satisfactory, and so I took a chance.

We worked together for several weeks, flew to Sydney to discuss contracts with lawyers, and generally began to organise our new venture. In the end, he went cold on the idea and wanted to reduce his financial involvement.

I responded by deciding to do the whole thing myself. I took the decision on an emotional basis to prove something. The result? I lost $30,000 in three months. But I learned that emotion and business seldom mix. I also learned that in the marketplace no one gives medals for bravery.

I learned that whenever a business proposal is brought to us we need to consider it from a business perspective. We need to calculate the extent of the cash receipts it is likely to produce either now or in the future. We need to ask: Is the profit worth the effort? Will we accept a small loss now for a larger gain later? Is there a credit risk involved? What is the background of the proposer? If we are being urged to do it now, what's the hurry?

Don't be overawed by marble offices, chandeliers and plush carpet. If you are being urged to put your money into anything, check the people behind the scenes—their track record. Ask for other opinions and not necessarily those of a lawyer or an accountant; they are good at what they do, but aren't necessarily good business-people.

Talk to someone who's felt the pain of financial loss. Base your decision on business logic and on your own sense of fair play. Remember that the market can only offer you money. If you are not making any, why are you there?

On the other hand should the proposal be a promotion to assist a charity, by all means decide on the nobler course if your cashflow can stand it. On that point Peter S., a multimillionaire developer from Perth, Australia, says:

'I always look at any business deal in a detached loss and profit way. I never agree to a deal unless I'm sure it will add to the bottom line. But privately I would give you the shirt off my back. One's business, the other's private. That's the difference.'

Business survival is about realism—about the way things are. Until you build sufficient assets to feel secure, view your business dealings through the looking-glass of the bottom line. Trust but verify. Once you have decided on a course, proceed with honour and integrity, with Personal Excellence.

If in doubt about potential partners, why not follow Harvey Mackay's advice detailed in his book, *How to Swim With the Sharks Without Being Eaten Alive?* He suggests:

'The second most important term [to add to a contract] is the right to inspect all their books and records, including tax records, etc., pertaining to the agreement. Once that clause is in there, people with a tendency to get cute usually don't.'

Hire people smarter than yourself

You can't succeed without help from others so it's important to check references because good people are found, not made. Good people produce good work; bad people produce bad work. Ask yourself: 'If they were going to work for my competitor, would I feel threatened?'

By hiring people who are smarter than yourself in their area of expertise, your company will grow. Hire those who are less smart and you will be fighting to keep your business from shrinking down to their size. In the words of Harvey Mackay:

'Winners surround themselves with other winners. A winner knows he's a winner. He doesn't need second raters and yes-men around to feed his ego. He knows he'll win more, and go further, with associates who not only can keep up with him but who are also capable of teaching him something.'

People smarter than you will keep your instincts sharp, but only if you get out of their way. Don't give them a job only to take it away from them by telling them how they should do it. In my consulting business I have worked for three developers who did not understand that point. Two were in different states of Australia and one in City X. All had the urge to hire experts, and then to interfere. Once their project was set up and running well they each formed the impression that it was easy to do, and so decided to save the cost of my services by running the projects themselves.

In the two Australian cases, both developers made such a mess of the projects that they lost millions. In the case of City X, the developer managed to run the project well for a time but had to put in so much of his time that his other companies suffered. In the long run he lost far more money than he saved. Trying to do everything yourself is not win–win. It's lose–lose.

You can't be a pal and a boss

Managers who try to win their employee's friendship are often despised for it. Moreover, business decisions need to be based on rational thinking and logic. They should not be influenced by personal feelings for people you like or dislike. Yet how many managers still make decisions based on favouritism?

That immortal Greek slave, Aesop, tells the story of a fox who meets a lion for the first time. At first the fox is afraid of the lion and keeps its distance. The second time it is not so afraid, and walks a little closer. The third time it walks right past, ignoring the lion completely. The moral Aesop gives is that 'familiarity breeds contempt'.

While an Air Force officer I found Aesop's principle correct. That does not mean you can't be cordial and treat everyone with friendliness and respect. What makes familiarity difficult is the fact that in a group of employees each has reached a different level of maturity. While some can handle familiarity well and not take advantage of it, others cannot, and do take advantage. The result can destabilise the group.

Learn the art of self-promotion

When an attractive career change is offered by your corporation you might have to decide to transfer to another State (or country). If you want to be promoted fast, you need to be prepared to move geographically as well as vertically. And if you are prepared to move, make sure the right people know about it.

Of itself, working hard won't move you up the corporate tower. You might not even be noticed. So to be promoted fast you've got to promote yourself by letting people see what you can do. Be a strong Self-leader. Go the extra mile. Think of ways to improve your job, or to improve practices in other sections. Research them, and put in suggestions with copies to the right people.

Show you are thinking beyond your brief—beyond today. Show interest in what your company does. Volunteer. Always put top quality into your submissions, including evidence that you have thought things through (e.g. listing the consequences and outcomes,of your recommendations, including, for example, a cost/benefit and SWOT (Strengths, Weaknesses, Opportunities, Threats) analysis).

There is no magic formula for ensuring a fast track career. Nevertheless the possibility of climbing the management tower faster 'than usual' is a challenge that few success-minded individuals can resist. And what is a very effective way to meet a challenge? By converting it into a procedure! Here are some guidelines for fast tracking the rise and rise of your corporate career:

■ You never know when the opportunity for advancement will come. For example, it can result from the unexpected resignation of a superior, expansion or a new corporate requirement. When that happens, to whom will senior management look as the ideal person for the job? You are right—to the person who is best prepared for the higher position and for the corporate game. So the first rule of giving your own career prospects a boost is: prepare yourself for the position you want.

■ As has been mentioned in Chapter 2, 'The "success book of rules"', read the books! This means to self-educate. Attend courses, seminars and meetings relevant to the area or level you want to enter. Remember that when preparation meets opportunity, most often the result is success.

■ Join management institutes or similar organisations that offer courses, programs and opportunities to meet leaders in business. Constant exposure to that environment can be energising.

■ Get the 'I've got to know' bug. Accumulate relevant information on your work and on anything that deals with the level or position you want. Get to know, understand and remember the pertinent facts, and then look for opportunities to make the people who count know that you know.

■ Think 'personal development'. Believe in it. Push for it. This includes the personal development of your staff too. Your staff's regard for you will be a key factor in any decision on your promotion.

■ Join a professional association for your area of expertise. Support the programs and efforts introduced by your organisation. Become known as 'a corporate person'.

■ Get to know the power groups in your organisation. Who influences what? Do you need to align yourself with one of those groups so they will act as your 'sponsor'? Even if you don't, you would be wise to know who they are.

■ Don't be afraid to make mistakes in your efforts to be innovative and to apply solutions; but avoid making the same mistake more than once.

■ Be seen and be heard—in a consistently positive, encouraging and willing way. Be first to volunteer and to offer assistance. Above all, establish a reputation for getting the job done. This means you do more than is asked of you, do it exceedingly well and on time. Don't offer excuses for late reports or late arrivals. Get the work done instead.

In daily situations you can 'promote' yourself as easily as writing to a person to thank them for a job interview. How many people do that? Whose resume will they remember more readily?

Why not take the time to list those things you can do to fast track the promotion you want? Remember that when opportunity comes you can't say to it: 'Give me another year to get ready.' If you do it will simply move on to someone who is prepared. So when is the best time to start preparing?

Play 'the game' to win–win

Unfortunately, playing 'the game' in some countries means adopting some of the corrupt practices that have ensured power remains with the powerful. Even those who strive to get things done fairly will probably fail more than succeed unless they too play by the 'rules'.

For example, City X is a city where poverty and corruption coexist. If the officials who have to approve your proposal do not receive a 'kick-back', they will delay and frustrate you so much you can go broke while you wait.

Here is a true account of what corruption did to someone I know in City X. The government awarded the entrepreneur a licence to collect a certain type of tax. The entrepreneur set up a large organisation including collection vans, computerised systems, 2000 staff, and so on.

The project cost him well over US$7 million to organise and run. He did it with borrowed money. The venture was successful. Very successful. Too successful.

A very highly placed official drooled at the success. He had the power to revoke the entrepreneur's licence and take it for himself— which he did. The result? The entrepreneur can do nothing but pay off the enormous interest bill from his setting-up loan. To take other action could cost him all his other businesses.

Here is a different example. An official with heavy political clout bought out the country's distributorship of US movies. US movies are all the rage in City X. But he refused to supply any movies to cinemas that he did not own.

As each of the starved cinemas closed, he bought them for a fraction of their value. Currently he controls virtually the whole country's film distribution industry. As for locally produced films, the industry is all but wiped out, ensuring irreparable damage to the country's culture.

But many of us are much luckier because we live in an open society where, even though some corruption exists, we have laws against monopolies and some recourse to legal processes which, if we are lucky, can give us satisfaction. Also, we can enlist the aid of our free press to expose shams.

What I mean by 'playing the game' in the context of achieving and maintaining holistic success is that we need to regard our personal and business life separately. Business is a 'game' with rules for losing and winning, and we need to know those rules to enhance our chances of winning. However applying business rules to our personal life rarely makes for a happy outcome.

For example, as a member of a football team you would strive to win. You would tackle hard. You would risk pain, run frantically and break through to a goal. Your opposition wants to do the same thing. Like you, they want to win. They have trained for it. Get in their way and they'll knock you down. Head for a goal and they'll do everything to stop you.

There is nothing personal in this. It's all part of 'the game'. The important thing is to go for a win (which may contradict what you might have been taught at Sunday school). Yet off the field you wouldn't dream of tackling an opposing player. The action would be irrelevant and out of context.

Business is very much like that. At work you're tackling, running, pushing and striving to kick goals (ensuring every deal is profitable). Privately you can invite your competitors to dinner. When you 'go to work' you step onto the 'playing field' and you do that to win. You can develop your instinct to win by putting on your 'player's hat' whenever you are at work. In their book, *Super Leadership*, Dr Charles C. Manz and Professor Henry P. Sims Jr write:

> 'A recent study of many of our nation's [United States] top artists, scholars and athletes indicated their success resulted more from determination and practice than from natural, inborn talent.
>
> 'They had been encouraged early on to value hard work and to be inquisitive learners, and over time they blossomed into great performers.'

The same principles of determination and practice also apply to developing your instinct to win–win. But it takes more than a willingness to do it. It takes effort—Self-leadership.

Personal success formula refresher

$$S = \frac{Asl^2}{PE}$$

Success equals Attitude times Self-leadership squared over Personal Excellence.

Practice is preparation in progress. As we have noted, when correct preparation meets opportunity (e.g. your moments of truth, a business proposal, a sales call) the result most often is success. But as for any player, you are a hero only when you win. Lose, and you might get sympathy from friends—sometimes—but not usually from your employer. When you lose in business you can get bankruptcy.

If you feel strongly about winning in business remember that the person you are up against probably feels the same way. Therefore there cannot be a winner at all unless both are satisfied with an outcome—unless both win in some way.

Warm-up before the event

Athletes warm up physically, emotionally and mentally before a game. They think through their strategy, visualise success and work to their game plan. Many business leaders, top flight salespeople and entrepreneurs adopt the same 'warm-up' strategy before conducting a business deal, staff meeting or sales call. Here's an example.

Before he meets a client, David R., the top sales representative for a large insurance company, plays each sales call on the 'movie-screen' in his mind. He imagines the interview, what he will say, the client's response and what he will reply.

More often than not it results in a 'sale'. Through his system he is able to approach each sales call with positive expectations for success, giving him an air of total confidence. This confidence influences the client and helps establish trust.

The result? David R. not only enjoys a very high income and the respect of his colleagues, but the respect and recommendation of his clients as well!

Become your own university

Despite how good you are to people or how much they like you, in the end none of them will pay your overdraft, mortgage or rent. You are the only person on whom you can rely totally. Develop your own workable philosophy and a set of core values for your personal totem. Increase your bank of knowledge. Update. (Would you be confident about a surgical procedure if you knew that your surgeon had been trained 40 years ago and had not updated his or her knowledge?)

The better your knowledge, the better your decisions. Read. Talk. Listen. Get ideas. Write them down. Review them. Learn from your own experiences, from the experience of others, and from books, tapes and videos. Learn from failure as well as from success. Observe.

Authors regard libraries as their second office. That's where many of them get ideas and background material (i.e. knowledge). Why not learn from their example? By changing your thinking you can change your life.

Sharpen your instinct to win–win by making self-education one of your major goals and a life-long endeavour. Become a serious scholar of life. Draw inspiration from English painter John Turner. During a tempest he had himself tied to a ship's mast so later he could paint the full onslaught of the storm.

Why not buy an indexed note book and head it: 'Success Journal'. Take it with you to work, to seminars and to meetings. Keep it with you whenever you're travelling. Have it beside you when you read. Record all your good ideas, the good ideas of others and your experiences. It might only cost you a trifling but what will it be worth when you have filled it? Why not let your completed Success Journals take pride of place in your success library? Let them form the core of your self-education and self-development resources.

Get the numbers right with Self-leadership

Out of·100 per cent, how well do you score in the following eight key success areas?

Score out of 100 per cent

1.	Regular saving and investment	___ per cent
2.	Daily reading of 'the books'	___ per cent
3.	Being faithful to your personal totem	___ per cent
4.	Self-leadership	___ per cent
5.	Goal setting	___ per cent

Score out of 100 per cent

6. Personal Excellence   _____ per cent

7. Steering towards your specific
Major Life Goal   _____ per cent

8. Associating with achievers   _____ per cent

TOTAL SCORE (out of a possible 800 per cent)_____ per cent

If your scores are low, the problem is not with the government, taxes, your mother-in-law or the weather; it's with your low scores! With Self-leadership you can increase your scores straight away and begin to change your life immediately. This is how easy it can be:

Score out of 100 per cent

1. Let a part of what you earn be yours to
keep and invest (10 per cent to 20 per
cent each week).   <u>100</u> per cent

2. Read success books, how-to books and
skill books. Take notes.   <u>100</u> per cent

3. Be faithful to your personal totem.   <u>100</u> per cent

4. Lead yourself to improve your work
habits (give your best instead of holding
back).   <u>100</u> per cent

5. Set short- and long-term goals; design
your future for the next ten years,
for retirement and beyond.   <u>100</u> per cent

6. Commit to a specific Major Life Goal;
write it down.   <u>100</u> per cent

Score out of 100 per cent

7. Achieve your Major Life Goal a minor
goal at a time through Self-leadership
and Personal Excellence.   <u>100</u> per cent

8. Disassociate with negative people; mix
with people who have high expectations
for their future. (Ask: With whom am
I mixing? What am I letting them do
to me? What have they got me
reading, thinking? What have they got
me becoming?)   <u>100</u> per cent

TOTAL SCORE (out of 800 per cent)   <u>800</u> per cent

Even if you only improve by 30 per cent you will have increased your chances for success by at least that much! All you need is Self-leadership.

While writing *Les Miserables*, French author Victor Hugo had difficulty finding the Self-leadership to write each day. But he knew it was vital, and ordered his servants to steal all his clothes in the morning so he couldn't go out. John Bunyan wrote his classic *The Pilgrim's Progress* while he was serving a 12 year sentence for preaching without a licence. Self-leadership made the difference. Admiral Nelson, Britain's great naval hero, suffered from severe sea-sickness all his life. Self-leadership enabled him to cope.

In 1990 the Dachau Symphony Orchestra comprised 16 musicians of the original 65. These survivors of the horrors of that concentration camp played for the people of Dachau. Their Personal Excellence refused to empower brutality to rob them of their dignity and of the dignity of their fellow victims.

Mouthing motivational phrases, affirming that you're positive, improving, and so on, is pointless if you cannot lead yourself to act decisively. Without Self-leadership self-motivation leads to disillusionment. For example, controlling emotions when something goes wrong is very important. You'll think far more creatively and clearly. But it takes Self-leadership to do it.

Here are a few personal moments of truth to help you see how strong you are as a Self-leader: If you smoke; stop! If you are excessively overweight, consult your doctor and reduce! If you don't exercise moderately and regularly, consult your physician and if he or she approves, start today! If you hold back at work, give all you've got!

Set yourself a goal of 14 days. Just 14 days! In any one of those areas. If you don't have the Self-leadership to achieve in those areas, where will you get it to persist in the make-or-break world of business? Of corporate reality? I have said all along that success takes effort. It demands persistent effort—the kind of Self-led effort that will keep you from paying the price of low achievement.

We can all draw inspiration from the most Self-led species on Earth—the ant. It heads relentlessly towards its goal. It keeps going until it finds it. Block its path, and it will go over, under or around you. Its instinct to win is indomitable. In summer it prepares for winter (i.e. analogous to downturns in supply, recessed economy, tough times). In winter, it focuses its goal on summer (it is positive, it knows winters don't last). It will succeed, or die.

Arguably the world's greatest ever male dancer, Rudolph Nureyev, grew up in desperate poverty in Russia. As a boy he dreamed of becoming a great dancer but his father, a political commissar in the Soviet Army, would try to beat this 'absurd notion' out of him. His father's storyline for Rudolph scripted a life of an engineer or doctor. Yet Rudolph Nureyev faced his moment of truth at every beating and conquered not only himself, but the world of ballet—a world requiring utmost Self-leadership.

In comparison, you are encouraged to succeed in Self-leadership for 14 days. In trying to achieve this you will soon discover what determination you have for your personal success journey. The urge to achieve is the same as the urge to know. You've just got to!

Get high on results

We are paid for the results we produce, not for the time we spend at work. The better the results, the bigger the reward.

If you are a sales manager and you require your sales people to make 12 calls per week, what will you expect from them at the end of the week? Will you want excuses? Will you accept eight calls per week? Won't you expect that at the very least the minimum number of calls are made even if no sales are achieved? If you expect results of your staff, what results do you expect of yourself? Reverse the role for a moment. What if you had to report to your staff about the results you achieved each week?

In business the result that matters is cash receipts. We need to set goals and procedures that give us the cash receipts to remain viable.

Developing your instinct to win–win in business is as easy as developing a passion for cash receipts. It doesn't matter how good your point of sale material is, how splendid your presentation, or how beautiful your letter-writing. Cash receipts are the arbiters of business success. Without them you have no cash-flow and all you are doing is financing your staff's livelihood through a burgeoning overdraft. Eventually, you will be the one to pay it back.

But results need time. How long would you give a child to learn to walk? On the other hand, how many years should your children stay in grade 5? We need to aim for reasonable results in reasonable time; to check we are heading in the right direction; to avoid making the same mistake more than once. Develop an instinct for checking the major result areas each week. Whatever you find will give you a chance to smile, or to frown. Either way, you've got to know.

Handle complaints to win–win

As we have seen, to win does not have to mean 'to beat'. Developing your instinct to win–win means that we need to sharpen our skills in bringing about situations where the other person can win too.

An area where some people lose is in handling complaints. They view a complaint as something to beat down; to crush; in any case to ensure their company is absolved. Yet few areas give us the opportunity to display our Personal Excellence as does the challenge of handling complaints in a win–win way.

I failed miserably in that area when, as a trainee manager for a large department store, a woman brought a complaint about a sweater she had purchased. She wanted a refund. It started with a call over the loudspeaker for me to attend our 'returns' desk. The employee handling the complaint was clearly flustered and at a loss about what she should do.

The customer stood to one side, clutching her sweater and fuming at the delay. At first, I adopted a friendly, empathic style—which did not last. Looking back at the whole thing now I can see many reasons to smile at my amateurish handling of the case. You be the judge.

I walked over to the lady, introduced myself and smiled. I asked the employee, who was obviously upset, to explain the situation. Then I asked the customer, whose age I guessed at 50 years, to tell me her side of the story.

Customer: 'This sweater here. The collar is all creased and won't iron out. I want my money back,' she demanded, her face flashing red.

Me: I didn't recognise the article as one of our line, and so I asked her: 'Where did you buy it?'

Customer: 'I already told the lady, at Target.'

Me: 'Do you still have the receipt?'

Customer: 'Of course not. I bought it two years ago.'

Me: 'I see. And has it been worn?'

Customer: 'I haven't worn it once. I've kept it in this bag. So just give my money back.'

She raised her voice an octave with every reply, and staff congregated to see how 'the new trainee manager' would handle the matter.

The event attracted the attention of other shoppers, something that did nothing to help my stress levels. But I think I managed to stay calm. I said, 'It's not quite as straight forward as that, Ma'am. I can't identify the garment as being one of our lines. And you say you do not have a receipt . . .'

At that polite, but officious reply, rage glowered in her eyes, swelling them moist and red. She fired: 'If I don't get my money back right now, I am going to have a heart attack!'

The thought of a customer having a heart attack in front of me turned my mouth into a desert. I sputtered: 'If you aren't feeling well we can call a doctor . . .'

My 'concerned' reply made things even worse. She took a deep breath and literally screamed, petrifying everyone in the store, especially me. She warned: 'I'm going to count to ten, then I'm going to have a heart attack . . . ,' and proceeded to count.

'There is no need for that, Ma'am. We will refund your money,' I replied, signing a refund voucher. I couldn't resist adding: 'On the condition that you never shop in this store again.'

Instead of creating a win–win situation I managed to bring about a lose–lose one—all by myself. The lady was an exceptionally highly strung person who managed to infect me with a little of that quality too. But I was green (it was my first week in the job).

So if handling complaints is an area of weakness for you too, why not use our formula for meeting challenges? Namely, convert the challenge into a procedure. For example:

- Acknowledge that regardless of how trivial the complaint might appear to you, it is important to the complainant.
- Hear the complainant out. Resist cutting in or second guessing what they are going to say. Listen with empathy.
- Remember they are complaining about a product, item, system or mistake—not about you personally. It's senseless to become defensive, to lose your cool or to insult their intelligence. If you do any of those things their reaction will only make matters worse by magnifying the complaint.
- Show you are taking their complaint seriously by taking notes.
- If it is a major complaint, agree on a time when you can investigate it and report back to them. In the meantime consider whether you should inform your superiors.
- Do something about the complaint quickly. Don't let it fester into a feud.
- If the complaint arose because your company was at fault, make amends and apologise. If it is the client's fault, handle the matter tactfully and explain the procedure.

Remember that to win–win, both parties must be satisfied with the outcome.

Win–win with power play

Have you noticed how powerful some individuals can seem, even though their 'power' is not backed by any position or authority? They seem to have 'presence'—or command.

Frequently power is perceived rather than substantive. Even so, if you want to create win–win situations you will be far more successful if you learn to project personal power—to play the power game skilfully.

How can you win–win by developing and projecting power? By our method of converting a challenge into a procedure. Namely:

▪ Recognise that power is a two-edged sword. It can be used for positive as well as for negative ends. In the philosophy of holistic success we are only interested in the positive use of power to bring about a win–win outcome.

▪ Develop your personal power by feeling confident and positive about using it.

▪ Be seen and heard. In the section on self-promotion we discussed the importance of ensuring that the 'people who count' see you and your abilities. Take an active role in meetings. Suggest. Innovate. Translate every problem into a challenge; every negative into a positive. Do things. Self-lead.

▪ Don't react subjectively to criticism.

▪ Develop contacts in and outside your business/work sphere of life—contacts who have influence and who can help you by supporting you or by helping you get things done.

▪ Read the books! Self-educate. Get to know your field better than anyone else in your peer group. Speaking knowingly imparts confidence and power by enhancing your personal influence over others.

▪ Reject negative self-talk and conditioning drag. Self-confidence is an indispensable quality of personal power.

▪ Recognise that you have been empowered to achieve—to lead. Act from this premise and project it. The world will stand aside for the people who know where they are going.

▪ Don't give up. Persist. Apply Self-leadership.

▪ Achieve and maintain Personal Excellence. Honesty and integrity are a tremendous source of personal power recognised by everyone.

▪ Help others; assist them to win and to convert their challenges into procedures. Share your know-how. Teach. This helps to give you even more power: the power of loyalty.

▪ Be seen to be fair and just in your treatment of staff and in any comments you make about other people. Treat everyone with courtesy and respect.

▪ Before you act, consider how other people feel. That will enhance your personal power even further because you will win the respect of others.

■ Be consistent.

Remember that as power is most often perceived rather than factual, the way other people see you will determine the extent to which they will empower you to influence them.

Develop your instinct to win–win with power play by ensuring the outcome of your actions will benefit everyone involved.

Win–win with stress

Our efforts to achieve and maintain holistic success through Self-leadership and Personal Excellence invariably will create stress. That is because the success journey demands action, consistency, effort and steady navigation towards our specific Major Life Goal.

Personal success formula refresher

$$S = \frac{Asl^2}{PE}$$

Success equals Attitude times Self-leadership squared over Personal Excellence.

But stress can be a positive force—an ally. It depends on how we view it and whether we respond, or react to it. (Reminder: stress is not pressure. Pressure is something we experience and is external. Stress is something we create internally.)

Causes of stress can range from our values, attitudes, lifestyle and even sickness. Symptoms vary from the most common (e.g. putting on too much weight) to far more serious illness. However we need to create some measure of stress to get us moving. The question is: How much and in what way?

If you have been reacting to 'bad stress', changing your life-style and focusing on achieving and maintaining holistic success can produce positive, healthy stress—the stress of the challenge we enjoy; the triumph of achievement; self-acceptance; satisfaction; and personal victory.

But life is not usually so straightforward and even the best plans and efforts can run foul of all manner of roadblocks. It is in such times that our 'good stress' has the potential to hurt us if we convert it into 'bad stress' by reacting negatively to the situation. If you are prone to reacting to stress, don't worry. There's a way out. Simply use our formula for meeting any challenge. Convert it into a procedure. For example:

■ Ask yourself: 'What is happening that I don't like? What am I letting it do to me; to my family? What has it got me becoming? How am I personally affected?'

■ Look for the causes of the stress.

■ Check your work pattern. Has conditioning drag stopped you from organising your work so you control it instead of letting it control you? Have you stopped using the Priority Planner (see the end of Chapter 12) or a similar system. Have you stopped tackling one job at a time?

■ Check what you are doing is in line with your specific Major Life Goal. Has your goal changed? Do you still have a burning desire to achieve it? If not, it could be possible that you have lost your way.

■ Discuss your pressures and stress with someone you respect and/or care about. Don't be reluctant to accept good advice. No one person is the fountain of all knowledge—neither you nor I.

■ If what is happening at your work is leading you to create 'bad stress', remember to take your frustrations out on your work— on its system. Do not take it out on your family or friends.

■ Recognise that strong drink is no solution and is likely to create even more pressure and stress—even if only in the financial sphere of your life.

■ After checking with your doctor, take up moderate, regular exercise. It is a great stress reliever. Play a sport you enjoy because if you work out at a gym and you don't enjoy it, it will probably add to your stress rather than reduce it.

■ If other people are the cause of your 'bad stress', check that you are not projecting your own storyline on them and are reacting because they don't fit the picture you have created. Try not to judge. Don't expect too much of others; they will rarely live up to your expectations because they are not you.

- Don't empower the things that are beyond your control to hurt you.
- Mix with positive, supportive people who have high expectations for their future.
- Take regular, short holidays—even if they only last a week-end at a time.
- Don't make mountains out of mole-hills. What seems critical and earth shattering to you right now may not seem like such a big deal tomorrow, next week, next year or next century.
- Remember that life is 95 per cent thought and 5 per cent form. You control thought so you can control the level of stress you create.
- It could help to connect with your spiritual dimension. It is a great source of serenity, power and strength. It can put every-thing into perspective so you don't react to things in isolation and see them looming larger than life.
- Remember that holistic success is win–win. You can reduce your own stress greatly by helping other people win. Do something unselfish. None of us is the centre of the cosmos and the major support that we have as a buttress against the misfortunes of life is each other.
- Accept that happiness is internal—that it starts from the moment we decide to be happy and to act accordingly.
- Enjoy life. A good friend of mine takes the view that every day above ground is a great day regardless of the pressures we face.
- Add variety to your life. Change your daily routine.
- Keep things in their true perspective. If you think you have pressure, compare it to the pressures of your brothers and sis-ters in war-torn Bosnia Herzegovena, of those suffering under the yolk of corruption in City X, or those who fled the killing fields of Rwanda.
- Be mindful of the good things and of the good people in your life. Empower them to win–win.
- Rather than seeing it as the enemy, treat stress as an ally and empower it to help you achieve all the good things you want for yourself and for those you love.

Having considered all those issues, list those that you can weave into a daily, weekly and monthly routine. It will be your win–win, stress-defeating procedure. Then simply apply it. If you are still subject to 'bad stress' symptoms, meditation can be a great help.

In December 1993 the Stress Management Centre of the University of Sydney announced they had developed a system to teach executives to manage stress by showing them how to decrease their heart rate. This system is available for purchase. It works.

An interesting note is that Yoga has been teaching a similar method for centuries. It is another glimpse of the helpful power of connecting with your spiritual dimension. (By programming the system into a computer it becomes more acceptable because it is tangible and people can measure progress in a visual way.) Whatever works in a win–win way!

Make win–win a habit

Instincts for winning can be developed by playing to win. Whether it's a game of cards, tennis, golf, a meeting at work or a sales call, develop the habit of taking it seriously enough to go for a win. You might not take home the prize, but you won by trying and therefore by reinforcing your success patterns.

In your work you win whenever you list tasks in priority order and do them one at a time. You win any time you can say you completed a job to the best of your ability. You win whenever you do willingly those jobs you don't like to do.

You win when you produce quality work, give encouragement or display a positive mental attitude. You win when you go home knowing you got from the day, not through it; and when you played to win–win, and everyone involved won in some way.

KEY POINTS

■ Developing your instinct to win–win is a fundamental of personal success. There are a number of 'philosophies' that will help refine your instinct to win–win.

■ The first is to treat business as business. By all means be generous in your private life. However the aim of business is to produce cash receipts. View all business transactions through the point of view of the bottom line. Look at life as it is. Trust, but verify.

■ Hire people smarter than yourself. If you hire people less clever than you, you'll be fighting to keep your business from shrinking to their size.

∎ You can't be a pal and a boss. Managers who try to win their employee's friendship often are despised for it. Business decisions must be made on a logical, impartial basis, and not on personal feelings you might have for your staff. From the staff's point of view, familiarity breeds contempt.

∎ Learn the art of self-promotion. Join a professional institute. Get to know your field better than any of your peers. Get involved in company activity. Find out who are the power groups in your company. Work on personal development. Above all, prepare for the job or level that you want.

∎ Play 'the game' to win–win. Training—physical, emotional and psychological—are as important to the Success student as they are to the athlete. This training is preparation for opportunity.

∎ Warm up before the event. All athletes warm up before they begin to play. They warm up physically and psychologically. Before each meeting or talk 'warm up' for the event by playing the situation through on the 'movie screen' in your mind—what you'll say, their replies, and so on. Then see yourself emerging with the result you want.

∎ Become your own university. Study. Attend success seminars. Make prolific notes in your Success Journal. Develop your own philosophy and code to live by. Get the 'I've just got to know' bug. Knowledge is the beginning of Success. We can only make decisions based on what we know. Incorrect or insufficient knowledge can lead to incorrect decisions. Become a Serious Scholar. Read 'the books'.

∎ Get the numbers right with Self-leadership. How do you score in the key areas that prepare you for success (saving and investing, daily study, attending seminars and courses, goal setting, Self-leadership and Personal Excellence, associating with positive people, commitment to a specific Major Life Goal)? If your numbers (scores) are low, so will your chances of success be low. Change your numbers in those areas and you'll change your life! Develop an 'ant' mentality—do or bust!

∎ Get high on results. In business all results rely on sufficient cash receipts. Without results, knowing how to succeed is of little relevance. Get excited about each win; those are the 'bricks' that build the 'big result' of your Major Life Goal. Remember that results need reasonable time to accomplish.

- Handle complaints to win–win. Regardless of how trivial a complaint might seem to you, it is serious to the complainant or they wouldn't be making it. Listen with empathy. Focus on fixing the problem, and not on beating the complainant. Complaints give us an opportunity to exercise our Personal Excellence.

- Win–win with power play. Recognise that power can be positive as well as negative. Often power is perceived rather than substantive. Personal power comes from self-confidence, knowledge and energy. Be seen and heard. Don't take criticism personally. Develop contacts. Persist. Learn to express your views directly and calmly. Be consistent.

- Win–win with stress. Stress can be positive—an ally. Stress is something we create internally. If you are suffering from 'bad stress', consider the areas that affect you. What are the causes? Check your work pattern. Are you organising and controlling your work, or is it disorganising and controlling you? Take regular exercise. Keep things in perspective.

- Make win–win a habit. By playing to win in sport, meetings, calls, and so on, you develop winning as a habit. That will enhance your winning instincts. However remember there can be no real win without honour for all concerned.

10

Negotiating to win–win

W HETHER you want a discount, a job or a meeting, to choose a restaurant, a car or a house, or to gain agreement on a deal or to cancel it, the process is one of negotiation.

I am not talking about tricks, manipulating others or of the 'win at all costs' brand of negotiation. Negotiation is not confrontation. It should be a process of meeting needs and wants in a manner satisfactory to everyone.

A successful negotiation is one where all parties are satisfied. The outcome might not be the one they had sought, but one that they can accept with honour. Psychologist, author and speaker Dr Dennis Waitley says in *Personal Success Magazine*:

> *'Bullies make poor negotiators. That applies to verbal bullies as well as physical ones.*
>
> *'Contrary to popular belief, negotiation is not won by intimidation. That only makes the other person defensive and resentful.*
>
> *'The rules to successful negotiation are based on the principles of communication and co-operation. First, you want the other person to talk to you and, second, you want him to work with you. In other words, negotiation is the gentle art of persuading the other fellow that you can help him achieve his goals if he helps you achieve yours.'*

This principle works on any level. For example, at City X selling for the project I set up involved a lengthy presentation to each client. The people of City X are accustomed to bargaining and negotiating for even small purchases. So almost always they came back with a counter-offer.

If the sales manager had refused to negotiate, clients would have walked out. That's because he would have created a dead end. But by training the sales manager to send the salesperson back with a counter-offer, sooner or later a compromise decision was reached and sales satisfactory to all parties were made.

The proposition is this: in a successful negotiation all parties need to feel involved in setting the rules. While it is true that sometimes threats and intimidation will work, generally they only succeed in postponing a problem until a later time when it might come back as a far larger issue. (Such was the case with the terms of settlement imposed on a defeated Germany at the end of World War I. Deprived of its major resources in the Rhur Valley and Alsace Lorraine, Germany became bankrupt. The result? World War II.) On an individual level major errors in negotiation occur when you:

- fail to consider the ability of the other party to negotiate
- don't consider what is acceptable to the other side
- fail to take into account cultural differences regarding negotiation, manners, their system of 'doing business', protocol, and so on
- fail to consider the pressures being applied on the other party by interest groups, lobbyists or politicians, and the possible need of the other party to appease those groups
- escalate the problem or your commitment to it
- are overconfident about the outcome
- mistake silence for agreement
- view a successful negotiation as 'win all or nothing'.

The matter of cultural differences must not be overlooked. Your approach in City X would only work if you modelled your negotiation to fit the way they do business. Many Western companies have gone in there with a 'frontal approach', only to fail. They mistook politeness and smiling faces for agreement.

In City X the way to get a proposal through is to use the multitude of back doors. You would make an approach to the very senior levels of the organisation as well as to those who would need to implement the decision but who may be lower down the scale.

Most importantly, your chances of success would be increased greatly if you had a local 'sponsor'—someone who had the back-door contacts and who could open those doors for you.

Finally, you would need to take into account the high probability that unless the decision makers will benefit through some form of kick-back, your chances of success would be slim. It's called corruption. In City X and other cities like it, it's called reality.

But most of us are lucky because, where we live, if the deal is attractive enough we can reach agreement without having to suffer corrupt imposts such as those in City X. So what excuses can we make for ourselves if we fail to negotiate successfully? Because relatively speaking, we have far more opportunities than do most people who live in developing countries.

Nevertheless to be a successful negotiator anywhere you will need to consider the other party's position and have alternatives that could be acceptable to both of you. (Also, it would be wise to include 'demands' that you are willing to remove by way of compromise.) You will also need to work out the terms acceptable to you before negotiations begin and to ensure they can be modified in light of additional information gained from the negotiation itself.

A particularly good (and common) way to begin is to ask for more than you really want. This works at almost any level of negotiation. It gives you the opportunity to make counter-offers and, consequently, provides room to manoeuvre.

Do such tactics really work? Let's see.

When Jan C. Scruggs was planning his negotiation strategy to build Washington's Vietnam War Memorial, he decided to ask for two acres (almost 1 hectare) of prime real estate. Everyone else told him that it would be impossible.

He didn't need two acres. He asked for more than he wanted so he would have a point on which to compromise.

The result? To his amazement no one questioned the demand. The memorial was built on two beautiful acres of rolling lawn in front of the Lincoln Memorial.

Effective negotiation begins when you listen, when you listen with empathy, and when you listen with a view to understand, not to reply. Personal Excellence requires that both parties focus on beating the challenge, not on beating each other.

To achieve that outcome and avoid negative emotional reaction we need to understand the key elements of negotiation technique, which are:

■ information
■ time
■ power.

Gather information

The more you know about the other party's needs, wants, deadlines and strengths, the more you will be able to influence the proceedings towards an outcome acceptable to you. It is to your advantage to know more about what they need and want than for them to know what you need and want. Yet few people take time to get as much information as possible about the other party before negotiation begins. I am talking about research.

One way to do this is to send in a proxy—someone who has no power to make decisions but who can start negotiations. This gets you more information and can encourage the other party to show their hand or to tell you where they stand. You can get involved later armed with vital intelligence and unfettered by prior involvement.

At the first meeting you can get additional information by asking 'open-ended' questions.

Consider a simple case of everyday negotiation: the case of Peter M., a recently appointed salesperson with a large insurance company.

Peter arranged an interview with Tom and Margaret B., a young couple who, unknown to Peter, were intent on saving enough money for a down payment on an apartment.

> *Peter M.*: 'There's a great deal of interest in pension plans these days. My company has the best in the market, earning (X per cent) interest.'

> *Tom B.*: 'I think we're OK for now. Actually we're more interested in savings and . . .'

> *Peter M.*: 'There are no better savings than pension plans. They give healthy tax deductions, and you can retire in comfort . . .'

> *Margaret B.*: 'Tom and I have thought about providing for a retirement income. But at the moment . . .'

> Peter M.: 'I know what you mean. There's always another bill to pay. But let me show you the cost of postponing your decision for just one year . . .'

Do you see the problem? Peter is trying to negotiate a sale without first obtaining information about the other party's needs or wants. His approach will result in a frustrating experience for everyone. The following approach would be more productive.

Peter M.: 'What is your main financial goal at the moment?'

Margaret B.: 'To be rich,' she jokes.

Peter M.: 'I can relate to that. But if you had enough money now, what would you do with it?'

Tom B.: 'I'm tempted to say, go off on a great vacation. But we're wanting to buy an apartment, actually.'

Peter M.: 'When have you planned to buy, Tom?'

Tom B.: 'With a bit of luck, we'll have a down payment by the end of next year.'

Peter M.: 'I can see that buying an apartment is very important to you. My company has a tax-advantaged savings plan that could really help. May I show you how it works . . .?'

In this case, Peter obtained information about the couple's wants and their deadline. With this knowledge he was able to negotiate a sale that satisfied his client's needs.

Without knowing the needs and wants of the other party any negotiation will reduce to flogging a product, service or idea that might be totally unsuitable for them. The result? No deal—or one that will cancel sooner rather than later.

To obtain information, questions are the answer. These can be classified broadly into two types—fact and feeling questions. Fact questions are used to obtain details such as age, size of company, location, quantity or date required. Feeling questions provide information about philosophy, feelings, wishes, aims, wants, dreams, and so on. For example, if you were negotiating to provide an office cleaning service, in your research phase you could ask:

Fact question: 'Who provides the service for you now?'

Feeling question: 'Are you happy with the value you are getting for your money?'

The fact question is important because it can tell you with whom you are competing, while the feeling question can give you vital information about the other party's level of satisfaction.

Once you have this information you can propose your own deal. Negotiation can begin in the knowledge that you are on the right track. A win–win situation becomes possible.

The same applies when you are negotiating to win co-operation. First get information on what 'they' want, how they feel, their present constraints—in short, as much information as you can get. Lead with open-ended questions.

An example: How to negotiate a better deal when buying a car

Simply knowing how another party works can be a great advantage. For example, assume you want to buy a new car. Knowing that most dealers work on monthly targets and their cars (in Australian dealerships) are 'owned' by finance companies can help you get a better deal. By postponing your negotiation until the last day of the month, dealers will be more likely to be flexible because they need to make their sales target and to put another 'dot' on the sales board. But does it really work? You be the judge.

Recently I bought a brand new car by applying the principles we are discussing. I went to the car dealer literally on the last day of the month. By talking casually to the salesperson I found out it had been a very slow month for them, and so I asked him: 'If I were looking to get the best deal from the new cars you have in stock, which car would you recommend for me?'

He showed me the car he thought represented the best value for money. After asking him to explain what made that car the best deal, I said that I would be prepared to make an offer today, pay cash today and take the car off the lot today provided I could get it at my price. He had to talk to his manager.

I entered the sales office armed with the following information:

■ It was the last day of the month.
■ The dealership was having a quiet month, making them eager to trade.
■ The new car in which I was interested had over $2500 worth of extras already included.
■ The average profit margin a dealer has on a new car is about $3000.
■ I had the cash to buy it that day.

My first offer was not accepted. They made a counter-offer. I responded with a compromise offer, which was accepted, and got a great deal. But was the result win–win? Here's how it wound up:

- *The dealer* sold a new car, which meant they had one less overhead on which to pay interest. The sale helped make target, which means the state distributor would be less likely to apply pressure. In my estimation, they made a net profit of about $500, which I do not begrudge them at all.
- *I* got a great deal with many extras, saved at least $3000 off their list price, and am enjoying the comfort of my new car.

Used-car buyers can also take the same approach. Dealers allow approximately $1000 to bring any trade-in 'up to scratch', another $1000 to defray costs of floor space and interest charges and a further $1000 for profit.

Therefore, it is a reasonable guess that on an average used-car a dealer will try to sell a trade-in at $3000 above his or her purchase price.

Armed with this information of approximate profit margins and the sales manager's end-of-month pressure, if your timing is right you should be able to negotiate a better deal. However, the car industry often uses its own variation of 'negotiation' technique. And as so many of us need cars, it's worth mentioning some of the more infamous of these practices.

High-balling
High-balling a prospect means the salesperson will estimate a much higher value for your trade vehicle. You will be pleasantly surprised and more receptive to start negotiating.

In the meantime their assessor is looking your car over. That will take time because, the salesperson having obtained your interest, will try to get you to invest as much time as possible so you will be more anxious to finalise a deal.

The assessor will inform the salesperson that the car has a few problems and that the original estimate was way too high.

However the salesperson has already 'worked out a deal' based on the original estimate, had you drive the car you want and got you seeing yourself as its new owner. You will be reluctant to get back into your old car.

The salesperson will rework the 'deal' and show you that in the end it might make very little difference financially and they have offered you the best deal anyone could make, given the condition of your car. More often than not, you will take the offer.

Alternatively, high-balling allows them to give you an inflated price on your trade by taking less off the price of the car you want.

The point is that you will be so delighted with getting so much for your old car that you will think they are very fair people.

Low-balling

Initially you will be disappointed at their estimate of your car's trade-in value. They will ask how much you expected. Once they have your figure (which invariably will be higher than theirs) they will ask you to allow them to 'shop your car around' to see what they can get for you.

All the while they are giving you hope that 'something could possibly be done'. In the meantime the salesperson will take you into his or her office to 'see how the deal would look on paper'.

To your delight, they will come back to you with a deal that will give you the price you want for your trade. Having found it so 'difficult' to get the price you wanted in the first place, you are likely to grab the deal while the grabbing is good.

De-horsing

This is a common tactic. Usually it follows low-balling or a deal that the salesperson can't convince you to accept. Because it is so 'difficult' to get you the trade price you want they will need your car for a day or so to take it around to various wholesalers. In the meantime they will let you drive the used-car you want, home.

You get to show the car to your family, keep it overnight, and feel the pleasure of being rid of the annoyances of your old car. (The idea is that having become used to the better car, you will be reluctant to get back into your old car.)

When you go back to the dealership you have already made a big investment in time, effort and ego. More often than not they will offer you a higher value for your old car than at first mentioned, and you will be more willing to make the deal.

During the entire process of the sale you, the 'prospect', deal with the salesperson. The salesperson is a 'proxy' with no power to make decisions. Their priority is to obtain a commitment from you, no matter how unrealistic, under which you will agree to buy today.

Your proposal will then be referred to the manager, who might accept it. Usually, the manager will send the salesperson back with a counter-offer.

The salesperson wants to go to the sales manager with a definite proposal like:

'I've got Tom S. who says that if we give him $XYZ on his trade-in he will pay $ABC for our car, right now, by cheque drawn on X Bank.'

If the salesperson does not go to the sales manager with an offer as specific as that, they are likely to be reprimanded and sent back for another try. (If all else fails they might de-horse you.)

The system of preventing direct negotiation with the decision maker maintains the manager's image of authority and allows the salesperson to foster the impression that he or she is on your side.

Understand the value of time

At Camp David former US president Jimmy Carter brokered the accord that brought peace between Egypt and Israel. The consensus of opinion was that he wore the protagonists down simply by using time—locking them into a process for weeks without an agenda so each felt they had to show their people something for their efforts!

As a general rule the party who has an urgent deadline usually makes the most compromises as the deadline draws nearer.

This knowledge is often shamefully exploited by negotiators at the highest level. By waiting until the eleventh hour they force compromise, often to the other party's detriment. It is also exploited in everyday life. Here's a true example.

Maria had five children. Her husband had preceded her on immigration to Australia in the previous year and now she and her children were to join him. To fund the voyage the family had to sell everything they owned, which included two houses, a blacksmith's shop and a small farm—all at post-war ravaged prices. She would need a considerable surplus to take to her new country because the rules were that immigrants couldn't bring towels, bed linen, crockery etc., and therefore many necessities would have to be bought on arrival.

The agent negotiating the sale knew that Maria had a deadline—her date of embarkation. Under instructions from the buyer the agent stalled, delayed, thought up excuses—anything to stretch out the payment of the balance of purchase moneys.

One week before her departure the agent informed Maria that the buyer had reduced his offer by 20 per cent. Maria knew it was too late to find another buyer. It was also too late to take any legal action. She had a deadline. She had no choice but to accept the offer and to borrow the balance from relatives to fund the family's voyage. The family arrived in their new country not only penniless, but in debt. (I know this story is true because Maria is my mother. We emigrated just before I was ten years old.)

That type of negotiation is the 'win at all costs' brand. It goes hand in hand with the belief that if you can disadvantage the other party, you win.

There is nothing wrong with using knowledge of a deadline to your advantage provided it leads to a win–win result. Remember your core values—your totem of Personal Excellence.

In his book *You Can Negotiate Anything*, master negotiator Herb Cohen describes an incident early in his career when he was sent to Japan to negotiate an important deal. The Japanese negotiators wined and dined him, entertained him and even enrolled him in a crash course in Japanese culture. They did everything except begin negotiations, insisting there was plenty of time.

Knowing that Mr Cohen had a deadline (a return ticket is a good clue) the Japanese negotiators skilfully delayed discussions until it was so close to the time of departure that Mr Cohen had to make concessions to return with a deal.

In his own words, his manager called it the greatest Japanese victory since Pearl Harbour.

Of the Japanese negotiating style, Donald J. Trump says in *The Art of the Deal*:

> 'I have great respect for what the Japanese have done with their economy, but for my money they are often very difficult to do business with.
>
> 'For starters, they come in to see you in groups of six or eight or even twelve, and so you've got to convince all of them to make any given deal. You may succeed with one or two or three, but it's far harder to convince all twelve.'

If you're outnumbered, make sure you're not outsmarted. Plan your strategy and build in alternatives on which you can fall back.

Determine where the power is

All too often 'power' is perceived, rather than substantive. Nevertheless our perception determines the approach, tone and conduct of negotiation.

For example, when you are negotiating for a new job, your approach to the interview and willingness to compromise would differ if you were the job giver and not the job seeker. That's because the job giver has the power to 'reward or to hurt'.

A basic point to remember is to ensure you negotiate with the decision-maker wherever possible. It is not uncommon to negotiate for hours only to discover that the other party has to refer to a higher authority. This has been many a salesperson's downfall.

Negotiating with intermediaries is quite common, especially at national level. The message is that: 'Oh well, we can't really decide anything anyway, so you'd better make your offer as attractive as possible for our bosses to consider.' There's no risk of an impulsive decision there.

Some negotiations are too complex to be settled in one meeting. Consequently it is vital to obtain as much information as possible (even about the decision-makers if you can) and to document the results of all meetings.

Following are some different aspects of power in negotiation.

Precedent

Car salespeople often meet customers who tell them that 'Better Motors' down the road offered them the same car at a lower price and with an additional $XYZ on their trade!

These customers are attempting to use precedent as a power factor. That is to say, 'Better Motors have done it, why can't you?'

You too can use precedent as a power factor in negotiation. Consider the following approach:

You: 'Your company is well recognised as a supporter of junior sports. Your donations to the junior league over the past five years have been of tremendous importance.' (precedent)

They: 'Thank you. Our firm prides itself on being a responsible community neighbour.'

> *You*: 'It's refreshing to deal with a company that has a social conscience. You might not have considered supporting the 'Youth for . . .' movement. However I believe its aims fit in well with your community neighbour policy.'

And another example:

> *You*: 'I don't know if I can arrange for 100 to be delivered by next Thursday. What if I can get 50 by Thursday and another 50 by the following Wednesday?'

> *Them*: 'That's no good. Wednesday's too late.'

> *You*: 'If I could ask my company to pull out all the stops, change its production schedule and deliver 50 by Thursday and the balance on the following Monday just as we did with that order two months back, could we go ahead with this order?'

In a successful negotiation, no one loses. Each person must feel satisfied or it will come back to haunt you.

Patience
Have you ever been subjected to a sales presentation or negotiation that dragged for hours? Many use this 'patience' technique to obtain a commitment favourable to them. It works because you have made a large investment in time and therefore are keen to wind up the process, or you buy to get rid of the salesperson or problem.

The more time people invest in a negotiation the more interested they become in concluding it quickly. Anyone who has experienced the Japanese style of negotiation will recognise the patience they display (i.e. getting you to invest as much time as possible).

If you want to negotiate successfully, don't be in a hurry. However for patience to work, the other party must also believe that you are in no particular hurry to conclude the deal.

'This is all I have'
The power of a last offer has clinched many deals. However it is best to leave this as a last resort.

> *You*: 'I know that your XYZ is worth more, but I only have $XXX.'

> *Them*: 'We couldn't accept that.'

You: 'I would pay more if I could but I don't have it. Would you at least consider my offer? Could you at least ask the boss?'

Them: 'I'll check, but you're wasting your time.'

Does this approach really work? It won't work every time but it's worth trying. For example, some time ago I saw a beautiful painting for sale. The original price was $4500 but it had been reduced to $2500.

Me: 'I'd love to own it. But my credit card can only carry another $2000.'

Gallery owner: 'It's already been reduced by $2000. I can't do better than that.'

Me: 'I appreciate that. It's so beautiful and worth more than I can pay. But $2000 is all I have.'

Gallery owner: 'In that case I don't know that I can help you. The artist . . .'

Me: 'Won't you ask him anyway. I'd pay more if I could. I know it's worth more . . .'

The gallery owner telephoned the artist who, tempted with the offer to make a sale that day rather than risk waiting several more months, approved the sale. Worth a try, wasn't it? I saved $500.

It can work because the demand first trumpeted by the other party might not be what they are willing to accept.

Winning in round two

Imagine an advertising agency carolling the virtues of their new campaign—account executives full of commitment, enthusiasm and hype delivering their presentation. At the end, wide-eyed and brimming with expectation, they ask:

Them: 'Well? What do you think?'

You: 'Sorry. But I didn't quite get it. Could you explain it again please?'

Them: 'Which part?' they plead, dismayed.

You: 'The whole thing!'

Can you guess the effect? Who could go through a lengthy proposal with the same enthusiasm and commitment a second time to the same audience? The same technique can be used in negotiation.

Ask the other party to explain their whole proposal and reasoning again. You might find their demands a little less firm and their willingness to compromise, enhanced.

Rapport
Establishing rapport and identifying empathically with the needs of the other party can provide you with the power of 'kindred spirits'. That is to say, being helpful, genuinely interested in the other party's problems and needs and 'being on their side' will encourage the other party to compromise.

Whatever proposal or counter proposal you put, always point out how your offer or suggestion will satisfy their needs and wants. Foster the approach that sends the message: 'By helping each other we can beat this thing and get the result we both want.'

Keep on keeping on
Most people quit negotiating too easily. In Bali the salespeople who ply their trade on beaches and tourist venues are natural negotiators. They have great persistence and really believe in keeping on. Selling anything from copy watches to sculptures of Garuda they make offers and counter-offers as naturally as they breathe.

One occasion Gayle (my wife) and I were enjoying an evening walk along Batubelig Beach. We were approached by a group of salespeople, many of them young. I was impressed by the virtuosity of one man in particular.

'Allo. You Italian, yes, Mister?' he asked, smiling. He added in Italian, 'Questi sono molto buoni' (these are very good) and opened his case of copy watches.

'I'm Australian,' I replied.

Changing 'gears' as smoothly as an automatic transmission, he declared: 'These are bloody good watches, mate,' right down to the Australian idiom. It was a command performance.

In his own way he was first trying to get information that he could use. He then switched his approach to suit his prospect, backing it up with sheer persistence. He followed us along the beach for at least 100 metres, all the while carolling the virtues of his product. I bought.

Later at a lookout overlooking a volcano we were approached by another salesperson who also must have 'studied negotiation techniques'. He was intent on selling me a wooden carving of a Balinese dancer. The interesting thing was the way he understood a key point of negotiation intuitively. He started off with: 'Beautiful Bali dancer, Mister. You buy. $50.'

'I have one already,' I replied.

'You buy. $40,' he offered, accompanying Gayle and me along the footpath.

'It's not the price. I really do have one.'

'Okay. How much you pay? We do deal.'

'I don't need it.'

'$5, you buy?' he persisted.

The statue was worth at least $30. He had no intention of selling it for $5. What he was trying to do was to get my agreement on a smaller point so he could win on a larger one.

He knew that if I committed to buy at any price, it would be easier for him to negotiate an int₀ease because the decision to buy had already been made.

The Balinese street vendors know that persistence and determination are essential. They too have a deadline—the length of time the tourist will be in front of them.

While often there are lengthier deadlines to consider, determination to 'see it through' can signal to the other party that you must be taken seriously. This itself can give you power—the power of purpose. .

Sometimes a successful negotiation can depend on the technique you use. For example, you could use the Balinese salesperson's technique. Namely: if you can't get agreement on a major issue get agreement on the minor issues first. You can return to the major issue later. They will have invested more time and energy, which encourages a willingness to conclude the negotiation.

Some final hints on negotiation

Generally speaking, in negotiation all parties bring their own baggage of needs, wants, deadlines, instructions, prejudices and limitations. So acquiring and developing negotiation skills is essential because so much depends on our ability to persuade, put our case, minimise losses, enhance gains, obtain support, get a good deal and avoid being disadvantaged, all in the face of the other party's paradigm.

I have found that effective negotiation is not necessarily a process of logic. You can have all the logic of an Immanuel Kant yet fail to persuade anyone because your logic does not provide what the other party wants. Often, what the other party wants can be related more to feelings, ego and emotion, than it can to logic.

Many salespeople fail because they do not understand this point. They try to overwhelm their client with facts and figures and performance specifications when all the client could want is something that works, but something that will also match their decor.

Neither is negotiation a battle. It is a process of finding that point where conflicting positions can meet and agreement reached.

So if you are ever faced with a negotiation involving a person you dislike, separate the person from the problem and focus on beating the problem, not on beating the person.

Remember to take cultural differences into account. What seems 'the right thing to do' for you might not be so for them. Insults and cultural bad manners will only put the other party off side and hinder the chances of a satisfactory outcome.

Learning and developing the art of negotiation can be a life's work in itself. Those who have learned the skills best are often sent abroad to deal with issues ranging from trade to diplomatic bungles to avoiding war.

They are people who know that getting a first 'no' is the signal for negotiation to begin, not for them to quit. They have learned that 'no' really means 'not yet'.

Finally, always try to put yourself in the other party's place. If you were they, how would you like to be approached? What offers would you find acceptable or at least worthy of compromise?

If there are two golden rules in negotiation, they are these:

■ To get what you want, help the other party get what they want or what they can accept with honour.
■ Sometimes it is wiser to say 'no', and walk away.

KEY POINTS
■ There are three cardinal points of negotiation: information, time and power.

- The aim of negotiation is a win–win outcome. Remember your totem of Personal Excellence. Negotiation is a search for a point of agreement. It is not a confrontation.
- Techniques of negotiation such as using precedent, persistence, working to a deadline, delaying decisions until all facts are considered and researching the other party for information are all valid if it results in a win–win outcome.
- 'No' means 'not yet'.
- Put a proposal aimed at satisfying their wants, not what you perceive to be their needs.
- Logic is useless if it cannot be shown to fulfil the other party's desires in the context of their cultural background.
- Show sympathy with solving their problems. Build rapport. Treat the other party courteously. Listen with empathy.
- The objective of negotiation should be victory over the problem, not victory over the other party. That's Personal Excellence!
- If personal feelings are involved, separate the person from the problem and focus on solving the problem.
- Always analyse the entire situation—all the pros and cons—before entering a negotiaticto.
- Be ready with a number of options that could be acceptable to all parties before you begin negotiation. Add features you would be prepared to remove.

11

Speaking in public for reward and profit

S KILLED public speaking is an effective method of furthering your standing in the community and promoting your business or career. Through it you can:

- inspire confidence in yourself
- make valuable contacts
- earn additional income
- maintain a sharp edge to your clear thinking, organisational and persuasive skills
- practise an enjoyable and rewarding skill.

Speaking in public can be a lot of fun. Doing it well is a mark of the accomplished Self-leader. Yet many people shudder at the very idea of it. They fear it. They don't understand that the audience is not against them—that people are there to enjoy their talk, not to watch them squirm.

A public talk is not a performance on which you are to be marked, so why be afraid of it? It can be money-making good. Here's an example.

At the end of my address to an international conference in Bangkok I was approached by a number of developers who wanted to utilise my consulting services. I accepted one offer that led to a lucrative contract which, in turn, led to other valuable contacts in Asia. Had I stood there squirming—unprepared, bungling and timid—how many offers would I have received?

There are few (if any) 'natural born speakers'. There are those who can talk to groups all day long and who might tell you that you do not need to learn technique to give a moving oration. They are talkers—not necessarily effective communicators or persuaders.

More than likely you could give a straight-from-the-heart talk that would be enjoyed by many. Every one of us has a great story to tell. However the issue here is about communicating effectively; about persuading; about influencing people into taking action not just once, but repeatedly; to communicate effectively not only on one topic, but on many.

Without knowing, practising and applying the 'rules' of effective public speaking the chances of communicating effectively are greatly diminished, even though your audience might enjoy your talk. But practice and application require personal effort—they require Self-leadership.

Personal success formula refresher

$$S \;=\; \frac{Asl^2}{PE}$$

Success equals Attitude times Self-leadership squared over Personal Excellence.

The ability to speak well in public is a vital part of the ability to lead. As no Self-leader would want to be counted among those who whimper, blush and cower from talking in public, these fundamentals of effective—and enjoyable—public speaking could be of compelling interest to you.

Analyse your audience

Are they businesspeople? A group of elderly lawn-bowlers, teenagers, musicians, salespeople? Many speakers do not find out and so disgorge a torrent of information that is neither relevant nor of interest to their audience. The result: audience fatigue, boredom, impatience, 'mental drifting' and polite applause.

If you don't know the make up of your audience in advance, find out. Talk to the conveners and ask them for:

■ details of the composition of the group, including age-range
■ their interests—what would they want to know?
■ any current issues (humorous or otherwise) to which you can refer
■ the key people in the audience (get their names and titles right).

Use the information to frame and set the tone of your talk. Build in references to key people. This will add relevance, interaction and interest to what you have to say. Your audience will be more attentive and you will have communicated far more effectively.

Determine your aim

Ask yourself: 'What am I trying to achieve from the talk? Is my aim to:

■ entertain
■ gain support
■ call to action
■ inform
■ sell a product at the end of the talk
■ promote my business?'

If the group's objective in having you is not in keeping with your aim, you might want to consider whether you should accept the invitation. Whatever you decide, do avoid opening with a 'guess what my talk is going to be about?' session where your audience doesn't grasp the point of your talk until it is almost finished. That only produces frustration. It's a trap you could fall into if, before you start preparing your material, you do not have a clear aim.

Prepare for your presentation

Research your topic. Find interesting things about it. Get to know it well. Prepare an outline of your talk organising your material in a logical sequence. For example, divide it into three main sections: introduction; body; and conclusion.

Bear in mind that people tend to remember the details said at the beginning and at the end of a talk. Therefore it is a good idea to prepare interesting material to 'lift' the middle. To ensure you get your main points through, add them to the beginning (introduction) and to the end (summary) of your talk.

In your *introduction*, include:

∎ a warm, empathic opening statement with a strong message
∎ what's in it for the audience (what benefits will they get from listening to you?)
∎ what the talk will cover, what you hope to achieve
∎ when you will take questions (at the end of your talk, or throughout?)
∎ historical information on the topic (key points—be brief)
∎ a vision of the future.

In the *body* of your talk, outline the key points. Support each point with information. For example:

∎ Key point 1
  — Support information A
  — Support information B
  — Support information C
  — Section summary statement

Repeat this formula for each key point or major section. (Note: Try to limit your talk to no more than seven key points or ideas. Research shows that for most people the mind cannot retain more than these at 'one sitting' in short-term memory.)

In your *conclusion*, include a:

∎ brief recap of the main points of your introduction
∎ brief summary of the seven key points or ideas
∎ concluding statement
∎ call to action or exhortation.

Check what you have prepared

When you have completed your outline ask yourself:

∎ Does the material address the topic?

- Is it relevant to the interests of the audience?
- Does it flow logically?
- Does it meet your aim?

Determine the need for visuals

Research shows we absorb about 10 per cent of information through the ears, 20 per cent through the eyes and 64 per cent through the eyes and ears simultaneously.

Colourful, well-prepared visuals can help your audience learn more. Visuals can enliven any talk—provided you do not have so many that your talk becomes a 'slide show'. (Recently I attended a two hour presentation where a speaker had far too many visuals. Moreover, his visuals had far too much information on them. The audience could read the information much faster than he could speak, but he insisted on reading each word and line and took what seemed to us an eternity to finish.)

Visuals are there to support, not to replace, your talk. They can include one or more of the following:

- overhead projection transparencies
- slides
- video tape/film
- flip charts
- whiteboard
- products or models.

The most common visual tools used are the overhead projector and whiteboard. Whichever you use will depend on the situation and on the aim of your talk. Here are some tips:

Use of the overhead projector:
- Switch it off as you change transparencies.
- Use a pointer on the transparency not on the screen (i.e. face the audience, don't turn your back to them).
- Use masks (a sheet of paper will do) to reveal complex information point by point; otherwise your audience will read ahead of you and will not listen attentively.

Overhead projector transparencies:
- Keep one idea to one transparency if you can; otherwise mask your transparency to reveal one idea at a time.

- Use colour where possible.
- Be brief.
- Use diagrams or graphics where possible.

Video / film:

- Don't let the video or film take over your talk. Use it only to illustrate specific sections (especially where movement is required). A humorous film of two or three minutes can be a great ice-breaker at the start of the talk (they are available for hire). An emotive film can be used in the same way to focus attention on a theme.

Whiteboard:

- If you have not used a whiteboard before it is a good idea to practise on one so you can write straight across it and can fit all the information you want on it.
- Again, reveal information point by point. Be sensitive to the possibility that your body will block some of your audience's view, so as you finish writing one section, step away and let everyone see what you have written.
- Whiteboard markers are available in various colours, and using a variety of the colours that are easy to see (e.g. black, blue, red, dark green) will add visual interest.

Choose a presentation strategy

The strategy for your talk will be determined by your aim. For example, if you want to entertain as well as to inform, you could choose a humorous opening or plant some 'hecklers' in the audience.

Even in a more serious talk it helps to use creativity. By tailoring your approach (e.g. serious, flippant) to your audience you will not only entertain them, but maintain their interest in what you have to say. You will communicate effectively, and will be remembered.

Using creativity need not be a daunting prospect. Most people can think of interesting 'attention grabbers'. For example, if your talk were about 'violence in society' why not arrange an 'incident' and let the audience think it is really happening? You could then walk onto the platform and begin your talk using the 'incident' as your starting point.

If you were talking to music buffs, an amusing story such as the one where Louis XVI of France asked his composer to invent an unusual instrument for the amusement of the court could also amuse your audience. (The composer brought seven pigs that could squeal in a different octave. By pricking each pig in sequence he was able to play a tune.)

I used these principles when I worked as a lecturer at the Air Force Officers' Training School. For example, to demonstrate the charging of an airman for insubordination and subsequently to demonstrate the correct summary hearing procedure, I arranged 'an incident' where a corporal would be insubordinate to me in front of a group of newly appointed officers. As far as the audience was concerned, the 'incident' was genuine.

Everyone was uneasy as they witnessed the corporal's remarks, my answers and my order to a sergeant to place the corporal under arrest. Once the 'theatrics' were over and the murmurs in the group settled, I explained the situation and we proceeded to show the steps of preparing charges, arraignment, summary hearing and sentencing. By using imagination in this way, everyone became involved and enjoyed our presentations of Air Force law much more than they could have if we had lectured at them.

Whatever you do also will be influenced by how you decide to handle the presentation—by the tone you want to establish.

A word of caution here: be careful not to offend through risque humour or 'bad taste'. Also, it's unlikely the audience will be completely ignorant of your topic. They want you to acknowledge that fact. So don't talk 'at' or 'down' to them.

Effective public speaking is similar to 'talking the topic over with the audience'. You add sincerity, conviction, enthusiasm and a bit of yourself to bring the talk to life.

Address your audience as if you are speaking privately with each individual because:

- they can only listen to you as an individual
- each individual is listening to you for their own idiosyncratic reasons.

Prepare a plan for your talk

Even a five minute talk should have a plan if it is to succeed in communicating effectively. Many people try to skip planning their talk because it is too much trouble. Unless they are so experienced in public speaking that they can create a plan in their mind and stick to it, I would suggest their talk would otherwise fail in its primary objective of effective communication.

Even the most experienced speakers plan their talks. The plan need not be a novella. It could take the form of key phrases written in logical order on a sheet of paper or on palm cards. It could include:

- notes to yourself (e.g. smile, OHP, W/board, anecdotes, film, joke)
- key sentences or words numbered sequentially
- timing for each section.

Writing or typing should be bold enough so you can read it from a distance. (I find the use of highlighter pens very helpful in separating sections of my presentations.)

Rehearse for practice

By rehearsing your talk you reduce your dependence on notes. This allows you the freedom to express yourself so naturally and confidently that by the time you deliver your talk you should only need a brief outline to keep you on 'track'.

Mark Twain quipped that it took him three weeks to prepare a good impromptu talk.

Rehearse for delivery

This can only be done when you have rehearsed and you know your material. Then you can concentrate on delivery. Here are some tips:

- Be 'conversational'. Don't preach.
- Deliver your talk in a 'friendly' way.
- Pause for effect. In other words, use silence to accentuate a main point. For example: 'To achieve (pause . . .) That is the alternative to despair.' It creates a 'phrase that pays'. Well-placed pauses punctuate a talk, add interest, and heighten our sense of expectation. They focus attention on the phrase following the pause. Consummate actor Sir Ralph Richardson said: 'The most precious things in speech are pauses.'

Do's and don'ts
Everyone appreciates:

- friendliness
- cheerfulness
- enthusiasm
- tasteful humour

- sincerity
- modesty
- good visuals.

Few people like:

- being talked 'at'
- being talked down to
- sarcasm
- criticism
- unpreparedness
- ridicule
- arrogance
- preaching.

When you 'rehearse for delivery', check you have not acquired any of those negatives because how you approach and deliver your talk will determine how well it will be received (in some instances, to a greater extent than what you say).

It is important to 'establish your credentials' as a speaker from the outset. Here are some guidelines:

- Start with a warm, empathic opening, then strengthen it. You can do this by:
  — throwing down a challenge (e.g. 'After today, none of you will be the same person you were yesterday—except by choice. If you have the courage, you can change your life.')
  — using an anecdote (e.g. for a talk on fitness: 'A friend of mine has this exercise thing beat. Every time he feels like exercising he lies down until the feeling goes away.')
  — asking an 'overhead' question (e.g. for a talk on financial security: 'How many of you could write a cheque for $10,000 right now—and not have it bounce?') A strong but empathic opening focuses the attention of your audience and gets them involved from the outset.
- Explain what the audience will get (benefits) as a result of your talk. In other words, tell them why they should listen. For example:

Opening: 'After today none of you will be the same person you were yesterday—except by choice. If you have the courage, you can change your life by applying what I'm going to reveal to you right now.'

Why should they listen? 'I'm going to share the secrets that have made people enormously wealthy.'

Tell them what you want them to do as a result of your talk: 'Take time to study the handouts. Apply the basics. Try. You've got to be here 'till you go so why not see how far your abilities will take you?'

Finish your talk with a strong, specific call to action: For example: 'The choice is yours. Success? Or mediocrity? Choose success. Make the commitment. Reach out. Success is your birthright. Claim it!'

■ Use the 'I' pronoun sparingly. Use 'we' or 'us' as much as possible. It conveys that you are one of the team.

Hints for making your presentations a success

The following suggestions will help bring your presentations to life.

Emphasise your strengths

Each of us has strengths. For example, you might have a friendly, warm manner, a great voice or a certain 'presence'. You will want to emphasise your strengths and minimise your weaknesses (through practice). Here are a few suggestions:

■ *Voice.* In public speaking there are few torments as great as a droning, monotonous voice. This 'quality' is an asset only to the hypnotist. To the audience it is a frustrating ordeal. (When Albert Einstein endured such a speaker, he leaned over to his friend and whispered: 'I've just come up with a new theory of eternity!')

   Vary your tone of voice. Talk loudly, softly, pause, add enthusiasm. Your audience will love you for it and you will enjoy doing it!

Take care with your enunciation. Pronounce your word endings. This is especially important when using a microphone. (If you are using a microphone, speak a little more slowly to prevent your words 'blending'.)

■ *Eye contact.* Effective speaking creates the impression that you are talking to each person individually. Eye contact is essential for that. Look at people individually at all areas of the room. Preferably, maintain your gaze for a complete sentence.

Reading your talk prevents eye contact and, hence, we do not enjoy what in those circumstances would be a lecture.

■ *Intensity, commitment, enthusiasm.* These are the elements that transform an ordinary talk into a dynamic oration. Be committed to your point of view. Be enthusiastic about the possibilities. Emphasise key phrases with conviction.

Use anecdotes

Relevant stories that illustrate the point you are making breathe life into a talk and help your audience remember what you have said. For example, if you were giving a talk on fostering 'better understanding' between people you might want to make the point that we can all look at the same object yet see it differently, by relating the story of Nasrudin.

Nasrudin was charged with undermining the security of the State because he accused their 'wise men' of being ignorant and confused. A court was convened to hear the charge in the presence of the King. Nasrudin requested that pens and paper be given to each of the seven wise men. He then asked the King to instruct them to write down the answer to the question: 'What is bread?'

When this was done, the papers were brought to the King who commanded that the answers be read out.

'Bread is food,' wrote the first wise man.

'It is flour and water,' wrote the second.

'It is a gift of God,' opined the third.

'It is dough, baked,' declared the fourth.

'It can change, depending on what you mean by bread,' said the fifth.

'A substance of nutrition,' wrote the sixth.

'Nobody really knows,' declared the seventh.

Nasrudin said to the King: 'When they decide what bread is it will be possible for them to decide other matters.'

While I try to use personal experience for my anecdotes whenever possible, sometimes it is difficult to think of one that helps illustrate the point I want to make. In those cases I refer to several books of quotations or humorous anecdotes, and perhaps those sources could be a help to you too.

Humour

Your audience will be grateful for the judicious use of humour (if it is appropriate to the topic and relevant to the point being made). Be careful not to offend. Don't use sarcasm, racial, religious or sexist jokes, ridicule or risque humour. There always will be people in the audience who might be offended.

When presenting to a group of managers for a large insurance company in Melbourne I made such a mistake. To add authenticity and a little humour to my anecdote I spoke just as the blue-collar worker in my example had spoken to me. This included the relatively common exclamation: 'Jesus Christ!'

At the end of the anecdote one of the managers interrupted and told me he was offended that I had taken 'the Lord's name in vain'. I was embarrassed not because I was interrupted, but because he was right. I should have known there might be someone in the audience who could take offence. I restored my credibility through a sincere apology. Since then I have been extra careful to avoid repeating the oversight. (Bear in mind that humour helps only if it illustrates a point or an irony. I have learned that it is best to leave unrelated jokes to comedians. You might be great at telling jokes and at getting the audience to laugh. To be sure, they will be entertained. But in the meantime, what about your talk?)

Ask rhetorical questions

Asking a question and pausing to let the audience think can be a great device for involving everyone. Questions allow you to 'talk' with, not to them.

Keep it brief

If you can't say it in 30 minutes, consider writing a book about it instead.

Smile

A smile beams friendliness. It is free. It is positive and healthy. Use it often.

Be original

Don't be afraid to use your imagination. For example, if you are talking about 'enthusiasm' consider making your first few minutes as boring and unenthused as possible. When you see the boredom on the audience's face, 'burst' with enthusiasm, demonstrating that enthusiasm makes all the difference.

Use word pictures
Use 'word pictures' to make a point. For example: 'Don't just wade in, take a belly flop.' Or, to explain the difference between involvement and commitment, 'It's like bacon and eggs. The chicken is involved, but the pig is committed.' Word pictures make the point in an imaginative and 'visual' way.

Build excitement
Varying the length of sentences is important. To build excitement use a string of short, sharp sentences. For example: 'Seize opportunity. Grab it. Use both hands. Achieve! Let nothing stop you!'

Use movement/gestures
Don't be chained to a lectern. Move to the front of it, to one side of the platform or to the other. Movement creates excitement. Use gestures sparingly and naturally. Don't 'force' them.

Overcome nervousness
All speakers are nervous. It helps make achievement possible by providing adrenaline for best performance. Controlling nervousness is not difficult. Apart from slow, deep breaths before you begin your talk, the best control is thorough preparation and rehearsal.

With everything prepared, what is there to be nervous about? The audience is on your side.

Use positive visualisation
Just before you give your talk, walk through the experience with your imagination. Imagine its resounding success. Imagine the applause of an appreciative audience. Then go out and make it happen.

Handle questions effectively
Tell your audience at the beginning of your talk whether you will take questions as you speak, or at the end.

There is no need to hurry your answer or buy time with 'That's a good question' or 'I'm glad you brought that up.' Simply pause, think and answer.

If you feel a question was not heard clearly by everyone, repeat it (especially as you have the microphone advantage).

If the questioner is emotional or angry, acknowledge the emotion before you answer. For example: 'I can understand why that would make you angry.'

Aim your initial gaze at the questioner, then as you proceed with your answer, if it is a lengthy one, look at the audience too so you do not exclude them.

Use the microphone effectively
Have your microphone positioned below your face, not in front of it. Don't blow into it, tap it or say 'Testing 1,2,3' etc. The equipment should be checked before you speak.

Speak a little more slowly and pronounce your word endings. Pronouncing the last syllable helps your audience distinguish between words.

Ensure seating arrangements are appropriate
If the room allows, you can say how you prefer your audience seated. For example, a 'U' shape encourages audience interaction. Theatre style discourages it.

Always check the equipment and your notes before the audience arrives (if you have no time, get someone else to check the equipment for you).

Write your personal introduction
Provide a brief 'resume' to the person who will be introducing you. This will save possible embarrassment for you, the introducer and the audience.

Use handouts
Depending on the aim of your talk, well-prepared summaries can be a great idea. Inform your audience that they will be available as they leave, or whenever is appropriate.

Remember: 'Thou art mortal'
Generally, we all engage in public speaking to some extent. Most successful people have learned to do it very well. It has been one of those skills necessary to their success. The social, career and business advantages you can enjoy by speaking effectively in public are well worth the effort and can enhance your reputation greatly.

By learning, applying and practising these fundamentals you can become an effective and sought-after public speaker. Amidst your triumph, try to remember that 'thou art mortal' and maintain humility when you speak.

Sir Winston Churchill knew this point well, because too much emotion can obscure the message and lose the audience. When a woman once said to the great orator: 'Are you not thrilled to know, Mr Churchill, that every time you make a speech, the hall is packed to overflowing?' 'Yes indeed,' he replied. 'It is quite flattering. However when I feel this way, I always try to remember that if, instead of making a speech, I was being hanged, the crowd would be twice as big.'

KEY POINTS

- Public speaking is an enjoyable method of furthering your standing in your community, business or career. It is a skill that helps you influence and persuade others to your point of view—to achieve and maintain Personal Excellence.
- Correct knowledge and preparation dispel fear.
- Master the basics. Analyse your audience. Determine your aim. Prepare your material, visuals, and strategy. Plan. Rehearse. Check facilities.
- Use eye contact, enthusiasm, anecdotes and visualise success.
- The level of audience retention is greater at the beginning and end of your talk. Build in some interesting points to lift the middle.
- Develop a strong opening and strong finish.
- Be friendly. Smile. Don't use sarcasm, ridicule or sexist jokes. Don't offend. Be cheerful and sincere. Use a conversational style.
- Tell your audience how they will benefit from your talk and what they are expected to do.
- Use pauses and rhetorical questions. Be brief. Don't be afraid to be original.
- Control nervousness. Everyone is nervous. The audience is not against you. They want to enjoy your talk, not watch you squirm.
- Answer questions simply and openly. Acknowledge any emotion such as anger or frustration.
- Place the microphone below your face, not in front of it. Speak more slowly. Enunciate last syllables.

■ Check room design and seating before your audience arrives. If this is not possible, explain what you need and have someone else do it for you.

■ If you are to be introduced, write a brief 'resume' for the person introducing you.

12

Managing your time and work flow

M ANY of the work practices in City X are an interesting example of people working in a time management vacuum. They
are centred around the national motto that 'time is elastic'. It is not
uncommon for appointments to turn up one or two hours late. Place
yourself into the picture for a moment. You are waiting to see someone
for a one hour meeting at 10 a.m. The person arrives at 3.30 p.m.
Because you still need to see them, your subsequent appointments
are delayed. The appointments and duties of those people, therefore,
are also delayed, and a chain reaction of time mismanagement
ensues.

Because everyone expects their appointments to turn up late
or not to be ready to see them on time, most people develop the habit
of showing up late anyway. So you can't plan anything precisely. You
don't know when anyone will show up. Consequently planning your
day and work flow with any accuracy is a formidable challenge.

Add the City X penchant for discussing decisions with a great
many people—even if those people have no expertise in the specific
area under discussion—and you get frequent, sudden calls to un-
planned meetings. Without knowing what is to be discussed you are
unable to prepare beforehand. You get further delays to appointments and work schedules and the time mismanagement circus
continues. (The sad thing is that in City X there is so much to be
done to improve the quality of life of the majority of people that this
inefficient, time-wasting system actually holds back their progress.)

On the other hand in developed countries many people have at
least heard of time management but do not apply it. The result?
They function in a state of perpetual hurry—rushing, bustling and

jostling but achieving comparatively little. They are stressed and constantly under pressure. They work harder than people who have a heavier workload but who are organised better.

The reason why the apparently busier people seem to put in so much effort for a lesser return is that they let their work control them instead of making sure they control their work. They have not learned that hard work and good intentions alone are no guarantee of success. Effective work, which needs effective time management, can be a vital part of the guarantee.

Rushing won't help. No one gets there faster than at the rate of 60 minutes an hour. We need to deal with constant interruptions, and with doing too many things at once. We need to prioritise, delegate and Self-lead.

The late Brian Epstein is known as the man who made the Beatles. However he failed miserably when it came to delegating. Even as his stable of artists grew, he couldn't bring himself to delegate. The result was a frantically stressful life.

In the end he died of a self-administered accidental overdose of pills, aged only 32. His failure to delegate only pressurised his life. (Of course, there were other factors that led to his insecurity and unhappiness, despite his considerable wealth.) Had he been able to manage time better he might have had the opportunity to live a more fulfilling life.

Managing time does not mean we have to organise every minute of the day. No one wants to work in a time straight-jacket. However to be effective we need to plan our day allowing for:

■ a quiet hour to ourselves
■ time buffers to cater for the unexpected
■ a prioritised list of tasks categorised into:
  — essential to do today
  — important but not essential to do today
  — desirable to do today
  — people to call today
  — meetings
  — reminders
  — personal matters.

(At the end of this chapter is a 'Priority Planner' that takes into account those primary areas. You could find it helpful for managing your time and work flow. While there are more complex systems for managing time, this chapter presents simpler methods that should serve you just as well and at a lesser cost.)

The benefits should be evident immediately the systems are applied. You will have more, not less, time. You will be more in control of your day, more relaxed and therefore less likely to make incorrect decisions. You will find time for long-term planning, recreation and concentration on achieving your specific Major Life Goal.

It is worth repeating that we are paid for the value we bring to the market place, not for the time we spend at our job. The more effective we become the more valuable we are and the more wealth we will generate for ourselves and for others. To achieve that we need to become effective managers of time and work flow.

The following framework and hints will help you to build a time management system that will work for you.

How much is your time worth per hour?

Facing death, Queen Elizabeth I cried: 'A million of money for a moment of time!'

Calculate how much your time is worth by dividing the hours you work into the personal income you generate in an average week. Assuming it is $X per hour, use this to ask yourself: 'Is this filing, routine phone call, photocopying, etc., an $X per hour task?' If not, delegate it to someone whose time costs less.

Limit phone time

Wherever possible limit each phone call to a maximum of five minutes. Learn and use polite ways to cut short a phone call, such as: 'I'll need to go very shortly. Before I do is there a final point you want to make?' Why not apply it to incoming and outgoing calls alike? (A mobile phone can be an excellent time saver provided you are selective about giving out your phone number.)

In City X, the irony was that I needed to encourage staff to use the phone more. Their culture dictates that 'it's not nice to discuss something without seeing them face to face'.

The result? Hours upon hours wasted with people driving through traffic-clogged roads to meet someone (who might not be there) to discuss something that could be settled in a four minute phone call.

Screen phone calls

If you have a secretary why not train him or her to ask: 'May I say who is calling? If it is a person you do not know you could train your secretary to say something like: '. . . is unavailable at the moment, but if you care to leave your phone number I'll be sure to give . . . your message'; or '. . . can't come to the phone right now and asked that you leave your phone number so . . . can return your call when free.'

These simple techniques can give control of your day back to you. The alternative is to relinquish control to others—to follow rather than to lead.

Do things in batches

If calls, letters and memos aren't urgent why not schedule a time in your day and do them in batches? That way you won't be jumping from one thing to another then back again. Your thoughts won't be as fragmented and it will help reduce stress.

Design simple systems that work

The humble manila folder can be a great help in organising your work, especially when you have loads of it. Try the following approach:

■ Divide your work into categories and raise a folder for each category. Place all the paperwork for each category in its respective folder. Prioritise and handle one folder at a time.

■ Raise a similar file for your key employees and superiors. You could call these 'Talk to' files. You will be able to place notes in them as matters arise without worrying that you'll forget to 'talk to so and so about . . .' Each morning review these files and schedule your calls or meetings in line with your Priority Planner.

■ On longer drives why not use a recorder to dictate memos or to give instructions? The important thing is to design a system for yourself, then use it.

Schedule leisure time

Fitness and health are important to good decision-making, productivity and to key elements of your personal sphere of life. If your work allows you, why not schedule some time for exercise or sport three times weekly?

Naturally, you'll make up for this time elsewhere. One hour per day should be feasible (even if you will have to take lunch later).

Write everything down
Much time is wasted because of poor communication or forgetfulness. Be a prolific note-taker. File your notes in appropriate categories. Accurate recall of previous discussions will keep you on track and save much exasperation and time.

Pay special attention to your letters and memos. If recipients don't understand clearly what you mean you will waste their time and yours unravelling unintended results.

Give little time to little things and big time to big things.

Learn to say 'no'
Do you believe that 'If you want a job done well you've got to do it yourself'? If so you could be in for a lot of frustration. The more you do the less effective you might become. A common time trap is taking on too much by not saying 'no', or not delegating.

Saying 'no' also applies for your managers. You can do it by reminding them of other tasks and priorities you already have and that taking on a new task might prevent you from completing them. (If you are the only one who can do those tasks ask to reorganise your current priorities, thus expanding your time frame.)

Delegate
Delegating is value for money. A good rule is: never do anything that can be done by an employee. That is good time and money management. Be prepared to let others make their own mistakes but anticipate and check for them. If you teach them to do something well in the first place you can be confident about delegating similar tasks later.

Don't become a workaholic
Workaholics are more addicted to work than they are to results. Instead of being good leaders of self, they let work lead them. Over time they become less effective, stressed and can ruin their private life. Workaholics generally are not regarded as initiators and seldom become the chief executive. They centre their existence on the work/business sphere of life often to the neglect of the other spheres.

The addiction to take on more and more, and work longer and longer hours, is unhealthy, as can be seen in the case of the late Brian Epstein. Workaholics get by at first through sheer volume of work and some results. However time often shows their results are mediocre overall. Workaholics are much too busy chopping wood to sharpen the axe.

Set aside time for yourself

Take a 'quiet hour' for yourself, perhaps first thing each day. This allows you to collect your thoughts and to plan ahead.

Famous achievers who believed in the principle of a 'quiet hour' in the morning include Charles Dickens. He said: 'There is something incomparably solemn in the still solitude of the morning.'

To start work, Beethoven got up at daybreak, winter and summer. John Milton (author of *Paradise Lost*) got up at 4 a.m. in summer and at 5 a.m. in winter. Goethe (German poet and author of *Faust*) started work early. He said: 'I have never worked at night. I work mornings, where the gold lies.'

John Wesley, fiery preacher and founder of the Methodist Church, began work at four each morning; so did Alexander Von Humboldt (scientist and oceanographer). Antoine Lavoisier (father of modern chemistry) began work at 6 a.m. and continued until 10 p.m. Mozart started his day at 6 a.m. German philosopher Immanuel Kant started work at 5 a.m., and so did Composer Brahms and author Sir Walter Scott. The list of early risers—of advocates of 'the quiet morning hour'—is extensive.

In his book, *The Technique of Getting Things Done*, Dr Donald A. Laird describes how John Curran, a famous Irish orator and judge, made sure he got up at 4.30 a.m. each day. He explains:

> *'Exactly over my head I have suspended two tin pans, one above the other. When I go to bed, which is always at ten, I pour a bottle of water into the upper pan, in the bottom of which is a hole of such a size as to let the water pass through it so as to overflow the lower pan at 4.30.'*

Julius Rosewald was one of the founders of the giant Sears Roebuck company. When he wanted to hire a lawyer he went to a lawyer's offices at dawn to see who came to work first. That was the person he hired and later took into the company. Perhaps you could take your 'quiet hour' at home, incorporating exercise and breakfast?

Solve problems brought to you by others—the smart way

Here's a helpful time-saving technique for solving problems that are put to you by your staff. Insist they put the problem in writing, clearly stating:

■ What is the problem?
■ What are the potential solutions?

- What suggestions do they have for solving it?
- Who is involved?

Many problems (especially minor ones) might never get to you because this technique allows staff a clearer perspective. Consequently solutions come to their mind and often they can deal with the problem themselves.

Make a hit list of frequent interruptions/interrupters
Identify your most common interrupters and work out a way to minimise their impact on your time.

Ensure your manager does not waste your time
Are you often called to a meeting where your manager keeps taking phone calls while you just sit there? Try slipping him or her a note saying:

> *'I can see you're busy. I'll come back when you have more time. Please call me when you're free.'*

Place it on the desk face down and leave quietly. (If you give it to your manager directly he or she will read it and signal for you to sit back down.) There is no need to be afraid to do this. Your manager will respect someone who is conscious of time and of the work to be done. Why not try it?

Be a good time estimator
When you are given a job to do, estimate how long it will take and plan a time to do it. (Remember that working fast is not the same as getting things done.)

Find a hideaway
Sometimes whatever you do to win some quiet time for yourself, fails. People get to know where you are and your daily habits, and plan their own visit accordingly. See if there is an area of your offices where you can work privately without being disturbed. Perhaps a seldom used training or meeting room?

Don't take on too much
Time will certainly run out if you overcommit and take on more work. Get to know what you and your section can and can't do. If

your manager insists on giving you more work, explain how taking it on will affect other work in progress.

Use support services
These days there are secretarial services, copying services, answering services, messengers, consultants, and so on. Consider using them to save your own time. The extra cost could be more than worthwhile if it enables you to devote your time to more important issues.

Write your replies on the original memo
Sometimes a memo or letter needs only a short reply. A yes or a no— or perhaps just a short comment.

In these cases it seems wasteful of time and energy to respond with another memo or letter. Why not write your reply on the original memo, keep a copy and send back the original?

Keep your watch fast
This old but effective tactic can work if you are apt to be late for meetings. By giving yourself a ten minute 'margin for safety' you could get there on time more often.

Have a place for everything
How much time do you waste in looking for that letter or memo that no one can find? Organisation really does save time. By keeping a place for everything and everything in its place you can save a lot of time and stress because you will not waste effort on searching.

Use faxes for brief letters
Because expense is an issue, some companies will discourage use of faxes as much as possible. However I tend to use them frequently because it saves time with envelopes, postage and getting the message through.

In this way I have found it is often better to let technology do the running around.

Play 'who's got the ball?' to win
A favourite trick of employees and managers is to keep passing 'the ball' to others. For example, an employee may come to you with a problem and leave it to you to take the next step. (You've got the ball!)

Try to end each meeting with the next action being theirs (give the ball back). You'll be amazed at the time this can free for you.

Keep deadlines visible
Write deadlines down and keep them in front of you until they are met. This device will remind you daily and help you apply your energy to more urgent tasks. Without deadlines, tasks can be done any time. As the old English proverb goes: 'What can be done any time is never done at all.'

Manage meetings effectively
We have all attended meetings that turn out to be great time wasters. Yet for the great part, business life is an ongoing process of one meeting after another. So to my mind it makes sense to get the most out of each meeting rather than to let meetings get the best of our time. Traps to avoid are:

■ *Having too many people at the meeting.* Before you convene the meeting, ask yourself: 'Who really needs to be there?' Keep the number of attendees as small as possible. Not all decisions require consensus (i.e. a result nobody wants but that everyone can accept).

■ *Calling a meeting with no clear objective.* Sort out what you expect to achieve before the meeting is called.

■ *Not having all the needed information at hand* for decisions to be taken.

■ *Choosing a venue that allows interruptions or that wastes time* because attendees have to travel some distance to get there.

■ *Not distributing an agenda in sufficient time* to allow participants to consider the issues and to bring relevant supporting data.

■ Where company politics or high levels of emotion are involved, *not discussing the issues with the key players beforehand* and winning their support.

If you must attend a meeting chaired by someone else and you are short of time, ask to be there only when issues relevant to your area are being discussed.

If you are chairing the meeting:

■ Express its purpose at the start.
■ Outline what you want to achieve by its end.

- Explain what contributions you want from delegates.
- Set a time for the meeting to end.
- Keep to the issues and don't allow side-conversations.
- Don't hold meetings up to accommodate latecomers. If possible, lock the door after the meeting starts. This encourages latecomers to be on time for future meetings.
- For short meetings, consider holding them standing up. Without chairs, the attendees will want to resolve the issue at hand and get back to their work.
- End the meeting on time.
- Follow up on any subsequent action that is required.

At the end of the meeting:

- Agree on the conclusions reached, and ensure you have everyone's support for them.
- Agree on what needs to be done, who is to do it, and when it must be finished.

(If you are preparing for a meeting take time to review the other notes on meetings in Chapter 6.)

Establish clear lines of responsibility
Make sure your staff know what they should be doing, where their responsibility starts and stops and to whom they report.

When this basic rule of management is not applied it can waste an inordinate amount of time through misunderstanding, bad communication and confusion.

Handle mail effectively
If you have a secretary you could arrange for him or her to open all but private and confidential mail.

Your secretary can divide the mail into urgent and non-urgent batches and set aside 30 minutes to discuss the mail with you. Give your instructions directly (e.g. file, distribute, bring forward in a month). Over a week this system can save you many hours.

Don't procrastinate
The only way to start is to start! Procrastinators must like time better dead because to procrastinate is to kill time. Yet no one has the power to give us even one moment of time when we have used it all.

If you must procrastinate, do it later. (If procrastination is a moment of truth for you, why not take time to review the notes on procrastination in Chapter 3?)

Reward yourself

Take a mini-holiday. Self-leadership also means self-reward. Go to dinner! Buy a new item of clothing.

We live and work for reward. So why not reward yourself when you complete a major task ahead of time?

Use a Priority Planner

The essence of managing time well is to:

▪ Plan your tomorrow, today.
▪ Set daily goals.
▪ Organise your time to achieve those goals.
▪ Control your activity during the day to focus on those goals.
▪ If you have a secretary, involve him or her in your plan (to help minimise interruptions).
▪ Accept that you are responsible for your day's outcome. It is up to you to lead yourself to get from, not through time.

The origin of the Priority Planner (or daily action plan) probably came from American efficiency expert, Ivy Lee. At a meeting with Bethlehem Steel's Charles Schwab, Mr Lee proposed a service that would help the company manage time more efficiently.

He suggested that after Mr Schwab had tried it, he could determine its value and send him a cheque for whatever he thought it was worth. Within a few weeks, Charles Schwab sent Ivy Lee a cheque for $25,000 (at a time when $50 per week was a lot of money).

The system was:

▪ Write on a piece of paper the six most important tasks you have to do tomorrow.
▪ Number them in order of importance.
▪ Tackle item one until it is finished, then item two, and so on, until they are all finished.

There it is! Simple enough, but it helped make Charles Schwab over $200 million! The Priority Planner is not new—just effective. It's where time management starts.

■ To start the system, at the end of work on the preceding day list all outstanding tasks on the Priority Planner.

Divide the tasks into 'Essential to do today' (those you must start or finish that day), 'Important but not essential to do today' and 'Desirable to do today' (the least important in terms of time deadline).

List these on the Priority Planner in their respective columns, and in priority order.

■ Add details of people that must be called that day, and any important reminders either for that day or for the next day.

■ Do the essential things first. On the day, work with the task designated Priority 1 until it is finished, with Priority 2 until it is finished, with Priority 3 until it is finished, and so on. As new tasks arise during the day, list them in the appropriate column.

■ As you complete each task, neatly rule a line through it. This will show the progress you are making.

■ Avoid handling a job more than once.

■ Transfer any unfinished task onto the next day's list before you finish work.

■ Check the items on your 'desirable' column. If any have been there more than four weeks consider scrapping them (they might not need to be done at all, or at least can't be too important).

■ Be prepared to alter your plan as priorities could change during the day.

Many things happen that are outside your control. Try to leave empty blocks of time in your day to allow for the unexpected.

These 'buffer zones' allow you to:

■ enjoy more flexibility
■ have more time to accomplish important tasks.

Use your diary with your Priority Planner as together they can serve you well. I recommend the Priority Planner on the following pages. It will help to maintain the Self-leadership required by the holistic success formula and to give back control of your day—to you.

Whether you use this particular format for your Priority Planner is not important. The vital thing is that whatever system you design, use it, because if you don't organise your day, it will disorganise you.

YOUR PRIORITY PLANNER

Date: _____

Tasks	Essential to do today	Important but not essential to do today	Desirable to do today	People to call
Priority 1.				
Priority 2.				
Priority 3.				
Priority 4.				
Priority 5.				
Priority 6.				

	Appointments	Reminders	Personal
8 a.m.			
9 a.m.			
10 a.m.			
11 a.m.			
12 p.m.			
1 p.m.			
2 p.m.			
3 p.m.			
4 p.m.			
5 p.m.			
6 p.m.			

Catch up if you are behind

As for most systems, the Priority Planner will work well in controlling the ebb and flow of your daily work. However it can be less effective if your work is way behind or your section has a large backlog of things to do. To maximise effectiveness of any time management system, first you need to catch up. A system that has proven of enormous help to me is a variation of the Critical Path Forecast.

I used this when newly appointed to a management role of an insurance company. The backlog of their accident and sickness division was daunting. Some jobs were still unfinished despite having been started two years earlier.

Before I could think of organising the day-to-day work flow, I decided my priority was to clear the backlog so we could at least see the horizon. I did this by:

■ noting down all the tasks
■ noting the job holder whose role it was to complete them
■ asking each job holder to estimate the time it would take to clear his or her backlog
■ determining which job holder would need additional assistance to complete the work
■ setting a specific date for all the backlog to be cleared
■ listing all tasks in priority order
■ drawing a Critical Path Forecast listing each task, the day it was to start, who was responsible for doing it, and the day it had to be completed.

The action sheet consisted of a vertical line for each day of the month, noting weekends and public holidays. As I listed each task in priority order from left to right, I drew a horizontal line from the point of the first day to the day that particular job had to be completed.

(On the horizontal line I noted the name of those who had to complete that job. By the time the sheet was finished, it resembled a descending staircase of horizontal lines noted with the job to be done, the days in which it had to be done, and those who had to do it.) I then moved to the next step by:

■ giving a copy of the sheet for the whole division to each job holder, and having them tape it to the wall beside them so that, as each job was completed, they could rule a line through it (that way, we could see progress being made)

■   supervising each job and ensuring it was begun on time, and finished on time.

By concentrating on this a job at a time, our backlog was totally cleared by the specified date, our agents were far happier because their new proposals and claims were attended to swiftly, our staff was much happier and I created an instant reputation.

Did the staff like my approach? Not in the least! They had a comfortable pace before I arrived, and they resented having to 'put in that extra effort'.

In fairness I must say that had I been better at winning their co-operation, there would have been less resentment. However I had just resigned from the Air Force and my Air Force ways hadn't yet worn off. Nevertheless they soon got used to the freedom of being up to date with their work, and the division did not slip back even years after I had left the company.

Essentially, 24 hours, 1440 minutes, 86,400 seconds—that's all we get each day, rich or poor.

What we do with our time, how well we use it and the choices we make ultimately determine the extent of our success.

Why not develop the habit of asking yourself: 'Am I using my time effectively right now?' Putting in long hours is not the important thing. What is important is what you achieve in them.

KEY POINTS

■   If you don't control your day, your day will control you. Managing time is self-management—Self-leadership.

■   Where possible limit each phone call to a maximum of five minutes. Find polite ways to cut short an unnecessary phone call. Make your phone calls in batches. Have your secretary screen calls for you. If you own a mobile phone don't give out your number to everyone.

■   If possible batch your letter and memo writing. This way your thoughts won't be jumping from one thing to another then back again.

■   Schedule leisure time during the week. Fatigue and lethargy are not friends of Personal Excellence. Remember to nourish your personal sphere of life.

■   Be a prolific note-taker. Don't rely on memory. Use a 'think' book or hand-held recorder.

- Learn to say 'no', even to your manager. Don't let others waste your time. Don't do anything you can delegate. Be a Self-leader.
- Work smarter, not harder. Workaholics are addicted to work, not necessarily to results. In the end they might become a liability.
- Set an hour aside for yourself every day. Use this 'quiet hour' to plan your day's activity. Don't allow interruptions during that time.
- Solve problems brought to you by your staff the smart way. Before you meet with them, insist they put their problems in writing with suggested solutions.
- Find a hideaway—somewhere you can get away to work alone for awhile. Don't tell people where it is.
- Don't overcommit. That is, don't take on too much. Get to know what you and your section can handle.
- Use time-saving services such as messengers, phones, facsimile machines, secretarial and answering services.
- Where possible write brief replies on the original copy of a memo or letter.
- Keep your watch fast. This can help you get to the meeting/ finish that job on time and give you a little breathing space.
- Have a place for everything and everything in its place. You will save time in looking for things you can't find—as well as saving stress.
- Play 'who's got the ball' to win. Don't let others leave tasks for you to action. Wherever possible always leave the next step to them.
- Keep deadlines, goals and projects visible. Write them down and keep them right in front of you where you can see them.
- Control meetings. Attend only for the discussion that concerns your area.
- Make sure your staff know what they are supposed to do. Lines of responsibility should be clearly drawn.
- Reward yourself each time you complete a major task ahead of time. Establish a time management success pattern. Self-leadership also carries a responsibility for self-reward.
- Use a Priority Planner as an extension of your diary. For either to be effective, the two must work together.

13

Managing your money and making it grow

ON the main street that lines the facade of prosperity in City X there are many beggars. Some of them merely come up to your car at traffic lights and ask for a handout. For pathos, the women strap toddlers to their breast—toddlers who must stay in that position during the hours of a very long day, every day.

Children aged between six and 12 risk their lives daily by weaving in and out of traffic to beg for money. They show considerable enterprise. On each side of a short stick they nail flattened bottle tops. By shaking the stick the bottle tops clash to form a sound similar to a tambourine. Using this to provide a beat, at traffic lights they come up to waiting cars and sing a pretty song.

The point is they offer something in return for alms. In their own way they are working for their money and put in very long hours every day, seven days per week.

Many of the children not only support themselves, but provide an income to help support aged parents. They are their family's 'social security'.

In the luckier circumstances that favour those of us who live in developed countries, we have a social security net. It may not ensure living much above our relative poverty line, but at least we do not have to send our children to beg on our behalf. On the other hand, what is the point of a life of hard work if that life is one of financial struggle capped by a retirement at or below the poverty line?

You probably know of people who could be heading in that direction—people in their mid-fifties who have worked hard all their lives but have not yet paid off their mortgage. They might be hard workers, good workers and honest workers, but the best they can look to as a reward for a life of toil is the age pension. They are Mr and Mrs Average—the majority of the population in developed countries. They cite any number of reasons for their plight. From them too we can see that hard work of itself, regardless of how well it is done, is no guarantee of financial success.

Yet they had many more opportunities than did the people of City X where, unless you are a government worker, you are not even entitled to an age pension. The only social security they have in old age is the large number of children they beget in the meantime—which in itself can ensure they remain poor.

If most people in developed countries had to answer to those in places like City X for not achieving a measure of financial independence and security, what credible excuses could they give? Could an 'average' person in a developed country look an 'average' person in a place like City X in the eye and truly say: 'I didn't have the opportunity'?

A common factor to all would be the effects of conditioning drag. Their parents probably didn't know how to manage money. Therefore, they couldn't teach their children. But what stopped them from finding out?

Every day there is a report of a person creating a better system, a better program, converting a misfortune into an opportunity, or coming up with something entirely new. All you need are 'the eyes to see' and the 'ears to hear'. To obtain these you will need to overcome conditioning drag and to look at the community and world around you with new eyes, to utilise opportunity thinking rather than obstacle thinking, and to apply the many principles we have already discussed.

Can it really be done? You be the judge. As mentioned earlier, in its 1992 list of Australia's 200 richest people, *Business Review Weekly* shows that only 2 per cent inherited their wealth. The rest made it for themselves.

If you want more proof, why not schedule a meeting with your city's chamber of commerce? Talk to some of the people there. Become a member. Meet those who are succeeding and achieving. Then learn from them.

Nevertheless creating wealth is only half of the equation. Keeping it and making it grow is the subject of this chapter. And the exciting fact is that even those who do not have a successful business, who do not enjoy a windfall, or who can't create a better mouse trap, can ensure financial security if they know how to manage and grow their money and have the Self-leadership to apply what they learn.

Consider Mr and Mrs Average who have worked for 35 years. Even at $20,000 per year for one and $10,000 per year for the other (adjusted for inflation and allowing one of the partners a break from full-time work) they will have earned a fortune equivalent to $1.05 million. Yet most retire broke.

Where did all that money go? If they had saved and invested 10 per cent they would have over $100,000! Add compound interest and they could have doubled that amount.

Ten per cent of their earnings could have made the difference between retiring broke and retiring with dignity, means and hope—retiring not from something but to something better.

Didn't they know they could have learned how to handle money successfully? What happened to their plans? To their dreams? To their Self-leadership?

Were they cratered by financial time bombs?

Defusing financial time bombs

Life is littered with financial time bombs. Here are three of the most common.

How much will your car cost?
One day soon the car you are driving will have to be replaced. Assuming this will be six years from now, how much will you need on top of your trade-in to buy a suitable replacement? $10,000? $15,000? Where will the money come from? (This is 'Time bomb No. 1'.)

If you are anything like Mr and Mrs Average you'll borrow the money and repay interest plus capital for a term of four to five years. If you borrow $10,000, how much will you pay for your new car? Maybe half its price again? If so you'll be paying far more than the car is worth! By the time you repay this debt you might have to borrow again for another car and so create another 'time bomb'.

How much will your house cost?
Your mortgage of $100,000 over 30 years could mean repayments of over $250,000! That's $150,000 of your hard-earned after-tax wealth you are giving away to someone else.

However a house is necessary, can be an appreciating asset and you save on paying dead money for rental; therefore it is an acceptable reason for which to borrow. But this does not mean you should be giving $150,000 to your bank. (Note that you could take many years off your mortgage repayments and save many thousands of dollars by electing to repay your loan fortnightly rather than monthly.)

Other time bombs hidden in your house are the inevitable repairs, painting, and so on. Where will you get the money for those?

When will you need to replace major items?

How long will your carpet last? Curtains? Refrigerator? Washing machine? Television? You know they will have to be replaced, but where will the money come from? (More time bombs.)

The fundamentals of money management

Saving and investing your money will teach you to make your wealth grow. Without learning this skill even if you have a windfall you might be unable to keep it.

Some people who win lotteries or those in 'The Lucky Sperm Club' who inherit wealth can soon lose it because they have never handled a substantial sum of their own money. They never learned the basic laws that govern money management. Here are two examples:

Example 1: Bill W. is a diesel mechanic who won a $1 million lottery. He bought a $500,000 house on a canal at Surfers Paradise, a BMW for himself, a new car each for his wife and two children and spent the rest on travel.

The result? When the bills came (canal fees, rates, and so on) he couldn't pay. He had to sell up and move back to a less prestigious area. He lost thousands in legal fees and commissions, sold below market value and learned some of the fundamentals of how not to handle money.

Example 2: Under the headline 'Lotto winner stole to live', Brisbane's *Courier Mail* reported a 44 year old man who had won $450,000 in the lottery and lost it on failed property deals. To survive he embarked on a stealing spree to obtain money to live. Before his win, he was a successful personnel officer.

It might comfort Mr and Mrs Average to say they did not know how money should be handled—that they didn't know about the need to secure an income stream. Their lifestyle was sabotaged by financial time bombs. Instead of paying themselves first, they paid others first. They were part of someone else's plans for their future. They were followers, not Self-leaders. They lived a financial storyline written by others.

Through this chapter I hope I can spare you the pain of learning the hard way by showing you an easier way. Firstly, let's place the issue into perspective. Financially astute people achieve their security by:

- working out what they want (e.g. to own their home)
- listing their wants in order of importance
- starting with what they can afford and adding to it later
- protecting their family and income
- sticking to their plan.

They don't pay interest first and themselves last—nor do they put off making a start, no matter how humble that start might be.

Make a list of your 'personal beneficiaries'—the people you pay each week from your take-home wages. (If you are like most people, the grocery store will be first on your list. Then there is the gas station, the finance company, the bank, the credit card, the telephone authority, and so on.)

Have you completed your list? Good. Are you on top of the list?

- What do you pay yourself? $ _____
- How much of your wage is yours to keep and invest? $ _____

If you are like most people, probably not as much as you would like. However what is more important is what you will do about it.

The six rules for growing and managing money

Why do you need to be an effective manager of money? Because one day you will have to stop working but the bills won't stop coming.

That's the time you need money to work for you. That's the time people pay the price of following instead of Self-leading.

Applying the rules—even those as stimulating as for making money—requires persistence. It's always easier to enjoy an immediate gratification than to put it off for the sake of a future reward. To avoid that trap, focus on the reward rather than on the task.

Rule 1: Pay yourself first and invest it

You need to invest 20 per cent of your take home pay (and certainly no less than 10 per cent). By investing the money that is yours to keep, you make it grow in the following way:

> *Capital* (what you put in from your pay each week,) plus
> *Interest*, plus *Interest on interest*.

Suddenly you have two workers to help you accumulate wealth. You will be delighted at how quickly your money will grow. At 10 per cent compound interest (i.e. interest paid on interest paid on interest and so on), money more than doubles every seven years!

After a little time you will have accumulated enough wealth to convert it into an opportunity to make even more money (e.g. buy a property). In this way you will be adding a third worker to help your money grow—capital appreciation. Without accumulated wealth, how can you grab such opportunities?

Many people will say: 'But I need all the money I earn, to live. I barely earn enough now!' And that might be true. However that does not mean we shouldn't try to convert defeat into victory or to make the most of whatever our circumstances can offer.

For example, if you were unemployed you would have to survive on social security benefits! It would not be pleasant, but you would manage it.

How? You would economise. You would spend more wisely. You would cut back on non-essentials.

When you have no other choice it is amazing what you can live without—even without things that now you might feel are essential. For example, most smokers set fire to $20 or more each week. That's $1040 per year. Multiply this by 47 years (average working life) and by adding compound interest of 10 per cent to this yearly amount they have set fire to a potential $998,579.

No one is asking you to cut back to the level of unemployment benefits—far from it. However if you want to accumulate wealth there is an effort to make—financial Self-leadership. Don't spend first and try to save what's left; that's the method of the poor. Save and invest first, then spend what's left.

You can add yet another worker to make your money grow:

Future pay increases.

In Chapter 8, 'Dealing with your moments of truth', we discussed the need for quality in all we do and for 'putting in that extra effort'. By keeping to those principles you will become more valuable. The more valuable you become, the more you will be paid (even if you have to change employers).

The more quickly you achieve that the sooner you will earn more money. The more you earn, the more your personal pay of 20 per cent which is yours to keep and invest will be worth. By investing this greater amount you will earn more interest and more interest on interest, and so on.

Rule 2: If you want to build a house, consult a builder

Many of us have well-meaning friends who seem wise and knowledgeable in all manner of things—including money management. However if you wanted to repair a serious fault in your car, would you go to a carpenter or to a motor mechanic?

How wise is it to follow the investment advice of well-meaning friends if their job is not the daily investment of money? By all means hear them out. Consider whether they have created considerable wealth for themselves through investment (including losses). But before you decide where, how and how much, would it not be wise also to talk to someone whose everyday job is to invest money? Also, would it not be wise to spread your investments?

Rule 2 of growing money is to seek investment advice from those who are qualified by training, knowledge and experience, and whose full-time job is to invest money.

Rule 3: Manage your expenses

Don't confuse necessities with desirables. Before you spend, ask yourself:

▪ 'How will this item help my money to grow?'
▪ 'What return will I get?'

Obviously many expenses go to maintain the lifestyle you want.

Nevertheless with many of the major items it is possible to combine lifestyle with a dividend.

For example, you might want a fine house. Great! You deserve it! However be sure to choose a fine house that also has excellent prospects for substantial capital growth. Or, perhaps you want to decorate your house. Great. If you had the money, wouldn't you wish to choose paintings, for example, which did the job you wanted (lifestyle) and also appreciated in value?

Not everyone is in a position to take advantage of such dual opportunities. However that is not a valid reason to neglect money management. On the contrary, managing our money is even more necessary.

Next time you purchase a substantial item (say, for \$500 or more) ask yourself:

▪ Will this article appreciate in value?
▪ If I buy it, what is the opportunity cost (i.e. if the \$500 were invested at compound interest for X years, what additional income would it produce)?
▪ Do I really need it?

You might buy it anyway. But at least ask yourself the questions so you know what you are doing.

How do you rate as a money manager to date?

▪ How much have you earned since you started work? \$ _____
▪ How much of it do you have left? \$ _____
▪ What happened?

If you found that simple exercise depressing, don't worry. Managing money is a skill that can be taught easily to willing students.

If you don't learn to handle smaller amounts successfully, how will you handle larger amounts? (Remember the diesel mechanic who won \$1 million—and squandered most of it?)

Rule 4: Protect your capital

If you want 'your ship to come in' first send a few ships out. Better still, climb aboard and steer them. Your ships can be your capital. Whatever you do, make sure your capital comes back to you.

Here is an example. You want to invest \$10,000 in XYZ venture for 12 months. Before you decide to invest you would satisfy yourself as much as possible that:

■ There was no risk to your capital of $10,000 (by avoiding high risk adventures).

■ The worst that could happen would be that you would recover your $10,000 because the investment was fully capital guaranteed, or you held a mortgage or security against it.

■ If inflation ran at 8 per cent, you would earn at least $1200 interest because if you earned nothing, the value of your $10,000 would have been reduced by 8 per cent (inflation) and it would be worth only $9200 in buying power.

■ You could withdraw your capital whenever you chose or with minimum notice.

Obviously as your wealth grows so too will its earning power.

However it is futile to have the best plans for accumulating wealth if through some tragedy you were prevented from putting them into effect (e.g. if you became totally and permanently disabled or left your family penniless in the event of your death). This leads us to Rule 5 for growing money.

Rule 5: Provide for the unforeseen

A small amount invested each week can defuse unforeseen time bombs. See an accredited lifewriter from a major insurance company or bank. Also, it is strongly recommended that you have a will prepared. Accepting our responsibility to others in this way is also a part of Personal Excellence.

Although life insurance and wills might sound depressing they are an expression of love for those who matter most in your life. Could you achieve holistic success without them?

Rule 6: Borrow only for things that generate an income and/or appreciate in value

Wherever possible, borrow money only to purchase income-producing items. For example, borrowing to buy a rental property might be preferable to buying a block of land. The house produces rental income and capital appreciation, while the land takes up income (rates, taxes) and might produce capital appreciation over time. (Of course the perfect block of land might do better than a less 'perfect' house. Nevertheless the principle of borrowing for income-producing items still holds true.)

Borrowing to buy an established business is another example. Borrowing to buy a car (unless essential for your work) might not be such a good thing unless it is the type of car that appreciates in value.

It is not always possible to keep to this principle because our immediate needs often override the wisdom of saving and investing first. That is all the more reason to get to the stage where you don't have to borrow at all. You can do this by paying yourself first and investing it over time.

It is also important to be prepared for opportunities. It is an amazing thing that opportunities are attracted to those who have prepared for them.

Having a lump sum invested and watching it grow can give you a wonderfully secure feeling. The aim is to seek capital growth and a good return with minimum risk.

Don't be blind to opportunities (such as a good investment property). However exercise all the prudence we have already discussed.

Before making your decision, get the 'I've got to know' bug. Talk to those who are expert in handling investment properties. Talk to your accountant regarding the returns you would need. Study similar properties in the area and consider the average increase in value over the past five to ten years.

Satisfy yourself that your capital (plus a factor for inflation and tax) is not at risk.

Patience and time are also important. Just as a tree needs time to grow, so does your 'tree of wealth'. The magic of compounding interest needs time to work. Get-rich-quick schemes might work sometimes, but invariably are risky.

Your aim could be to increase your wealth in the short term (say, five to ten years), which will give you an opportunity to accumulate wealth at a faster pace after that.

Be happy to succeed in smaller goals at first. Ultimate success is the sum of your smaller successes.

Be reasonable with time and don't become discouraged. If you pay yourself first, thereby ensuring that 20 per cent of what you earn is yours to keep and invest, you can't fail to create wealth.

The remainder of this chapter deals with a basic money management system that can help ensure you defuse financial time bombs and obtain financial peace of mind.

If every family on limited income used a similar plan it would make a positive impact on their financial situation. In any event it is strongly recommended that all serious students of holistic success use this or a plan like it. By all means modify it to suit your personal situation. Only, start it now. Be a strong Self-leader. But don't focus on wealth creation at the expense of your other spheres of life.

The Money Management System

Whenever the words 'budget' or 'money management' appear, many people equate them with dieting or going without things they like. Nothing could be further from the truth. The idea of managing money is to get more of what you like much sooner with the freedom that goes with it. Here's how it works.

Step 1: Establish your surplus

Make a separate list of essential and desirable (but non-essential) items and their weekly cost. (You could use the cashflow analysis pages provided in Chapter 14.)

Total the costs for each group separately, then combine the totals.

Deduct the grand total from your weekly take-home pay.

Did you have a surplus?

If yes, you can invest this surplus as money 'which is yours to keep and invest'.

If it is less than 20 per cent look at your non-essential items of expenditure. Which can you do without to 'pay yourself first' at least 20 per cent? (If you are serious about creating wealth you should not feel remorse in doing away with some non-essentials.)

At the very least see if you can manage a surplus of 10 per cent of your take-home pay NOW and increase this to 20 per cent as soon as you can. (You are not losing non-essentials, you are gaining wealth that will grow!)

Step 2: Break down your expenses

If you are paid weekly, fortnightly or monthly you will have to calculate the yearly cost of each expenditure item and its proportionate cost, according to how you are paid.

For example, if you are paid fortnightly and your council rates are $1000 per year, divide $1000 by 26 fortnights giving you the fortnightly expenditure for your rates of $39 (to the nearest dollar). (If you are paid weekly you would divide by 52, and so on.)

Each pay you:

- pay yourself first the amount that is yours to keep and invest (20 per cent)
- allocate the rest of your pay to the categories of expenditure shown on your lists in the appropriate fortnightly, weekly or monthly proportions required.

For record keeping and ongoing money management you will need to follow these guidelines:

- Purchase a ledger (up to 18 columns or more as needed). See the example of the Money Management System on the next page.
- Identify your:
   — usual categories of expenditure from your lists
   — your future items of expenditure (time bombs)
   — the amount of money you have in cash now.
- Enter one category heading for each column in your ledger.
- Calculate how much money you should already have in each category to meet expected bills. For example, if you are paid 'monthly' and receive a rate notice for $600 in June, assuming it is now January, under the 'house' category you should allocate $300 for this item now.
- Allocate the cash you have in the bank to those categories, to 'catch' up on your monthly allocation to date. If you have any 'surplus', allocate at least 20 per cent of the surplus to the 'Mine to keep and invest' category and spread the balance over the remaining categories as you consider prudent. Don't neglect to provide for a replacement fund (financial time bombs).
- Each time you are paid, allocate your pay according to the need for each category by completing a book entry.
- Each time you withdraw money, complete a book entry.

Notes
The last amount in each column must reflect the cash held for that category at any one time. Therefore equations are cumulative.

Audit your calculations regularly to pick up arithmetical errors. Check your 'total' against your bank books.

Persist. Once set up it will only take a few minutes each pay-day to update. (To make things easier, if you have a computer simply set up your Money Management System using 'spreadsheet' software such as Lotus 1-2-3 or Microsoft Excel.)

THE MONEY MANAGEMENT SYSTEM

Date	Item	Withdraw	Deposit	House $200	Mine to keep and invest $110	Rates, elect., phone $20	Clothes etc. $25	Education $25	Life insur. $15	Entert./ gifts $20	Item replacement $50	Contingency reserve $10	Car $50	TOTAL Money held in at call accnt	TOTAL Money held in investment accnt
1/3/.	Initial disbursement of money in bank account		2500	500	380	300	250	150	200	150	120	250	200	2500	
8/3/	Allocation of pay		520	700	490	320	275	170	215	170	170	260	250	3020	
10/3/	Clothes	50					225							2970	
12/3/	Car	131											119	2839	
16/3/	Allocation of pay		520	900	600	340	250	190	230	190	220	270	169	3359	
17/3/.	Transfer to investment	500			100									2859	500
18/3/..	Dinner out	50								140				2809	
23/3/..	Allocation of pay		520	1100	210	360	275	210	245	160	270	280	219	3329	
28/3/...	Mortgage payment	1000		100										2329	
23/3/.	Haircut	35					240							2294	

Don't despair if you discover that you do not earn enough to pay yourself first and invest it. It gives you all the more reason to spend wisely and work to succeed as quickly as possible.

When the combined funds in the 'Mine to keep and invest', and 'Item replacement fund' categories exceed $500, you could transfer them to a capital guaranteed investment that provides access to your money, a good rate of interest and tax advantages. Remember to add other 'surpluses' and interest accrued from other sources.

Whenever you get a pay increase, allocate a least 20 per cent of the increase to the 'Mine to keep and invest' category first and spread the rest as you judge prudent. By managing your money in that way it will not only grow surprisingly fast, but give you satisfaction and financial peace of mind.

Do you want to update your wardrobe? Take the worry out of agonising whether or not you can afford it. Refer to the appropriate column in your ledger and if there is sufficient money allocated, enjoy yourself! Perhaps you would like to take someone to dinner? Again, refer to the appropriate column and bon appetit!

As time elapses and you need to replace a household item, refer to your 'Item replacement' column and you will know what you can afford.

By using this system you will control your money. You will be in charge—no more nasty shocks.

But beware the trap! A column may show an excellent deposit 'just sitting there'. Don't be tempted! It is there for a future expenditure (time bomb). The car will need replacing, and by paying cash you will save thousands of dollars in interest. Don't pay for the present by stealing from your future.

If you do nothing else, keep this rule: save 20 per cent of your take-home pay, and invest it. It can keep you.

KEY POINTS

■ Most people earn a fortune during their working life, yet wind up broke. Hard work and good intentions are not a guarantee of success. The majority who worked hard and had good intentions are old and broke because they never bothered to 'know' about creating and growing wealth. Ignorance is not bliss; it is poverty.

■ Provide now for expenditure later. Many people have been kept broke by financial 'time bombs' that cause them to borrow and pay interest to strangers. Don't share your wealth with strangers. They won't buy your groceries nor pay your mortgage.

■ Pay yourself first. Twenty per cent of what you earn should be yours to keep and invest. It will grow through compound interest. When you have a good sum set aside it will attract wealth-creating opportunities such as property investments.

■ Make a list of essentials/non-essentials. Cut down on non-essentials and pay yourself the savings.

■ Become more valuable by achieving and maintaining Personal Excellence and by putting in that extra effort. The sooner you earn more, the more you can pay yourself first.

■ Talk to experts. By all means listen to well-meaning friends or to relatives. But before you decide where to invest your money talk to someone whose daily job is to invest money. (You don't ask a pastry cook to build a garage.)

■ Manage your expenses. It is amazing how well you can get by even by cutting back one or two items. Our expenditure tends to increase in proportion to our income. You can avoid this trap by ensuring that 20 per cent of what you earn is *yours to keep and invest*.

■ Protect your capital. Don't invest unless you are certain your capital (plus a factor for inflation and tax) will return to you.

■ If you must borrow, borrow for an income-producing investment. Apart from your house, try to borrow for an item that produces income as well as capital appreciation (e.g. another house to rent). Don't borrow for depreciating items (e.g. cars, costume jewellery) as you will pay far more than the item is worth (its cost plus interest). Pay yourself, not strangers.

■ Be prepared for opportunities. As your wealth grows be on the look-out for wealth-creating opportunities (e.g. property), but talk to the experts before making your own judgment. Remember, don't risk your capital.

■ Be reasonable about time. It would be rare to 'make a killing' overnight. Money, like a child, needs reasonable time to grow. Avoid high risk adventures.

■ To manage large sums, learn to manage small sums. Use the Money Management System and it will save you thousands of dollars by teaching you prudence, planning ahead and money management. It will help you avoid the mistakes of paying for the present by robbing your future. It will also help you achieve financial peace of mind.

14

Designing your Life Blueprint for success

W OULD you board a ship if you knew the captain had no idea where he or she was going, had no navigational charts, had not checked to make sure there were enough fuel and provisions and did not realise the crew was about to mutiny? Would you build a house without a plan?

Isn't the principle just as relevant to someone embarking on a life success journey without a blueprint for its achievement? Self-leadership is all very well, but tcwhere are you going to lead yourself? And how? If you don't have a Life Blueprint for your success you will be part of someone else's blueprint for theirs. You will be living a storyline written by others with no guarantee of a happy ending. The Chinese philosopher, Confucius, said:

> *'In all things success depends upon previous preparation, and without such preparation there is sure to be failure.'*

Your blueprint for your success needs to be a storyline written by you. It is your definite plan to live life by your own design, not by default—a plan that will be 'conditioning-drag proof'. It needs to be flexible enough to accommodate change as you and your needs change. It should enable you to check progress regularly so you don't lose sight of who you are, where you are going and why you want to go there.

Before you start on this vital task, consider what the master strategist himself—Napoleon—had to say about planning:

> *'Men take only their needs into consideration—never their abilities.'*

You too will have many abilities to take into account.

Plan to do—to lead yourself to your destiny. It is pointless designing the best looking Life Blueprint for success if it comprises a catalogue of promises that you don't intend to keep. Someone once said: 'Goals are dreams with a deadline.' Make your goals big enough to excite you into action, but be realistic about their achievement. Be reasonable with time. Before you proceed, here's a refresher on the art of goal setting.

Goals—the basics

Many businesspeople have confided to me that they actually took the time to work out their goals. They even divided them into short-term, medium-term and long-term goals. But shortly afterwards they abandoned them. They found that for them, goal setting didn't work. A major reason? Conditioning drag! It is difficult to work to goals if you have worked without them all your life because you will be resisting conditioning drag all the way. But it can be done.

The second major reason why so many people abandon goal setting is that the goals they have set are not the goals they earnestly want—that stir a burning passion within them.

Professor Fred Hollows had goals—not self-serving goals but goals that, even after his death, continue to restore the sight of people in many countries. When he was diagnosed as having terminal cancer did he abandon his goals? In a recent interview on SBS Television his wife, Gabi Hollows, said that he actually redoubled his efforts to do even more for his program. His goals set him afire with ambition to achieve them.

On the other hand many people set goals only for work, even when they don't like the work they do. And if they like their work, it might not be a major passion in their life. So it is little wonder that so many of them try, fail and then give up goal setting entirely. They set goals they really don't want or in which they do not passionately believe.

In designing your Life Blueprint for success we are talking about real goals in all the major spheres of your life. Not lip-service goals. Not desired goals, but goals that you really want and are determined to achieve. Why? Because you will be doing it not to please an employer, not to pass a management course, but for yourself.

The third major reason for goal-setting failure is that most people set goals that are inflexible. They do not allow for personal growth. As they grow, their goals might change. So instead of replacing superseded goals they scrap goal setting completely. The result? The following experiment will provide the answer.

Inflate a balloon as much as you can without bursting it. Hold its neck tightly for a moment. Consider the air you blew into the balloon as representing all the enthusiasm, energy, positive mental attitude, extra effort and Self-leadership that you can muster. Now let the balloon go. What happened?

If it behaved as do all other balloons under the same conditions it would have zig-zagged across the room, turning and shifting direction with impressive agility.

Without the direction of a Life Blueprint for your success, your life journey could be as impressive as that of the balloon—full of enthusiasm and energy but without a place to go and deflation when you get there.

How to set goals that work

Whatever your past experience with goal setting why not take this opportunity to look at it afresh? Use our model or alter it to suit you. It won't matter if you change it. But, please try it. Here is how I would recommend you go about it:

■ Start with your specific Major Life Goal—that is, the goal that at the end of your working life you will be satisfied in saying you devoted your life to its achievement. Therefore, make your purpose a noble one. (All my research into personal success has shown that exclusively selfish goals may produce wealth, but rarely do they produce a balanced and happy life.)

■ Determine the spheres of your life in which you want success. Include the extent of the success you want for each sphere.

■ Divide your goals by time. Categorise them into long-term (to retirement), medium-term (five to ten years) and short-term (one to five years).

■ Face reality as it is, not as you wish it to be.

■ Don't hurry. Make sure these are the things you really want. What could you achieve?

In setting your goals, note the following guidelines:

- Each goal should describe a specific result and set a date for its achievement.
- A goal should be ambitious yet achievable.
- Don't use vague terms such as 'wealthy by the time I'm in my forties'. Be specific.
- Almost everything we have learned has required us to try, fall, adjust and try again. We learned to walk, talk, swim and drive in the same way. Prepare for and anticipate falls.
- Goals should need you to do more, or to do it better or differently.
- Your goals should be flexible enough to change as your needs change. In ten years you might not want the things you want now.
- Reward yourself each time you achieve a goal (e.g. a dinner, new clothing, shoes).
- Share your plans with someone you respect.
- Include family and personal time in your plan.
- List your reasons for wanting success.
- Question your motives for wanting each goal. Make them honourable—in keeping with your totem of Personal Excellence.
- Include nourishment for the spiritual aspect of your nature, thereby achieving wholeness, purpose and peace within yourself.

Your holistic objective is to achieve wealth, health and happiness through Self-leadership and Personal Excellence in a way that enriches others and benefits your community. Therefore your Life Blueprint for success is more than a wish list; it is your design for your future. It is the point where Self-leadership—and your better tomorrows—begin.

Personal success formula refresher

$$S \; = \; \frac{AsI^2}{PE}$$

Success equals Attitude times Self-leadership squared over Personal Excellence.

Your Life Blueprint for success

The following pages provide a framework to help you design your
Life Blueprint. Start it now. Invest a few hours into the rest of your
life. Let our model blueprint help you determine how you will achieve
holistic success. Begin your Life Blueprint by following these steps.

Step 1: Establish your specific Major Life Goal
You can begin this process by answering these questions:

- *Who am I?* (To help you answer this question, ask yourself:
  'What are the things I want other people to know about me?'
  and 'What are the things I don't want other people to know
  about me?' Consider what you have written, and then form a
  clear definition of who you are.)
- *Where am I?*
- *What are my weaknesses, strengths and opportunities?*
- *Where do I want to be:*
  — In the next five years?
  — In the next ten years?
  — By retirement?
- *How am I going to get there?*
  — In the next five years?
  — In the next ten years?
  — At retirement?
- *What is my specific Major Life Goal?*
  — How will I achieve it?
  — When will I achieve it?

Step 2: Determine the success you want in each sphere of your life
In this step you need to assess each sphere of your life, and determine
what you want to achieve and by when.

Your personal sphere of life
- I will have succeeded in this sphere of life when I have
  achieved: _____
  — How will I achieve it?
  — When will I achieve it?

Your family sphere of life

■   I will have succeeded in this sphere of life when I have achieved: _____
  — How will I achieve it?
  — When will I achieve it?

Your work / business sphere of life

■   I will have succeeded in this sphere of life when I have achieved: _____
  — How will I achieve it?
  — When will I achieve it?

Now that you have outlined the success you want in your work/ business sphere of life, consider and answer the two following questions:

■   Why did I choose (your type of work/job) as the vehicle to achieve my goals?
■   What are the opportunities for me to acquire the wealth I want through this type of work/business?

As your work/business takes up so much of your life and affects nearly every other sphere, now is the time to consider whether you are in the right job. If you conclude that you are not doing what you really want to do, you might not be able to change it straight away. However you can prepare for change. Completing the following table will help you determine your best plan of action.

How I plan to change my line of work/business

The line of work/business I want is: _____

The resources/qualifications I will need to enter my preferred line of work are: _____
_____

I want to enter my new line of work/business by (date): _____
Obstacles are: _____
I will overcome these obstacles by taking the following action: _____
_____

The work/business sphere of life is directly related to the financial sphere. If you have decided to change your work, take into account your present income as well as the income you plan to acquire in your new line of work/business.

Your financial sphere of life
■ I will have succeeded in this sphere of life when I have achieved: _____
   — How will I achieve it?
   — When will I achieve it?

Now that you have determined the level of financial independence you want, it will be useful to consider your present income and expenses in detail. That way you will have a realistic starting point.

   Don't skip this section. Use it as a tool to guide you. Once you have completed it, review your goals for your financial sphere of life to ensure they are what you really want.

Cashflow analysis

*Monthly expenditure on **essential items***

HOUSE
Mortgage/rent _____
Rates _____
Maintenance _____
Furniture _____
Insurance _____

CAR
Fuel _____
Parking _____
Repairs _____
Repayments _____
Registration _____
Insurance _____

UTILITIES
Phone _____
Electricity _____

Cashflow analysis—*continued*

*Monthly expenditure on **essential items***

UTILITIES—*continued*
Gas ⎯⎯⎯
Water ⎯⎯⎯

CLOTHING/ACCESSORIES
Clothes ⎯⎯⎯
Shoes ⎯⎯⎯
Accessories ⎯⎯⎯

COSMETICS
Hair care ⎯⎯⎯
Skin care ⎯⎯⎯

GROCERIES ⎯⎯⎯

EDUCATION
Self/spouse/partner ⎯⎯⎯
Children ⎯⎯⎯

HEALTH FUNDS ⎯⎯⎯

LIFE ASSURANCE ⎯⎯⎯

INCOME PROTECTION ASSURANCE ⎯⎯⎯

RETIREMENT INCOME SAVINGS PLAN ⎯⎯⎯

CASH
(fund for day-to-day needs—pocket money) ⎯⎯⎯

(A) TOTAL FOR ESSENTIAL ITEMS ⎯⎯⎯

*Monthly expendiure on **non-essential items***

ENTERTAINMENT
Travel, holidays, dining out, films,
theatre, concerts, etc. ⎯⎯⎯

Cashflow analysis—*continued*

*Monthly expendiure on **non-essential items***

MISCELLANEOUS _____

CREDIT CARDS _____

OTHER _____

(B) TOTAL OF ALL NON-ESSENTIALS _____

GRAND TOTAL
Add the amounts at (A) and (B) _____

**YOUR COMBINED MONTHLY
NET INCOME** _____

(C) DEDUCT GRAND TOTAL _____

SURPLUS _____

DEFICIT (if any) _____

Your community sphere of life
■ I will have succeeded in this sphere of life when I have achieved: _____
— How will I achieve it?
— When will I achieve it?

Your global sphere of life
■ I will have succeeded in this sphere of life when I have achieved: _____
— How will I achieve it?
— When will I achieve it?

Your spiritual sphere of life
■ I will have succeeded in this sphere of life when I have achieved: _____
— How will I achieve it?
— When will I achieve it?

Step 3: Determine the training and resources you need

No one can achieve their specific Major Life Goal without support and co-operation from others. Now that you know more clearly what you want to achieve and by when, consider what training and support you will need.

The training and support I need

Training   Date to be achieved:
1. _____   _____
2. _____   _____
3. _____   _____

Support needed from my partner/spouse:
1. _____
2. _____
3. _____

Support needed from my office/company:
1. _____
2. _____
3. _____

Other specific support and resources that I will need:
1. _____
2. _____
3. _____
4. _____
5. _____

General: _____
_____

How I plan to monitor my progress (e.g. write a weekly report to myself, discuss with my manager/partner/spouse): _____
_____

Obstacles to overcome: _____

How I will overcome them: _____

Step 4: Write your 'business plan'

By completing the foregoing you have detailed the goals that will form a part of your Life Blueprint for success. They will serve to point you in the direction you want to go. However to achieve each of your goals you will need to prepare a thorough strategy for its achievement—a detailed road map. Using your goals as a guide you will need to plan exactly how and when you will achieve all the good things that you want.

Whether or not you are in business, wish to start a business, buy one or expand one, you will need to add a 'business plan'. It will help you:

▪ determine if your goals, ideas or business ventures are viable
▪ itemise resources, determine funding, clarify concepts and detail a plan to achieve your goals
▪ determine 'signposts' to mark your progress.

If you need funding, your 'business plan' will be an excellent document to present to bankers, investors, accountants, prospective partners or to any party who might help you or who might want to become involved in your venture. Your plan will be the navigation chart for your holistic success journey.

As everyone will have different goals it is not practical to provide you with a ready-made format. However by regarding your goals as 'business objectives' you will be able to take a business-like approach to achieving them.

If you still have doubts about any of your goals, you could dispel them by completing this plan. Simply work with the following structure, substituting any headings that do not apply with headings that are relevant to you. Have it typed. Bind it.

Treat it as a serious document that you will present to yourself. Each time you review it the professional approach you have taken will remind you of its importance and value to the rest of your life.

Your plan should include the following sections.

▪ *The cover page.* This should identify the concept/subject of the plan and include your name and title as the plan's designer.
▪ *Contents page.* List the various sections of the plan. Later this will help you get to the information you want, quickly. It also gives your plan a professional touch and shows that you are really serious about its achievement.

■ *Summary*. State the nature of your venture (e.g. to achieve holistic success in the seven major spheres of life by (date)) and what it offers you (and, if it includes a business proposition, to any prospective investor). Usually, the summary takes up to one page, rarely more. (This tends to be the first page read by anyone who will be involved because it gives a precis at a glance.)

■ *Personal (or product) profile*. This section could contain the goals you have already identified. If you plan to achieve your goals through starting a business, outline the nature of your product or service. Explain its background and answer the following questions:
— Who invented it?
— What research was carried out to determine a need in the market?
— Do you have firm offers to manufacture or distribute it?
— Do you have orders to fill?
— What competition will you be facing?
— What are the opportunities for expansion, export, and so on?

■ *Management and organisation*. Describe how you intend to organise and achieve each of your goals. If you plan to achieve your goals through a business, provide information on:
— How will you run the business?
— Who will manage it?
— What is their background?
— What staff will you need?

■ *The finances*. This is the 'guts' of your plan. It forecasts cash-flow. For example, it needs to include details of:
— net income
— expenses
— current cash position
— forecast for the next three years or more.
If you plan to start a business, also include:
— sales income (projected)
— cost of product.

■ *Annexures*. In the annexures provide support information (e.g. your qualifications), documentary evidence and your resume. If you are starting a business add:
— resumes of managers and directors
— details of any research undertaken
— brochures etc.

No two plans are alike and usually their purpose is to provide an overview of your goals and expected benefits. (For business, the plan's purpose is also to show projected profits.) As almost nothing ever goes strictly to plan it is wise to build in reserves and leeway, to be modest with your forecasts and to give yourself more room than you might need.

KEY POINTS

- Don't build your house of success without a Life Blueprint. Determine the success you want in each sphere of life, and then develop a plan showing how and when you will achieve it.
- Build in flexibility. Your ideas and goals might change as you grow. Don't cast your plan in concrete.
- Most people fail in setting goals because they choose goals that don't set them on fire with a passion to achieve them. Once the initial enthusiasm wears off, they give up.
- It takes time to achieve your goals. Be reasonable with time.
- All your goals should be in line with your specific Major Life Goal, with your totem of Personal Excellence, and should require you to exercise Self-leadership. Aim high.
- Life is an obedient employer. It will pay you the wages you ask of it—in exchange for effort. Build in resistance to conditioning drag.
- Face reality as it is, not as you might wish it to be.
- Your plan should be ambitious yet achievable. Make it specific. Don't use vague terms. Give yourself short-, medium- and long-term objectives and deadlines.
- Don't be afraid to ask for support. No one ever achieved anything worthwhile by themselves.
- Reward yourself each time you achieve a sub-goal. Where you have 'failed' but learned, reward yourself then, too, because you will still have achieved a positive result.

15

Tapping into your spirituality

A FTER years of research I have concluded that no system of success embodying happiness can be complete if it is not connected to human spirituality. By-passing this deeper aspect of our humanity would have presented you only with part of the holistic success equation.

Many successful people are deeply spiritual. That does not mean that all successful people are regular visitors to a church, temple or mosque. Some spiritual people do not find the formal practices of 'mainstream' religions fulfilling. And so how we express our spirituality is a matter of personal preference. Such preferences can range from the ascetic to more conventional forms.

For example, while I would not recommend it, in the advanced stages of Hatha Yoga, one technique involves swallowing one's tongue to inhibit the breathing reflex. (That can be done after the tongue has been stretched by months of rigorous exercise and massage. The aim is to retain more carbon dioxide, thereby inducing a euphoric state where one becomes 'more aware' of the deeper meaning of nature.)

Another rigorous path to achieving a higher sense of spiritual awareness is that of asceticism. It has been practised since recorded history and involves disciplines such as ritual fasting. For example, some North American Indian tribes include a nine day fast in the induction of a shaman. That produces a 'state of feverishness' that enables the individual to see into nature, and discover what 'his medicine' will be. (I would not recommend this practice, either.)

People get in touch with their spiritual dimension in diverse ways. Their common denominator seems to be that regardless of the way they choose to express their spirituality, all have an inner power from which they draw strength, wholeness and serenity. They tend to be happier despite the level of achievement they might enjoy in their other spheres of life. Consequently this final chapter deals with spirituality in the context of achieving personal success and happiness, not as an apologia for religion.

Most of us do not need to go 'ascetic'. We can connect with our spiritual dimension simply by taking a walk along the seashore at dawn, listening to the roll of the surf, and feeling its sense of power and timelessness.

We can tap into our spirituality through meditation, by walking through a forest, experiencing the power of a thunderstorm, appreciating a beautiful painting, in a loving hug from a child or by letting music transport our soul to higher planes of feeling. Or, as my daughter Kerrie told me, we can connect with our spiritual self simply by taking a quiet hour at home alone.

Another common denominator of spiritual people seems to be the regularity with which they get in touch with their 'higher self'. Like our personal success formula for meeting challenges or to get a thing done, they turn it into a procedure. A church, temple or mosque does that for us. It could be one reason why so many successful, spiritually connected people value their affiliation with their church, temple or mosque.

Spirituality and holistic success seem to be inextricably woven. They are bonded in the knowledge, practice and philosophy required to succeed in the holistic success journey. For example, the central aim of most religious figures, including Jesus, was to teach people how to achieve and live a happy and personally successful life based on mutual respect, caring, integrity and, from a religious point of view, faith in the benign fatherhood of (God). However because so many organised religions have lost sight of this main theme many people are turning to other options, including psychiatry.

Psychiatrist Dr Claudio Naranjo makes this point in *The One Quest*:

> '. . . in reaching for a deeper understanding of neuroticism, psychiatry has become more and more concerned with matters such as authenticity and estrangement, the real self, responsibility and other issues that were formerly the concern of philosophy or religions. In fact, what psychiatry is presently doing is not just curing physical or emotional symptoms of

psychic origin, but helping the individual to find the good life for himself—as philosophy and religion had been doing for centuries, prior to becoming riddled with abstract speculation and authoritarian dogma.'

Even if you want success exclusive of spirituality, it might be of interest to note that were you to research success experiences from 2200 BC to the modern era, you would find the central precepts for achieving holistic success are contained in the Bible, the Vedas, the Qur'an (Koran) and in other inspired religious works. (As we noted earlier, the Qur'an links personal success to personal growth.)

To the best of my knowledge, no one on their death bed has ever been reported as saying: 'I only regret not having had time for more work.' It seems, as said by Leonardo Da Vinci, that even at the end most of us have an irrepressible feeling that there is more to life than 'consuming food and producing excrement'.

Dr Claudio Naranjo, quoting Happold, expresses the driving force behind our search for a deeper meaning:

'. . . to escape from a sense of separation, from the loneliness of selfhood, towards a closer participation and reunion with Nature and God, which will bring peace and rest to the soul . . . This urge has its origin, if one accepts the only thesis on which a case for the validity of mysticism is based, in the fact that man is in some way a sharer in the divine life. He therefore longs to return to that from which he feels he has come, to be more closely and consciously linked with it. He feels himself to be a pilgrim of eternity, a creature in time but a citizen of a timeless world.'

Despite the personal benefits of a spiritual connection and the many successful scientists, businesspeople, corporate chiefs and other outstanding achievers whose spiritual values are a matter of public record, in my research I encountered several recurring themes in arguments against the existence of a spiritual dimension.

I will list those I encountered most frequently and will outline my own ideas about them. However please note that I am not claiming my ideas are correct for you, nor am I trying to convince you of any specific point of view. Each of us has to determine our own philosophy of life, and there could be philosophies other than mine that would serve you far more effectively.

Technology and affluence have made spirituality irrelevant

For many 'modern' people, technology is the 'divine power' of today. In developed countries we revel in it. It produces wealth (i.e. ownership of 'things'). Some people take this concept of material wealth to their grave.

For example, in Vienna must be the crypt of all crypts. The burial place of the Hapsburgs is indeed impressive. So is the crypt of the Hapsburgs and Bourbons at the El Escorial palace in Spain. Lavish marble coffins are trimmed with silver and gold. Splendid columns rise to vaulted ceilings decorated with the finest architecture, art and sculpture. The trappings of past glories and wealth adorn every corner.

However the point is that all those wealthy people are just as dead as if they had been poor. Were their lives any happier for their great wealth?

Maximilian 1, the man who built the great Hapsburg empire, towards the end of his life cried: 'God, please give me death . . . for I have been spared nothing . . .'

In much of the developed world we have increased wealth for most people. But have we produced a happier society as a result of our progress? Are we any better at getting along with each other? Are we more fulfilled as human beings for what we have achieved? Or has our modern hunger for material wealth, pleasures and power replaced our need for meaning?

Despite having a home and a car, do not most people play the 'Who's got the biggest house and most expensive car' game? Do we not keep wanting more and more? And even if we could provide them, what impact would it have on the Earth if every one of the world's people owned a private motor vehicle? (That is not to say that we should not use and enjoy the many benefits of our technology. The point I am making is that its proliferation needs to be balanced against the wider needs of humanity, not only against the needs of commerce.)

We are so enthralled with our own achievements that I often wonder if humankind were removed from the Earth, what would the Earth lose that it could not do without? What have we humans really contributed to the Earth's well being?

Apart from having created a degree of material comfort for about 40 per cent of the world's population, has our technology helped the progress of better human relations? Let's see.

The ultra-sound machine that allows doctors to peek into our body has proven a boon to medical treatment. However as recently as 1994 many pregnant women in India used ultrasound to determine the sex of their offspring so they could abort female babies.

In 1993 it was estimated that over one million female babies were killed each year in India, mainly for the 'crime' of being female. This is at least one case where even everyday technology has been used to worsen rather than to help our human relations. But what about in more developed countries?

In an interview on SBS television on 1 December 1993, former prime minister of Britain, Lady Margaret Thatcher, was speaking on the serious spread of crime and social disorder in Britain. She noted that:

> 'As prosperity has increased people have taken the freedoms but not the responsibilities that go with them . . . A great issue into the twenty-first century will be increased wealth and with it, increased temptations. How will people deal with them?'

Not too long ago the 'average' person in developed countries could not afford to buy a gun. Consequently there was a chance that a person consumed with hatred would cool off rather than react in a murderous way. With increased wealth, people have the money to buy the same type of automatic weapons that are used by today's modern armies. Despite the price tag of US$4000–$6000 each, gangs and individuals bent on violence manage to acquire these weapons. In many incidents they are better armed than are the police.

In December 1993, two ten year old boys in England were found guilty of kidnapping a four year old boy from a shopping centre, leading him to a railway yard and callously murdering him by bludgeoning him with bricks. Subsequently a British member of parliament accused the Churches of failing to teach modern children the difference between right and wrong. (Of course, the primary responsibility for those lessons must rest squarely with the parents.) Shortly after the trial Mr John Major, prime minister of Britain, launched a campaign to promote higher moral values throughout Britain.

During the murder trial it was revealed that the father of one of the accused boys had hired some 300 violent videos in the previous two years. Apart from the conditioning and role model this must have provided for one of the young murderers, it shows how misused technology and wealth can supply the means and opportunities to degrade human dignity, even in the home.

If you doubt that, just take note of some of the messages emblazoned on T-shirts these days. In Brisbane, Australia, I saw one T-shirt that read: 'Rape the whore Christianity'. Even if they are not Christian, why would anyone set out to offend and debase a belief held by over a billion people? This is quite apart from the central message of violence inherent in their statement. What messages are these people sending to our younger children? To those who are emotionally vulnerable?

That type of behaviour reminds me of the anguished cry of many parents who say they cannot control their teenage children. But are their children that much different from those born two decades earlier? I suspect they are pretty much the same. It is the parents who have changed.

How? Generally speaking, in developed countries many post World War II 'baby boomers' have been more reluctant than were previous generations to impose rules and discipline on their children. Their drift away from spiritual values has failed to provide children with a philosophy that they belong and that they are valued.

That may not cause serious problems when the children are of elementary school age. But children grow into adults. Many children who have not grown within a framework of clear, positive guidelines react negatively to attempted parental and societal discipline when they are teenagers and young adults. As a result, innocent people and the community, generally, suffer.

If nurturing spiritual values can redress many of our social dilemmas, how can technology have made our spiritual dimension irrelevant?

Living a spiritual life can be viewed as the antithesis of antisocial behaviour. It provides a caring and humane perspective for life— a celebration of our existence and a joyous sense of approval and of belonging.

Neither in my research nor in my experience have I found any one or any community that has derived any lasting benefit from living in a spiritual vacuum. Conversely I have met people who are not spiritually inclined and who, by their own admission, live a shallow and unfulfilling life—a life without a sense of hope, direction or purpose. (Yet they are materially wealthy—that is, they own lots and lots of 'things'.)

In the 1960s the great psychologist Dr Carl Jung observed:

'Man is lost in the cosmos because he has severed his spiritual connection with nature . . . He has freed himself from super-stition but in the process has lost his spiritual values to a positively dangerous degree.'

I conclude that what Dr Jung was telling us is that many people have sacrificed their human soul (i.e. what it means to be human in the best sense), to the quest for more money, pleasures, material comfort and technology.

When we get away from our spiritual dimension we seem to move away from our higher self and from what it means to be who we really are. For example, primitive tribes everywhere use masks and dance as a way of connecting with their spirituality. If the mask is of a bird figure, while they dance with it they actually 'become' that bird figure in a spiritual sense. The ceremony reinforces the people's self-identify and what it means to be who they are.

In many 'civilised' countries masks are still popular at carnivals, feasts and social events. It seems that hiding our faces releases us from the 'public persona'—the person we present to the world—and allows us to express our inner selves.

I am not advocating that we should all wear masks. I am noting that the society we have chosen to develop tends to emphasise materialism and to suppress spirituality without producing a happier people. More often the result is a spiritual void in which lonely, disconnected souls live out hum-drum lives in the anonymity of the suburbs.

It might have been such an outcome that, in 1994, led the Australian prime minister, Paul Keating, to launch a nationwide campaign to fight negative attitudes and to promote community spirit and cohesion. Corporations weighed in with generous support, including millions of dollars of free television time to screen the positive attitude advertisements. Why was such a campaign needed at all?

The irony is that many 'non-spiritual' people who trade faith in a supreme power for faith in technology revert to superstitions. When we diminish a central belief in the one supreme power all manner of superstition, cults and sects can fill the vacuum. For me, a vacuum in spiritual belief raises far more questions than it answers.

Evolution versus spirituality

It is interesting to consider the view of a noted professor of mathematics who states that the laws of physics make consciousness inevitable. He sees it reflected in the growing complexity of the universe. For example, its beginning in void, then the appearance of matter, expansion, the appearance of chemistry, then biology and, ultimately, consciousness as the inevitable next step in the 'design'. He concludes that this sequence—this ordered evolution—implies a deeper meaning underpinning the universe.

Whether or not you agree with him is not important. The issue is whether you can achieve a deeper happiness that will accompany you through life by connecting with your spiritual dimension.

While I accept the theory of evolution in explaining the major mechanics of most physical progress, I do not believe it can explain all physical progress. For example, why did the human brain advance far beyond its present needs? If the function of natural selection is to maintain the physical traits required to survive, what part does music play in the survival of the human race? When you cut off a finger then photograph the hand with Kirlian photography, why is there a human energy field that shows the outline of the missing finger? (The same phenomenon occurs when you cut a piece off a leaf.) What has that to do with our ability to survive 'the battle of the fittest'?

I am not aware that anyone has come up with an all-embracing theory of spiritual evolution. Yet spirituality is a feeling that most of us seem to acquire from a very early age. It's as if there is a part of our brain that 'manufactures' our spiritual inclination.

It gives us an inner sense that there is something more to life than what we can see through the electron microscope or the Hubble telescope. It enables us to feel a spiritual uplifting when we behold a beautiful panorama. It invites us to explore an outer space that is patiently waiting to welcome us back to the stars.

Importantly, spirituality expresses itself in most people through an underlying sense of what is right and wrong. It is that part in so many of us that takes pity on those less fortunate, on those in distress and on those who are suffering.

It is the power that creates a Francis of Assisi, a Florence Nightingale, an Albert Schweitzer, a Mahatma Gandhi, a Martin Luther King, a Fred Hollows, a Mother Teresa and many other people like them.

Compare such people with the likes of Mao Ze Dong, Lenin, Stalin, Pol Pot (they denied a spiritual dimension and actively suppressed any belief in it), Kim Il Sung, Hitler and the Klu Klux Klan (they pervert religious belief to justify racial hatred and murder), and you have the two ends of the spiritual spectrum. (Yet two of the greatest spiritual teachers, Jesus and Buddha, taught moderation. They knew that few of us could be 'saints' and hopefully still fewer of us 'devils'.)

Those who expound natural selection as the only imperative for humankind's progress need to reconcile many unanswered questions. What do they make of the force that drives us beyond satisfying our physical needs for survival, comfort, social needs for recognition and prestige? Because even when we have those things and have met the dictates of physical evolution, the spiritual force urges us towards still greater improvement—to strive for spiritual freedom, and to improve our humanity beyond physical boundaries.

To my mind physical and spiritual evolution are fellow travellers in the cosmos. We are still evolving physically, socially and spiritually. As our knowledge increases we can set aside old superstitions and connect to a far deeper spiritual meaning, thus finding our own place in the universe—a place in which we are an integral part of the glorious whole.

Spirituality is superstition

It always puzzles me that many of the people who tout this objection refer to their horoscope in the daily press. Some of them believe in the 'power of the pyramid' and of 'crystals' (perhaps a prettier version of the old magic stones).

As inspired teachers taught people to put aside their idols, talismans and sacrifices, superstition evolved too. Initially, it served the purpose of providing primitive people with a sense of control over the things they feared or did not understand. We can still find it in the games that children invent when they are placed in a threatening environment for extended periods.

For example, during the plague that decimated the population of Europe, children's perception of the world around them must have been bleak indeed. Intuitively, they sought to devise a system of reassurance—to show they had control.

They did this by inventing a game still played by children today. It is a rhyme sung as children join hands and form a circle. Moving in one direction or another, they sing the rhyme, which usually goes something like this:

Ring around a Rosie
A pocket full of posies,
A'tishoo, A'tishoo,
We all fall down.

The rhyme mimics the environment and symptoms that beset the victims of the plague (a rosy rash, flowers at the bedside, sneezing and collapse).

In Hitler's holocaust, some children in concentration camps played a game of 'gassing a victim' and 'handing out the dead person's clothing'. By transforming their fears into a game it helped the children 'cope' with a cruel and brutish world.

Superstitions might have developed in the same way. We created the rituals of superstition to give us control over what we feared or did not understand. By offering 'a sacrifice', as people still do in the volcanic regions of Java, we sought to bring about a desired result (i.e. dissuade the volcano from erupting).

Our apparent ability to influence outcomes (e.g. to bring on plentiful rain, a good hunt or a good harvest), even though coincidental, 'proved' to us that we could be in control, and reinforced our superstition. (That was probably harmless enough until those with more cunning and malice recognised the power they would have if they controlled and manipulated the superstition itself.)

The interesting thing about creating superstition in the first place is that, intuitively, our early ancestors turned to a spiritual rather than to a physical solution. However by speaking of spirituality I am not speaking of superstition. Neither am I speaking of a need for endless ritual, tongue swallowing or self-flagellation (although some moderate ritual may be useful in expressing a spiritual thought, concept or emotion in a symbolic way).

Everyone thinks their spiritual view is correct

Most, if not all, organised religions hold that their model for tapping our spiritual dimension can satisfy every individual's spiritual needs. To my mind they are greatly mistaken because spirituality means different things to different people.

Some of us need a sense of ritual and ceremony to bind together as a community and to counterbalance the increasing estrangement of suburban living. Rituals help us become fully integrated into our world and with life. Ceremonies can also reinforce people's self-identity. Without them they could feel separated, isolated and disconnected. Other people connect with their spirituality in the privacy of their own home. It is a personal matter.

Most forms of spiritual expression are different road maps leading to the same destination. However the map is not the territory.

If there really is 'an intelligent force', why is there so much misery in the world?

Many people turn away from spirituality because of the suffering humans inflict upon each other. They ask: 'Why are there wars, why is there disease, injustice, and so on?' And in a moment of personal suffering and anguish, these questions are certainly understandable.

My own view is that 'the rules' have been established from the very first day. For example, if you put a flame against your skin, you will suffer burns and pain. If you hurt someone you also hurt your own soul because you diminish your humanity. Also, you have to live with the consequences of what you have done, thereby eroding your self-esteem and peace of mind.

If you see an injustice and fail to act, you will live in an unjust world—a world you have helped to create by your inaction. If you do not treat others as you would like to be treated you will help to produce a selfish and cruel society. If you pollute the water, you will cause disease and perhaps death.

In other words, for every action we perform there is a personal, social and spiritual consequence. But while many people will understand this point, their frustration lies mainly with the apparent absence of 'divine intervention'. They want to see 'The Lord smite the wrongdoers'.

They yearn for a 'superperson' to right our wrongs. But the solution is and has always been in our own hands.

For example, Hitler's holocaust is probably the worst example of our inhumanity to each other. I am sure that, during the horror, many of its 13 million dead prayed fervently for divine intervention. Yet the power to end it was already in our hands. But the allies chose not to act. Even as pressure for intervention mounted, the allies did not act because 'it would divert military resources away from the central mission of prosecuting the main war'.

The tragedy of Sarajevo, Gorazde and many other Bosnian towns where civilians were subjected to relentless Serbian bombardment are other examples of our apparent inability to act decisively as a world body.

It is not surprising that many people wonder if there really is a 'divine being'. But the 'divine being' has nothing to do with, such events. We have the power to stop such injustices. The Western world could have stopped the Bosnian tragedy early in its development. However its increasing moral weakness delayed intervention and, hence, the injustices continued.

Soon afterwards, an even more appalling tragedy unfolded in Rwanda. Warlords took comfort in the apparent lack of resolve of the major powers to act decisively.

The lesson is clear. It's up to us. If as a global community we never want to see such atrocities again we will have to take action as they arise. We have the means, and the resources. Sadly, where economic interests are not threatened, we tend to lack the will. So the blame does not belong to any 'divine being'. It rests with us collectively.

We could also fix many of the problems within our own society. The reasons we do not do so is that most of us are not yet ready to accept the restrictions that such a move would place on individual freedoms.

For example, if we wanted a more caring and non-violent society then we would need to ensure that children—who are, after all, the future of humankind—are brought up in a caring and supportive environment. That means that 'would-be parents' would need to be screened to determine their psychological readiness to have children.

They would need to demonstrate the financial ability to support the children and to provide them with a sufficiently high standard of living and education. They would need a health clearance.

They would also need to have adequate qualifications for parenthood (i.e. they would need training in child care). Vetting their attitudes might also be important to ensure that ancient prejudices, racial and religious hatreds and bigotry would not be passed on to their children.

Does such an idea sound preposterous? If so, take a moment to think about it. Does it follow that because people are born with the physical equipment to beget children they also have the psychological aptitude and quality of character to bring them up well? If the high levels of divorce, domestic violence, child abuse and anti-social behaviour are any indication, it appears that many of us are simply not equipped to be good parents. (However many more could become good parents with adequate training and social support.)

While many people might agree that thorough 'pre-natal' preparation of intending parents is highly desirable, what would civil libertarians cry? They would scream that having children is a fundamental right, regardless of the parent's ability to support them or to care for them. And so we stand still.

The result? Many brutalised children who grow into brutal teenagers and desperate adults. (This argument supports the 'nurture' view of social behaviour. However it must be stated that an individual's genetic makeup (the 'nature' view) plays a strong role in determining character and, therefore, behaviour—especially when placed under pressure.)

My point is that to solve our problems, intuitively we were given 'the rules' and physically we were given the intellect, the ability, the resources and each other. The 'divine being' does not 'cause' the child abuse, the violence and the cruelties that we inflict on our fellow human beings. Nevertheless many people yearn for 'divine retribution'. But were such intervention granted we would ask for it at every disagreement.

Has it not been our practice to abuse our resources? Even if that intervention were simply a matter of 'influencing' others to act in a better way, would it not diminish our freedom? What would life be like if we were mere puppets who had no choice but to act according to the way the 'divine being' influenced or forced us to act (i.e. we would lose our free will)? What would be the point of creating a human race without free will? (Robots would be far more efficient—and less trouble.)

To my way of thinking, 'the rules' are clear. If we don't want injustice, we must act to eradicate it. If we don't want wars and conflicts then one of the major reforms we need to implement is a fairer distribution of global and national wealth. (In some countries, 90 per cent of the wealth is in the hands of 3–5 per cent of the people.)

Neither must we, the people, give our leaders the right to start wars or conflicts as the means of conflict resolution.

As for individuals, humankind also needs to accept responsibility for its own life. There is no superperson to do our work for us. The holocaust and the tragedies in Cambodia, Bosnia and Rwanda should have made that abundantly clear.

Finally, as for disease, many of the major diseases have been self-caused through our close association with animals, our own pollution and our ignorance of causes and treatment. Just a few major diseases that are largely self-caused are most lung cancers, heart disease and cirrhosis of the liver.

The effect of smoking is a case in point. Although smokers know their habit causes many diseases, including 97 per cent of all lung cancer, they persist with it. Can that be blamed on the 'divine entity'?

For diseases that are not of our own doing we have been endowed with the intellect to conquer them. Had we spent even a small portion of the resources we have wasted on weapons and channelled them to curing disease and suffering, by now incurable disease would be a scourge long passed into history.

'I'm not spiritual, and I'm OK'

But who wants to be OK when you could be wonderful? I have yet to meet a holistically successful person who is not spiritual in his or her own way. (They might exist, but I have not met them.) Are there negative consequences to being spiritually disconnected? Of having no deep sense of human value? One answer could lie in the following example. In the United States hundreds of thousands of children take loaded guns to school. In 1994 it was reckoned that before North American children left elementary school they will have witnessed 8000 killings and 200,000 acts of violence on television.

It is estimated there are over 240 million firearms in private hands—some 160 million of those are pistols. In 1993 United States, over 10,500 people were murdered by guns (compare that to 60 for the same period in Canada). In the United States there are more gun shops than there are garages.

The most popular video games are games showing explicit violence—as if it carried no human consequences. One violent game or film may have little or no effect. One violent toy may have little or no effect. However we barrage young minds with an on-going stream of information showing heroes solving problems through violence, winning through violence and being admired for it. Are we not 'conditioning' the more susceptible of our young to solve their problems through violence too?

What messages are we sending to our children in place of the spiritual messages of responsibility, of courtesy, of caring, of love and of a high regard for the humanity and dignity of others?

Some negative manifestations of 'violence conditioning' are becoming clear. In Los Angeles many children sleep on the floor to avoid being shot by random 'drive-by' shootings. Add the abuse and violent upbringing of so many children and it is little wonder that violence is such an escalating problem.

Even those who are not in the 'susceptible minority' are affected because, having seen so much violence on film, they can become desensitised to real violence.

Of course, spirituality of itself will not solve all our social or political problems. Neither will it alleviate our economic woes, diminish an individual politician's lust for power or prevent the misuse of religious devotion as a pretext to take another person's property, go to war to take someone else's country, force terms of trade, and so on.

However we are discussing holistic success, and how a spiritual connection can help individuals—and collectively, society—lead a healthier and happier life.

In her book *Feel the Fear and Do It Anyway*, psychologist Dr Susan Jeffers says of spirituality:

> 'I believe that what all of us are really searching for is this divine essence within ourselves. When we are far from our Higher self, we feel what Roberto Assogioli has so aptly called "Divine Homesickness". When you are feeling this sense of being lost, or off course, the thing to do to find your way home again is simply to use the tools that will align you with your Higher Self—and thus to allow the good feelings to flow once again.'

It is true, of course, that one can accumulate wealth and enjoy physical health without being spiritual. However how many of those who have done so can be said to be holistically successful? Did they achieve happiness? Did they discover fulfilment?

The former Soviet Union made itself a non-spiritual State by law. It forbade any form of spirituality and actively persecuted adherents for 75 years. Were its people happy? Did they become wealthy individually or as a nation?

Of course, there were many other factors responsible for the misery and deprivation suffered by the Soviet people. But having denied a people's spirituality, no compensating benefit became apparent. Brutality, however, increased and was practised systematically by the State. For instance, under Lenin and Stalin, 50 to 80 million Soviet citizens were murdered, or worked and/or starved to death.

'God is dead . . . isn't (He)?'

Whether or not you believe in an intelligent force that pervades and sustains life is a matter for you. It is not my intention to proselytise. However it needs to be said that for many successful people spirituality seems to provide a solid foundation for their life—a sense of 'partnership' with a 'Life Force', a strong sense of human value and purpose, of a higher self, of the quest for Personal Excellence.

In his eighties, Dr C. G. Jung was asked if as a young man he believed in God. He replied that he did. He was than asked: 'And what about now, after a lifetime of exploring the human psyche?' Dr Jung replied: 'Now I don't have to believe. I know!'

Helen Keller, the famous blind, deaf and mute girl who captured so many hearts with her courage and strength, when asked about God said: 'I knew Him. But I didn't know His name.'

They called this deeper meaning 'God'. However if you asked them to define 'God' you might not get a common definition at all. Likewise if you asked me whether I believed in God, firstly I would have to ask you to define 'God', then I could tell you if I believed in your version of (It?).

Nevertheless spiritual people seem to handle life's major crises with more courage and strength. They tend to be more resilient and in times of trouble find sources of power within themselves. However the frenetic pace of modern life tends to distract many others from seeking deeper truths.

Howard Crago, noted Australian journalist, writes in *Spare a Minute*:

> *'Modern life is against looking out of the window or, as some would say, looking into life. It's pace constantly accelerates.*
>
> *'Demands on our time continually increase. Much of this action aims to increase the possessions that satisfy our physical and emotional needs. Yet it can deprive us of the chance to grasp other, less tangible, but more satisfying and durable possessions.*
>
> *'These include buried memories we can be too busy to recall; ideals and aspirations we do not stop to define; and an appreciation of "the mysterious affinity binding together . . . religious truths, aesthetic beauty and moral goodness".'*

And it might be that the frenetic pace of life in the guise of 'modernity' makes so many people look upon spirituality as 'old hat', as out of context or simply as irrelevant.

A joy of researching is that one often savours many ironies of spiritual wisdom. For example, Australia's Aborigines are probably the oldest surviving race who chose not to develop a material culture beyond the level of the stone age. (They didn't have to. Instead of our modern approach of changing our environment to suit us, they changed themselves to suit their environment, and lived in perfect harmony with it.)

The Aborigines developed a complex theory of the universe and creation they call the 'Dreamtime'. According to noted anthropologist David Maybury-Lewis, their explanation of the creation is much closer to the theories of our most eminent theoretical physicists than are the beliefs held by most 'modern people'. How does one explain such 'intuitive' wisdom that can bridge a 60,000 year chasm?

You proved for yourself that life is 95 per cent thought and 5 per cent form by trying to 'snatch a moment of it' in your hand. Given that truth, is it really any wonder that life itself should contain a spiritual dimension and, with it, an intuitive spiritual wisdom?

In the end we are all fellow travellers on a voyage of growth, learning and discovery. Our paths might diverge, but our destination is a common one. Each system provides its own road map. The fools who stop their journey to claim they have a better road map than someone else are fools indeed. They have forgotten that the map is only a map. It is not the territory.

A personal note

I have been a spiritual person as far back as I can remember. My childhood ambition was to become a priest. I even saved my pennies to prepare for that day. However I abandoned that idea by the age of ten. I think the attraction was that the priest in Caraffa, the village in Southern Italy where I was born, was a man of charisma. Everyone looked up to him. He was the guest of honour at all the festivals and parties so I thought: 'That's for me!'

I continued to have an interest in religious affairs until the age of 30. Up to that time I had been involved—off and on—with various churches. At times I took an active involvement. However it wasn't until January 1977 that I changed from being a 'religious' person into a spiritual one.

Some would describe the event as a 'born again' experience. At one moment I experienced a coalescence of insight. For the first time I understood there really was a higher purpose. I realised that dogmatic religion inhibits a deeper—almost intuitive—understanding of our spiritual dimension and can turn into fanaticism. I understood theological concepts far more clearly and in a more exhilarating way. Blinkers fell off. I no longer needed to believe. I knew.

Did I feel the urge to tell everyone about my experience? No way! It was mine. I wanted to keep it. I was so elated at this boon, at this mysterious infusion of 'grace' that I couldn't sleep well for days. The awesome thing was that I seemed to know its source and felt a strong connection with it.

From that time my life changed dramatically. I feel a sense of partnership with my spiritual self. I feel as if I am walking with a spiritual companion who guides me and helps me see that trials and setbacks are merely learning experiences, that life is mostly thought, not form, and that to overcome the physical trials of this world we have been given our talents and each other.

I know how easy it is for those engrossed in their work/financial sphere of life, especially those who operate a business, to block sensitivity to spiritual issues. That is not necessarily intentional. The nature of competition and the daily struggle to survive can soon disconnect them from deeper issues. I can only speak for myself and as far as I am concerned I have been blessed with a precious gift that, despite what cynics might say, I would rather have than the offerings of all the 'modern rationalism' they can muster.

Is my experience common? Apparently, yes. And many people are restored to health by it. For example, renowned psychologist Abraham Maslow states in *Religious Values and Peak Experiences*:

> 'To have a clear perception (rather than a purely abstract and verbal philosophical acceptance) that the universe is all of a piece and that one has his place in it—one is a part of it, one belongs in it—can be so profound and shaking an experience that it can change the person's character . . . forever after . . .
>
> 'I have two subjects who, because of such an experience, were totally, immediately and permanently cured of (in one case) chronic anxiety neurosis and (in the other case) of strong obsessional thoughts of suicide . . . the person himself tends to move toward fusion, integration, and unity and away from splitting, conflicts and oppositions.'

What seems particularly common to spiritual people is that when they tap into their spirituality for strength, they get it! Spiritual people know that forms are not what they seem because we can see only their reflections. They know that everything in life is in motion—on the way to becoming something else. They know that even on a scientific level there exist other dimensions of life that our eyes cannot perceive. So they look beyond the merely visible. They search for spiritual truth.

Spiritual people know that humankind's ultimate arrogance lies in rejecting the likelihood that there could be a higher intelligence than ours. They know. They do not merely believe. They connect with their spiritual source and draw from it strength, peace, goodwill and sure footing for life's journey. They are part of the wholeness of the life experience.

Edward Carpenter expresses this feeling best in *The Drama of Love and Death* when he says:

> '. . . it is to wake up and find that the "I", one's real, most intimate self, pervades the universe and all other things— that the mountains and the sea and the stars are a part of one's body and that one's soul is in touch with the souls of all creatures . . . So great, so splendid is this experience, that it may be said that all minor questions and doubts fall away in face of it; and certain it is that in thousands and thousands of cases the fact of its having come even once to a man has

completely revolutionised his subsequent life and outlook on the world.'

I don't think I could express the benefits of connecting with our spiritual dimension more eloquently than this:

'I prosper because I know what gives me purpose on this Earth.'

You have embarked on a personal journey of holistic success. You will need the power of Self-leadership and the strength of Personal Excellence. Take encouragement from the fact that health, wealth and happiness are your birthright, as is your right to spiritual wholeness. Why settle for less?

References

Araron, Daniel (1990) *Franklin: The Autobiography*, Vintage Books, NY.

Berne, E. (1968) *Games People Play*, Penguin Books Australia, Melbourne.

Bromberg, M., Fier, L., Greene, J. E. & Kirsch, P. J. (1967) *100 Great Thinkers*, Simon & Schuster, NY.

Carnegie, D. (1985) *How to Stop Worrying and Start Living*, Pocket Books, NY.

Carnegie, D. (1988) *How to Win Friends and Influence People*, Angus & Robertson, Sydney.

Carpenter, E. (1912) *The Drama of Love and Death*, Allen & Unwin, London.

Clason, G. S. (1988) *The Richest Man in Babylon*, E.P. Dutton Signet Books, NY.

Cohen, H. (1989) *You Can Negotiate Anything,* Angus & Robertson, Sydney.

Covey, S.R. (1991) *The Seven Habits of Highly Effective People*, The Business Library, Melbourne.

Crago, H. (1986) *Spare a Minute*, The Joint Board of Christian Education, Melbourne.

Eysenk, H. & Wilson, G. (1975) *Know Your Own Personality*, Maurice Temple Smith Ltd, London.

Hill, N. (1966) *Think and Grow Rich*, Wilshire Book Company, Hollywood, California.

Hill, N. (1979) *Law of Success*, Success Unlimited Inc., Evanston, Illinois.

Hill, N. & Stone, W. C. (1987) *Success Through a Positive Mental Attitude*, Angus & Robertson, Sydney.

Hollows, F. (1991) *Fred Hollows*, John Kerr, Melbourne.

Hopkins, T. (1982) *How To Master the Art of Selling*, Grafton Books, London.

Jeffers, S. (1990) *Feel the Fear and Do It Anyway*, Random Century Ltd, London.

Kassorla, I. C. (1988) *Go For It*, Futura Publications, London.

Laird, D. A., *The Technique of Getting Things Done*, McGraw Hill, New York (out of print).

Lee-Emery, B. (1990) *Stop Procrastinating!*, Hutchinson Australia, Sydney.

Mackay, H. (1991) *How to Swim With the Sharks Without Being Eaten Alive*, Ivy Books, NY.

Mackenzie, A. (1990) *The Time Trap*, The Business Library, Melbourne.

McCormack, M. H. (1990) *Success Secrets*, William Collins, Glasgow.

Manz, Charles C. & Sims, Henry P. (1989) *Super Leadership*, Prentice Hall, Englewood Cliffs, NJ.

Maltz, M. (1960) *Psycho-Cybernetics*, Pocket Books, NY.

Maslow, A. H. (1964), *Religious Values and Peak Experiences*, Ohio State University Press, Columbus.

Mitchell, S. (1984) *Tall Poppies*, Penguin Books Australia, Melbourne.

Mitchell, S. (1991) *Tall Poppies Too*, Penguin Books Australia, Melbourne.

Naranjo, C. (1974) *The One Quest*, Wildwood House, London.

Peters, T. J. & Waterman Jr, R. H. (1990) *In Search of Excellence*, Harper & Row Publishers, Sydney.

Peyser, J. (1987) *Leonard Bernstein*, Bantam Press, London.

Rohn, J. (1986) *Seven Strategies for Wealth and Happiness*, Prima Publishing and Communications, Rocklin, California.

Schaefer, H. & Brashear, M. A. (1989) *A Guide to Public Speaking*, The Berkley Publishing Group, NY.

Schwartz, D. J. (1959) *The Magic of Thinking Big*, Wilshire Book Company, Hollywood, California.

Shah, I, *The Exploits of the Incomparable Mulla Nasrudin*.

Stanton, H. E. (1988) *The Success Factor*, Angus & Robertson, Sydney.

Trump, D. J. with Schwartz, T. (1988) *The Art of the Deal*, Century Hutchinson, Melbourne.

Vogelaar, D. M. (1990) *How to Write a Business Plan*, The Business Library, Melbourne.

Watson, T. J., Jr (1991) *Father, Son and Co.*, Bantam Books, Sydney.